T0287038

SPYMASTER'S PRISM

SPYMASTER'S PRISM

The Fight against Russian Aggression

JACK DEVINE

Potomac Books

AN IMPRINT OF THE UNIVERSITY OF NEBRASKA PRESS

All rights reserved. Potomac Books is an imprint of the University of Nebraska Press.
Manufactured in the United States of America.

First Nebraska paperback printing: 2023

Library of Congress Cataloging-in-Publication Data
Names: Devine, Jack, 1940– author.
Title: Spymaster's prism: the fight against Russian aggression / Jack Devine.
Description: Lincoln: Potomac Books, an imprint of the University of Nebraska Press, [2021] | Includes bibliographical references and index.
Identifiers: LCCN 2020037025
ISBN 9781640123786 (hardback)
ISBN 9781640126015 (paperback)
ISBN 9781640124530 (epub)
ISBN 9781640124547 (mobi)
ISBN 9781640124554 (pdf)
Subjects: LCSH: Espionage, American—Russia (Federation) | Espionage, Russian—United States. | United States. Central Intelligence Agency. | United States. Department of State—Security measures. | Cyberterrorism—Russia (Federation) | United States—Foreign relations—Russia (Federation) | Russia (Federation)—Foreign relations—United States.
Classification: LCC JK468.16 D49 2021 | DDC 327.1273047—dc23
LC record available at https://lccn.loc.gov/2020037025

Set in Garamond Premier Pro by Laura Buis.

To my wonderful wife, Pat, and to our loving family

and

To all the dedicated men and women of the CIA—past,
present, and future

My last words to you, my son and successor. Never trust the Russians.

—ABDUR RAHMAN KHAN, founder of modern Afghanistan

CONTENTS

List of Illustrations - - - - ix

Acknowledgments - - - - xi

Preamble - - - - xiii

Introduction - - - - xv

List of Abbreviations - - - - xxiii

1. Our Strategic Intelligence Shortfall—Then and Now - - - - 3

2. Shaping and Reshaping the CIA - - - - 17

3. A Study in Russian Spycraft - - - - 31

4. A Spymaster President - - - - 57

5. Spies among Us - - - - 67

6. A Spymaster's Rules in Counterintelligence - - - - 87

7. Limits of Counterintelligence - - - - 107

8. Agents-in-Place - - - - 119

9. Policy Spies - - - - 139

10. An American Covert Action Playbook - - - - 155

11. Best Practice - - - - 179

12. A Cautionary Tale - - - - 193

13. Onward - - - - 211

Appendix: Russia's Known Elicitation Attempts in Trump's Inner Circle - - - - 221

Notes - - - - 225

Bibliography - - - - 251

Index - - - - 255

ILLUSTRATIONS

Following page 116

1. Yalta Conference
2. Oleg Penkovskiy's military pass
3. James J. Angleton at Allen Dulles's funeral
4. MRBM field launch site in Cuba
5. Arkady Shevchenko at the White House
6. Jack Devine boarding Soviet helicopter
7. Jack Devine in front of KGB headquarters
8. Jack Devine inside KGB headquarters
9. The arrest of Dmitri Polyakov
10. The arrest of Aldrich Ames
11. Sergei Tretyakov at the grave of Konon Molody
12. Vladimir Putin's Dresden ID card
13. Donald Trump and Vladimir Putin in Helsinki

ACKNOWLEDGMENTS

In so many ways the writing and publication of *Spymaster's Prism* was a team effort. In fact, I sought the support and advice of so many folks that it is hard to list them all. Let me begin where the process began by noting the outstanding support from my great literary agent, Andrew Wylie, who believed in the book from the outset and through thick and thin persisted in finding the right home for it—Potomac Books. In this regard, I would like to express my deep gratitude to Potomac editor Tom Swanson for deciding to publish the book.

Because of changing political events at home and in Russia, the book has gone through a major metamorphosis over the past three years, ending in a very different place from where I started. Throughout this process a dedicated team stayed with me in researching, editing, and conceptualizing the book. First and foremost, I would like to tip my hat to Victoria Kataoka, who spent endless hours researching the multiples cases and issues involved in the manuscript, as well as writing and editing her findings with her heart and soul. She was backed up by Conway Irwin, Susan Varisco, Amanda Mattingly, Aaron Springer, and Stephanie Danyi, who tackled various substantive aspects of the manuscript, adding their excellent thoughts, suggestions, and writing. Sarah Crichton and Michael Signorelli also contributed their thoughts and insightful feedback, especially relating to the thematic structure of the text.

In addition to conducting exhaustive research, I wanted to make sure that I had the facts just right and turned to several of the most respected CIA and State Department experts who had firsthand knowledge of the historical cases, personalities, and foreign policies described in the book.

These experts included Burton Gerber, Sandy Grimes, Jami Miscik, David Shedd, Mike Sulick, Tom Twetten, Marty Roeber, Paula Doyle, and Ambassador Frank Wisner. I also turned to many friends to get their valuable feedback, including Robert Dilenschneider, Joe Finder, Rollie Burans, David Ebershoff, Kathy Lavinder, Lisa Carroll, and John Hughes. I also would like to express special appreciation to my longtime friend and business partner Stanley Arkin, who provided great encouragement and support throughout the writing of the book.

Finally and above all, I would like to give loving praise to my wonderful wife, who put up with all of the time I carved out of our hectic life to write *Spymaster's Prism*. And, as in the writing of my earlier book, *Good Hunting*, I found priceless her abundant and unvarnished critique of the manuscript, albeit painful at times. She provided the unique and blunt critique that no one else would contemplate offering.

Thank you all.

PREAMBLE

Spying is not for everyone. It takes a unique DNA to fit the mold of a spy. It requires a willingness and ability to navigate ambiguous terrain fraught with acute risks that can sometimes be fatal.

The best spies have and maintain a steadfast sense of mission. They provide highly valuable and sensitive national security intelligence that informs policy makers and allows them to undertake strategic actions against their adversaries. Foreign recruits to the spy service, though viewed as traitors in their own countries, are hailed as heroes in ours.

Spymasters are not spies. Their mission is to run and handle foreign spies and spy networks. They exist in virtually all sophisticated intelligence services around the world, including the more high-profile services such as the CIA, the Russian SVR, the British SIS, the Chinese MSS, the Iranian VAJA, and the Israeli Mossad. Without exception, these spymasters are highly trained and broadly experienced top-level government officials at the heart of the intelligence business. They make the life-and-death decisions. The vast majority of spymasters remain unknown to the world, but from time to time a few emerge into public view, such as legendary East German spy chief Markus Wolf and high-profile CIA Russian expert George Kisevalter.

The distinguishing characteristic of a spymaster is the ability to look at the world dispassionately through a prism that refracts political events into multiple nuanced dimensions, distilling centers of power, areas of leverage and risk, and the key dynamics that can determine the course of history. In this context what is most important is knowing how to manage and direct spies for maximum impact. It is a powerful and addictive skill and responsibility, which together bring forth a sharpened perspective or, on occasion, an imbalanced distortion that can conjure destructive paranoia. When a spymaster's prism brings clarifying and nuanced insight, it can illuminate the public debate on national security. As the 2020 presidential election approached, it was ever in my mind that public discourse on our country's intelligence and counterintelligence posture against Russia in the future must be enhanced. It is my hope that a look through this spymaster's prism will offer further occasion for discussions on that topic.

INTRODUCTION

Enduring Prism

Leaving the CIA on the last day of a long career is never easy. My turn came in late 1999. I departed alone by design. I wanted to savor the moment and reflect on my thirty-two years in the agency. I decided to walk the halls around the atrium on the ground floor and take in the many memories that were enshrined there and to reflect upon the present course.

The CIA building is impressive by any architectural standard, and there is great beauty in the graceful simplicity of its design. Just past the front door the CIA seal is richly embedded in the floor. To the left is etched in marble the rightful mantra of the CIA, a quote from the New Testament (John 8:32): "And ye shall know the truth and it will set you free." This profound statement is the foundation of the U.S. intelligence business: seek to see things as they are and report it objectively to policy makers. A statue of General William "Wild Bill" Donovan, chief of the Office of Strategic Services (OSS), the forerunner of the CIA, stands nearby.

Even before entering headquarters, one encounters a relatively small statue of Nathan Hale tucked to the side. Its meaning is self-evident. He was the first American hanged by the British for spying during the Revolution of 1776. His patriotic last words have been memorialized: "I only regret that I have but one life to lose for my country." It stands as a reminder to all spies of the high stakes of their enterprise, as well as the potential outcome if they are discovered.

Through the security control area and up the steps are imposing portraits of the twenty-six CIA directors who have led the agency since its inception. All but seven I knew personally, from Richard Helms to Gina Haspel. I stopped at each one and reflected on the challenges and transformation that the agency endured during their respective tenures, not always for the better. This special cohort of leaders served the agency and our country, shaped the culture and mind-set of the agency, and ultimately determined the path of the Cold War, as well as our current course.

On the right side of the atrium, paintings depicting key moments in CIA history have been added. One of my favorites shows OSS heroine Virginia Hall cranking out a secret communication while working behind enemy lines in France during WWII. Farther down the hall is a painting of the first Stinger shoot-down of a Russian helicopter in Afghanistan, which took place during my time as chief of the Afghan Task Force. Nearby is one portraying Tony Mendez, a talented agency undercover tech officer, preparing false documents for embassy officials holed up in Tehran after the fall of the Shah. With his help, these officials were able to exit Iran undetected, as depicted in the movie *Argo*. These were indeed key moments in the agency's history, but I can think of countless more of great merit and will cover many in these pages.

As I drifted toward the front entrance, I was drawn to contemplate the treachery of Aldrich "Rick" Ames, a mediocre man with an outsized self-image. He was ultimately identified as the traitor whom I believed existed inside CIA ranks. It was frustrating to leave the critically important task of hunting down another key mole, but it is a reality of the intelligence world that the work is never really done. (FBI special agent Robert Hanssen, who like Ames was remarkable only for the depth and impact of his perfidy, was eventually exposed in 2001.) In the last moments before my departure I thought about the victory over the Soviets in Afghanistan and the many high-level spies we ran inside the Soviet Union: Soviet agents such as General Dmitri Polyakov and Adolf Tolkachev, who paid with their lives to deliver critical Soviet state secrets.

Still, I didn't appreciate at the time how our critical victory in the Cold War would not put an end to Russian aspirations and how our struggle with Russian intelligence would endure to this day. Russia never abandoned its spying program or its active measures operations. It has become increasingly clear, ever more so since former KGB operative Vladimir Putin's power has become more entrenched, that Russia's aggressive behavior has ramped up to an unprecedented level, breaching long-standing norms and actively seeking to subvert the Western democratic order. Furthermore, Russia has capably shifted the struggle to a new arena—cyberspace—where the SVR and GRU and their proxies have managed to develop powerful capabilities and wage asymmetrical warfare to great effect.

With my last long walk through the agency halls as an active-duty officer behind me, little did I know, little did the U.S. intelligence community know, that Russian covert action and espionage against the United States would continue unabated, taking forms both familiar and new. I walked out the front door of CIA headquarters with these deep-seated memories and my personal spymaster's prism—a unique and intelligence-seasoned way of looking at the world.

Intelligence Matters and Moscow Rules

The last few years have seen a steady flow of new information and intelligence community conclusions about the extent of Russia's ongoing efforts to penetrate and influence the U.S. government and its democratic processes. Although these conclusions have been the subject of some debate, a Senate Intelligence Committee report released in April 2020 confirmed the intelligence community's findings that Russia intervened in the 2016 U.S. presidential election.[1] However, it would be naïve to think that having its activities discovered would trigger Russia to rein in its political meddling in the United States and elsewhere.

Russia's dramatic loss of global clout in the wake of the Soviet Union's dissolution has obscured the fact that for most of the last three decades it has not only sustained an aggressive stance toward collection and even active measures in the United States but also aggressively sought to regain its sphere of influence. As recently as February 2020 news surfaced that Putin was renewing pressure on Belarus to accept a long-standing proposal to "merge" with Russia by threatening to sharply raise prices for oil and gas unless Belarusian president Alexander Lukashenko acquiesced.[2] While Russia today isn't trying to spread communist ideology, Russian nationalist objectives are quite similar. They seek to undermine the U.S. strategic position in any vulnerable theater around the world and increase Russian influence wherever possible: in Syria, Venezuela, Libya, Afghanistan, and Ukraine and other countries in proximity to Russia. Its newest course of action has been to interfere directly in our internal politics and defense industry and double down on its quest to delegitimize and undermine the democratic and Western order.[3] Putin's game plan remains to promote Russia's long-standing strategy, which is unlikely to deviate significantly, no matter what President Donald Trump's overtures might be. Although every U.S. president since 1999, when Putin became Russia's president, has endeavored to progress toward a cooperative rather than adversarial relationship with Russia, all learn eventually that any unlikely support from Putin for reconciliation will be ephemeral and shallow and the price to be paid too high.

Because Russia's assault on Western democracy has primarily been predicated on what can be traditionally considered intelligence actions, it is helpful to consider the term "Moscow Rules." The phrase refers to a set of unwritten norms meant to limit operational activity that would upend the balance of powers and potentially lead us closer to testing the tenets of mutually assured destruction. Both Russian and U.S. intelligence services have followed these norms since the height of the Cold War. Under this understanding, Russian and U.S. intelligence services have refrained from assassinations, terrorism, or strong-arm tactics directed against each other's officers, as well as from engaging in counterfeiting operations or direct interference in each other's internal political processes. On rare occasions during the Cold War, CIA and KGB representatives would even meet to sort out thorny issues regarding the Moscow Rules. This concept of the Moscow Rules is a very useful framework to consider, as it has become clear that Russia violated an important political threshold when it interfered in the 2016 U.S. presidential election. And it is this interpretation of the Moscow Rules that is relevant to the analysis in this book.[4]

The Moscow Rules had been adhered to by both sides for decades, out of self-interest as much as anything else. So when the media first reported that the Russian government had interfered in the U.S. elections, I was skeptical that it had happened, especially on such a large scale. The hack of Democratic National Committee computers was plausible, since that sort of thing is done by most countries with cyber capabilities. But actually attempting to sway the U.S. election was a seismic shift. I couldn't make sense of why Putin would choose to blatantly abrogate a long-standing red line and, what's more, in favor of a then-unpredictable candidate who would be difficult to calibrate on national security issues. And yet he did. Understanding why Russia breached this important threshold will be the only way to know how to respond and how to try to walk back the breach of the Moscow Rules.

At the time of the Helsinki summit in 2018, Trump seemingly had little appreciation for the importance of challenging Putin on breaking the Moscow Rules. By contrast, Putin took advantage of the forum, in true Russian intelligence tradition, as an opportunity to muddy the informational waters about what in fact happened and to posit alternative, barely plausible explanations. In a rather self-revealing statement, he went so far as to say that as a former KGB officer he knows how "fake news" is developed and therefore can assure the U.S. president and the public that the charge against the Russians was groundless! Putin abrogated the Moscow Rules and needs to be held to account. What's more, Putin's calculus on this issue makes him a far more dangerous, high-risk gambler than is generally perceived. He is indeed a formidable opponent.

It is worth recalling that President John F. Kennedy performed poorly in his first encounter with First Secretary Nikita Khrushchev in Vienna in 1961. Khrushchev sized up Kennedy as inexperienced and naïve, and he boldly decided to put nuclear-armed missiles in Cuba, which precipitated the Cuban Missile Crisis and brought us to the brink of nuclear war in October 1962. Fortunately, by then Kennedy had gained a solid international footing. Armed with highly valuable satellite imagery and critical, sensitive intelligence provided by Soviet spy Oleg Penkovskiy, he was able to get Khrushchev to back down and withdraw his missiles from Cuba. We do not know what Putin's mind-set was after the Helsinki meeting, nor do we know his subsequent intentions toward the Trump administration. However, we do know that Russian collection and interference efforts continue, and a recalibration of U.S. policy and actions will take time and significant effort. Joe Biden's election will not deter Russian cyber intelligence operations against the United States. Quite the contrary, it's a good bet Putin will ramp up aggressive cyber attacks while the new administration is trying to get its sea legs. These attacks are not fundamentally political but rather derive from twin strategic goals of undermining and weakening U.S. democratic institutions and using cyber capabilities to acquire our secrets and debilitate our military and strategic infrastructure. They are now and will continue to be a national security problem that is crying out for a counterintelligence and disinformation strategy. And I am afraid we may not have modern-day, Penkovskiy-like sources helping us in this task.

The purpose of this book is to provide a unique spymaster's analysis of how to effectively respond in light of Russia's (and others') ongoing intelligence assaults on the United States. We know that Russia has the plumbing in place to conduct further cyber assaults on our democracy, and the U.S. intelligence community warned Congress in a February 2020 briefing of Russia's intention to interfere in both the 2020 Democratic primaries and the presidential election.[5] Furthermore, our intelligence agencies believe that Russia is taking things a step further by seeking to foment unrest among white supremacist groups and to exacerbate existing political cleavages.[6] Armed with this knowledge, we must formulate effective offensive and defensive operational plans to counter such aggression. In evaluating the different aspects of Russia's current actions and our sometimes flawed responses to them and in offering a comparative analysis with key historical intelligence cases, we can develop a prescription for action to help us navigate the current state of play between Russia and the United States.

These observations are organized under thirteen key intelligence lessons. Some lessons may have been the bedrock of U.S. policy for decades, but they bear reiterating today. First among these is that Russia is our strategic adversary, regardless of how we might like things to be, and second is that the ambition and ingenuity of Russian intelligence operations are unrelenting. Others are universal truths about spying that are particularly relevant today as they pertain to Russia. These include the understanding that as long as there is human frailty, people can be persuaded to spy for Russia, and as long as there is an autocratic government in Moscow, there will be people willing to spy for the West. Fundamentally, though, the ultimate lesson to take away is this: never trust the Russians.

All these lessons are founded upon the historical experience of the CIA and other intelligence agencies, and we would be wise to heed them. As you will see in the following pages, our current contest with Russia is very much a continuation of our intelligence dueling with Moscow since the end of World War II. However, our strategic shortfall and dearth of tactical readiness to confront Russia resulted from a series of clear policy pivots, often in response to larger geopolitical developments. On the heels of World War II the United States was already late to the game in terms of sophisticated intelligence collection and covert action capacity. The Russians had been well practiced in spying operations for generations, and it would take the United States a decade of concerted effort and funding to achieve parity, if not superiority, during the Cold War. But such diligence would only ever be temporary. An irresistible complacency toward Russia would take hold in policy circles and the United States in general in the aftermath of the Cold War; our attention was directed elsewhere. As Russia gathered its strength and found new tactics, we were slow to react to their resurgence and distracted first by the drug war and then by the scourge of transnational terrorism.

The unprecedented attack against our democracy in the 2016 presidential election could be seen as an inevitable result of our wrongsighted policies toward Russia. Given what we have learned from the Mueller Report, the congressional testimony of the report's compiler, former FBI director Robert Mueller, in July 2019, the 2019 Senate intelligence report on Russian interference in the 2016 U.S. election, intelligence briefings to Congress in February 2020, as well as ongoing news reports, we have every reason to believe that this assault continues. Now, with a resurgence of this Russian aggression, a review and reiteration of the value of espionage and covert action directed toward Russia is crucial.

While it may alarm some to learn that Russia never ceased its relentless intelligence battle against the United States, it is important to grasp that Russia is not the powerful adversary it was in the Cold War. Many of the weaknesses that underpinned its failures in the Cold War endure, and we are well poised to exploit that vulnerability if we are willing and resolved to do so. Much of our success may lie in how we leverage our intelligence resources. Given the pace of world events, the militarization of our foreign affairs, and, perhaps most important, our sphere of action extending into the cyber world, the need for meaningful intelligence has never been more important, and we must best Russia's actions if we are to protect American principles and interests both at home and abroad. Our endgame should be twofold: we must first and foremost protect our democracy from the assault, and we should endeavor to stabilize relations with Russia by negotiating an updated version of the Moscow Rules, one that could lay the foundation for a return to a productive diplomatic relationship with Moscow.

ABBREVIATIONS

ADDO	associate deputy director of operations
BND	Bundesnachrichtendienst (West German intelligence service)
CAATSA	Countering America's Adversaries through Sanctions Act
CCTV	closed circuit television
CI	counterintelligence
CIA	Central Intelligence Agency
CIC	Counterintelligence Center
CKTAW	listening device attached to underground communications cable
CNC	Counter Narcotics Center
COPS	chief of operations
COS	chief of station
CPSU	Communist Party of the Soviet Union
DARPA	Defense Advanced Research Projects Agency
DCI	director of central intelligence
DDP	deputy director of plans
DEFCON	defense readiness condition
DGI	Dirección General de Inteligencia (Cuban intelligence agency)
DNC	Democratic National Committee
FARC	Fuerzas Armadas Revolunionarias de Colombia (leftist Colombian rebel group)
FSB	Federal'naya Sluzhba Bezopasnosti (Russian intelligence agency, successor to KGB)

FSK	Federal'naya Sluzhba Kontrrazvedki (Russian federal counterintelligence service)
FSLN	Frente Sandinista de Liberación Nacional (Sandinista National Liberation Front)
GRU	Glavnoye Razvedyvaatelnoye Upravlenie (Russia's military intelligence directorate)
HVA	Hauptverwaltung Aufklärung (East German First Intelligence Directorate)
ICBM	intercontinental ballistic missile
IED	improvised explosive device
INF	intermediate-range nuclear forces
IRA	Internet Research Agency (Russian cyber operation)
IRBM	intermediate-range ballistic missille
ISI	Inter-Service Intelligence (Pakistan's intelligence agency)
ISIS	Islamic State in Iraq and the Levant
IT	internet technology
KGB	Komitet Gosudarstvennoy Bezopasnosti (Committee for State Security, Soviet Union)
MRBM	medium-range ballistic missile
MSS	Ministry of State Security (Chinese intelligence service)
NATO	North Atlantic Treaty Organization
NKVD	Narodnyi Komissariat Vnutrennykh Del (People's Commissariat for Internal Affairs, the Soviet secret police)
NOC	non-official cover
NSA	National Security Agency
NSC	National Security Council
NSDD	National Security Decision Directive
OPC	Office of Policy Coordination
OSO	Office of Special Operations
OSS	Office of Strategic Services
PDVSA	Petróleos de Venezuela, S.A. (Venezuela's state-owned oil company)

RFE	Radio Free Europe
RNC	Republican National Committee
SDF	Syrian Democratic Forces
SIG	Special Investigations Group (CIA's counterintelligence operation)
SIS	Secret Intelligence Service (British foreign intelligence, MI6)
SVR	Sluzhba Vneshney Razvedki (Russia's foreign intelligence service)
TOW	tube-launched, optically tracked, wire-guided missile
UAE	United Arab Emirates
UFC	United Fruit Company
UNO	Unión Nacional Opositora (National Opposition Union, Nicaragua)
VAJA	Vezarat-e ettela'at jomhuri-ye eslami-ye iran (Iranian intelligence service)
VEB	VneshEconomBank (Russia's state-owned development organization)
WMDS	weapons of mass destruction
VPN	virtual private network

SPYMASTER'S PRISM

LESSON ONE

Russia is our strategic adversary, regardless of how we might like things to be.

The Cold War never ended. Before the collapse of the Soviet Union, the KGB had a list of three main adversaries: (1.) The United States (2.) NATO and (3.) China. After the KGB was disbanded and the SVR was formed, ... the SVR had three main targets: (1.) The United States (2.) NATO and (3.) China.

—KGB officer SERGEI TRETYAKOV, quoted in Pete Earley, *Comrade J*

1

Our Strategic Intelligence Shortfall—Then and Now

Coming into Focus

In the lead-up to the 2016 presidential election, troubling reports emerged of a seemingly unremitting and coordinated attack by the Russian state that caught the U.S. government and its intelligence community off guard. The Democratic National Committee, the Democratic Congressional Campaign Committee, and the presidential campaign headquarters of Democratic candidate Hillary Clinton were hacked, and sensitive information was leaked through WikiLeaks and DCLeaks. In the aftermath of the election it became clear that a preponderance of "fake news" and divisive stories had been placed on Facebook, Instagram, Twitter, and YouTube. The most jarring details of Russia's ambitious, multipronged, and complex hacking-and-dumping operations and sophisticated and targeted social media campaigns emerged from the investigation led by Special Counsel Robert Mueller III.[1]

We should not have been surprised. The Russians have been running such operations for decades, and Vladimir Putin has been honing his assault strategy on democratic institutions for years. The signposts were there to see, had we taken note of them. The first of these came sixteen years prior, when a Russian intelligence officer named Sergei Tretyakov told us unequivocally what Russian ambitions were.

In 2000 the deputy resident for the SVR (the modern-day KGB) in New York, Colonel Sergei Tretyakov, defected. He had been spying for the United States for three years as an agent-in-place, driven by disillusionment with the moral decay within Russia's leadership. During this time Tretyakov oversaw from his perch all clandestine operations in New York City and the strategically and intelligence-rich gathering pool of the United Nations. From the UN, the SVR recruited and ran diplomatic sources from all over the world.[2] Outside the UN the SVR was relentless in seeking to recruit spies who could provide privileged access to the political, military, economic, technical, and media sectors in U.S. society. Some of the SVR's top targets in New York City included the U.S. Mission to the UN, New York City political circles and financial institutions, the Council on Foreign Relations, and Russian and Jewish immigrant groups, among many others.[3]

Codenamed "Comrade J," Tretyakov revealed to the American intelligence community that the fundamental interests of Russia vis-à-vis the West had not changed since the end of the Cold War. And, accordingly, Russia had not ceased its efforts to gather intelligence to aid it in navigating a new era. Tretyakov's existence offered proof of Russia's continuing espionage.[4]

Tretyakov is thought to have shared five thousand top-secret cables, along with intricate details of Russia's intelligence operations in New York, over his period of cooperation. He revealed the identities of the SVR's agents and contacts in the United States and Canada. Most important, he provided information on Russia's global political and military actions, as well as its objection to the admission of former Soviet satellites into NATO.[5]

American policy makers did not fully comprehend the implications of what he had told us—that the Russians were still very much in an aggressive intelligence war against the United States and Western democracies. Tretyakov's revelations received attention in the intelligence and foreign policy realms but failed to change our priorities. At the time, U.S. policy was intensely focused on forging a post–Cold War order defined by a unipolar U.S. hegemony. Russian aggression on this scale did not fit that narrative.

Furthermore, at that time our attention was about to turn to a new and emergent threat: transnational terrorism. Tretyakov's revelations were only beginning to percolate across U.S. intelligence circles when Osama bin Laden and al-Qaeda attacked the United States on September 11, 2001. From that moment on, nearly all eyes turned toward this new, asymmetrical, stateless, ideological, and seemingly existential threat to the West. Any other policy priority was subjugated to it, and because of the military engagements that followed, intelligence-collecting covert action was modified to be used primarily in service of those military engagements. Twenty years on we can see the results of and the opportunities lost from this strategic posture. Because we didn't take sufficient note of Tretyakov's revelations about Russia then, we are now racing to catch up in the wake of Russia's interference in 2016 and to head off Russia's continuing and evolving efforts to interfere. We need to revisit what Tretyakov told us and see Russia as it truly is.

A New Tsar

Putin's strategic view of the world should be transparent to everyone. At his KGB core, Putin is a hard-edged, pragmatic opportunist whose fundamental foreign policy objective is to return Russia to what he believes is its rightful place as a world superpower—this time not as a communist Soviet power but as a Eurasian giant sprawling from the Korean Peninsula to Europe.

For the most part this means building dominant relationships with the countries that border Russia and expanding influence in the Middle East. In carrying out this mission, he will not hesitate to use military force or his intelligence services to accomplish his tactical objectives, as he did in Chechnya, Ukraine, Syria, and Afghanistan, where intelligence reports have indicated that Russia may have paid Taliban militants bounties for killing U.S. service personnel.[6] At the same time, he wishes to construct a counteralliance with other nations not in the Western orbit, especially China, Cuba, Iran, North Korea, Syria, and Venezuela.

A key strategy to achieving this objective is to weaken the integrity of the political systems and alliances of other nations, especially of Western nations, by any means, including political, economic, and military subterfuge. What's more, he has amplified his actions by interfering directly in the internal affairs of the United States and other Western democratic countries. In this regard it is useful to underscore Putin's KGB-rooted mentality of using covert power to accomplish short-term and long-term objectives.

Putin's strategy is not a new one. He has adopted the Cold War strategy of the communist Soviet Union and reinvigorated it with elaborate covert cyber operations and, despite Russia's military might, asymmetrical paramilitary actions to assert Russian strategic objectives internationally. In so doing, he has shown himself to be an effective and bold tactical thinker who is willing to take risks that the aging Soviets were unprepared to take before the collapse of the Soviet Union. Although Russia is no longer a communist state, Putin's efforts to centralize Russian governing power in his hands and exert influence abroad, wherever he can, have created an environment in which he, as a single person, holds more power than any one Russian leader other than Stalin during the Cold War struggle.

This tactical reliance on Cold War objectives has given his actions the veneer of strategic thinking. Putin seemingly has been successful in exerting power around the world in recent years, despite Russia's diminished post-Soviet territorial and economic base. But the world has changed dramatically since the Cold War, and with some perspective we can see Putin's actions as extremely risky. They resuscitate a tired Cold War strategy, this time based on authoritarian nationalism, which ultimately predestines a perpetual struggle between Russia and the United States, NATO, China, and many of its neighbors. The long-term negative implications of many of his "bold" actions do not bode well for his top-priority objectives of reducing Russian isolation on the international stage and undermining Western democracy.

A First Glimpse at Red

Our current predicament is not the first time Russia has made strategic intelligence gains under the radar of U.S. policy makers or exploited the openness of our democratic system of government for its advantage. Indeed, the echoes of history are particularly resonant today.

In the middle of the last century, after the end of World War II, it took the United States considerable time to fully register the degree and intensity of the Soviet threat to U.S. and Western security, especially domestically. Having long been focused on Nazi Germany and Japan, we did not perceive our purported ally as a strategic adversary.

However, following the 1939 Molotov-Ribbentrop Pact of nonaggression between the Soviet Union and Nazi Germany our perception of Russian intentions took a marked turn. And it then took a series of revelations—over nearly a decade—about Soviet spying within the United States to compel the government to see the need for cultivating a political intelligence capability that focused on Soviet ambitions.

Important disclosures that changed our perception included confessions from Whittaker Chambers and Elizabeth Bentley.[7] They and others, most notably Alger Hiss, had been spying for the Soviet Union for years.[8] These penetrations were discovered just as intelligence was emerging from the Venona Project, which decoded encrypted wartime Soviet cables indicating that "illegals," or Soviet deep-cover spies, were operating abroad without any sort of diplomatic cover and that the Soviets had targeted some key U.S. military and scientific development programs, notably the Manhattan Project.[9] The scope of Soviet penetration in the United States was dizzying. It is estimated that as many as five hundred people spied in some capacity for the Soviet Union throughout the 1940s and 1950s.[10]

Concurrent to these revelations, across the pond the British too were coming to terms with their own penetrations from within the closed world of Britain's privileged class. The treachery of the Cambridge Five spies—Anthony Blunt, Guy Burgess, John Cairncross, Donald Maclean, and Kim Philby—was jarring for not just British sensibilities but for its national security implications.

The legacy of their treason is stunning, particularly that of the infamous turncoat, Philby. Philby—previously head of Britain's Secret Intelligence Service (SIS) anti-Soviet section and the presumptive heir to the role of "C," or head of British intelligence—had passed highly sensitive information to the Soviets for years, including while serving as head of the SIS anti-Soviet section. Burgess provided key insights into the West's Korean War strategy. And it was Maclean who in the summer of 1941 provided his Soviet handler with the Maude Report, which was a British intelligence summary of all that was known on the German atomic weapons program. As legendary CIA spymaster and Soviet expert Burton Gerber emphasized, "Stalin had it before

Roosevelt! And directed his intelligence chief Lavrenti Beria to penetrate the American/British program."[11] But perhaps the most enduring
damage, also inflicted by Maclean, was the sharing of delicate correspondence between Roosevelt and Churchill, thus undermining the
British and U.S. strategic posture ahead of the 1945 Yalta Conference.[12]

Maclean's material, along with Hiss's access to policy secrets through
his advisory role for Roosevelt at Yalta, empowered Stalin by giving
him key insights into just how far the Allies were prepared to go in
accommodating the Soviets. Most critics even now see the Yalta agreement as a sell-out to the Russians. By failing to see the threat clearly
and having underdeveloped intelligence and counterintelligence capabilities, the United States and Britain allowed a Soviet spy to represent
the West in the delicate negotiations that would establish the postwar
geopolitical structure of Europe.

The Alger Hiss and Cambridge Five affairs were transformational
moments in the American and British collective conscience about the
possibility of Soviet infiltration in Western society and the devastating
effects such penetrations have. In a similar manner the 2016 hacking
of the U.S. presidential campaign may well go down in history as this
generation's moment of awakening to the reality of Russian spying. As
more and more information emerges about the unrelenting Russian
recruitment efforts across all sectors of American society, from members of the Trump campaign to the National Rifle Association (NRA)
to low-level political operatives on the right and left, it is worth bear-
ing in mind that the Russians may have such high-level spies in our
government today, just as they had during the Cold War.

While there are stark parallels to our current situation, unlike the
period just after World War II, today we have formidable intelligence
capabilities. But the focus of our intelligence agencies and the tradecraft skills that underpin them have been redirected largely toward
counterterrorism and, more recently, in support of our military engagements abroad. We need another major shift to recalibrate our intelligence priorities, which is happening, albeit slowly.

The cost the anticommunist witch hunt known as the Red Scare
exacted on the public trust was perhaps nearly as damaging as the

spying itself. In February 1950 Senator Joseph McCarthy of Wisconsin, the Red Scare's chief architect, made his famous and controversial speech claiming he had a list of 205 members of the Communist Party who were "working and shaping policy" in the State Department. He also alleged that the CIA was crawling with communists. Although he was never able to substantiate most of his claims and was eventually censured by the Senate, for more than five years McCarthy created an atmosphere of fear among government employees, members of the entertainment industry, labor activists, and members of the general public. He played his accusations out in the press and the court of public opinion. Much of what he alleged in specific cases was unfounded, and he was eventually discredited, which led to a decline that contributed to his premature death. But he wasn't wrong about Russian intelligence aggressively working to penetrate our government, just as it is today.

The media spectacles revolving around Hiss and McCarthy obfuscated the real peril presented by the Soviet Union. The politicization of the Russian interference in the 2016 U.S. elections has a similar risk of preventing us from effectively addressing the real threats posed by Russia while also distracting us from shoring up the integrity of and public trust in our foundational democratic institutions at home.

Indeed, we must not overestimate Russia's ability. Soberly assessing its interference and capabilities as well as its fundamental weaknesses is an essential exercise if we are to properly respond. Lastly, counterintelligence is a very slow process that includes targeting, recruiting, and vetting sources and information, giving attention to even the smallest minutiae of evidence, challenging prevailing assumptions, and recognizing threats—all work that is best done behind the scenes. Strident public accusations shed little light on the actual threat. Today, as in the early 1950s, there are real espionage threats, and they are best addressed rigorously and discreetly until resolved.

Deep Roots

To understand what the Russians are up to today, it is instructive to look at the formation and development of its intelligence services and understand how formally entrenched the intelligence function has been in Russian leadership circles for at least two centuries.

In contrast to the fledgling American intelligence posture after World War II, secret intelligence has deep roots in Russia, where there is a long history of spying organizations thoroughly embedded within government. Russia's tsars relied heavily on security organizations to keep them informed about treachery and plotting within the royal court and to keep an eye on dissidents and foreign representatives. One of the most notorious of these security organizations was the Okhrana, a secret police force established in 1886 and largely focused on tracking trade unions and revolutionaries. Its primary mission, however, was to prevent assassination attempts against the tsar, of which there were many. It is no surprise that when the Bolshevik Revolution erupted in 1917 following the ouster of Tsar Nikolai II, Lenin set up his own spy group. His Vacheka, or "Cheka," would later become the NKVD.[13] Its power and size dwarfed any intelligence apparatus that the tsars had used up to that time. The most infamous NKVD chief and spymaster, Felix Dzerzhinsky, was a hardened revolutionary who had spent several years in prison and on the run from the tsar's secret police. He was an authentic "hero" of the revolution and a strong ally of Lenin.

In the aftermath of the Bolshevik Revolution, Dzerzhinsky ran the intelligence service with an iron hand, and he thus acquired the nickname "Iron Felix." His intelligence service was responsible for indiscriminately arresting, torturing, imprisoning, and sometimes killing many thousands of Russians. At the same time, tens of thousands were put into forced labor camps, which were later consolidated under a formal nationwide system of infamous camps known as gulags. Nobel Prize–winning author Alexandr Solzhenitsyn would later write several works describing the incredible hardships of his eight years in the gulags.[14]

In 1924, after Stalin consolidated power following Lenin's death, he raised the bar even higher in repressing opposition, real and perceived, resulting in unprecedented levels of violence, including mass executions and the robust expansion of the gulags. Stalin had three intelligence chiefs—Genrikh Yagoda, Nikolai Yezhov, and Lavrenti Beria—spymasters who orchestrated bloody purges at his behest. His third head of intelligence, the Georgian party boss Beria, is renowned for a reign of terror that surpassed Dzerzhinsky's. Even the Kremlin's inner circle acknowledged that Beria was an irrepressible rapist and personally committed many other violent transgressions against his prisoners.

During a 1991 trip to Moscow on an official visit to meet with the KGB leadership, I had the eerie experience of staying as a guest of the KGB in one of Beria's many dachas. Sleeping there made me wonder just how many gruesome crimes had been committed within its walls in prior years of state-sponsored brutality. It's a stark reminder of the dark roots of the KGB. Like many ruthless intelligence chiefs, Beria met a violent death himself when he was on the losing side of Khrushchev's political maneuvering in the aftermath of Stalin's death in 1953. He was unceremoniously executed by a firing squad. If history teaches us anything, it is that tyrants and their strongmen should always have an escape plan because when their governments fall, their leaders invariably are sent to the chopping block. Finally, in 1954 the Soviet intelligence apparatus was reorganized, and the NKVD was renamed the KGB. It, along with the GRU (Soviet military intelligence), became the main adversary of the CIA throughout the Cold War.

The KGB, unlike the CIA (its modern U.S. counterpart), was a quasi-military service with responsibility for both external and internal intelligence operations. It also maintained a sizable paramilitary force set up for special operations, both outside and within the Soviet Union. What's more, the KGB had sweeping responsibility for guarding the international borders and providing executive protection for top government officials. In a way, the KGB was imbued with the combined responsibilities of the CIA, FBI, Secret Service, Border Patrol, and Special Forces. These responsibilities were all lumped together, resulting in a mammoth and very powerful intelligence organization.

With such extraordinary power, the KGB inherited a robust culture of fear, violence, and meddling in internal political affairs, a situation that endures to this day. This is different than the CIA, with its international focus. The CIA has always been barred from being involved in internal American politics and was never feared broadly by the American people, in large part because it doesn't have law enforcement authority to arrest or to interrogate citizens. The rigorous application of the rule of law in the United States also kept the CIA—with a few exceptions that will be discussed later—from engaging in domestic issues.

Americans have rightfully been concerned about U.S. intelligence organizations accruing too much power. Consequently, we have structured a strong legal system to keep our intelligence institutions out of internal political affairs. By contrast, the KGB was its own independent power center inside the country and played a very important role in every Kremlin power shift since its creation. Moreover—though it was reorganized and renamed first FSK then FSB for internal intelligence and SVR for external intelligence—in sum and substance the KGB endured relatively unscathed even after the fall of the Soviet Union. And of course the rise of Putin seems a fitting culmination of Russian intelligence power—power that migrated with Putin, the former KGB operative and former head of the FSB, into the position of head of the Russian state.

When I visited Russia in June 1991 as a guest of the KGB, I managed to have a photo taken with the then-head of KGB counterintelligence, with the Dzerzhinsky monument in the background. It was a moment of great historical flux. After nearly fifty years of the Cold War, everything in Russia was about to change. As the shifting political sands were apparent, the CIA decided to warm up its relationship with the KGB. The only safe topic to talk about with the Russians was the drug war, so we were seeking their possible cooperation on this front. Milt Bearden, who was chief of the CIA's Soviet Division, asked if I, then-director of the Counter Narcotics Center, would go to Russia with him to meet with the KGB leadership. Bearden and I arrived in Moscow in June 1991, only a few months before the collapse of the Gorbachev government. I was supposed to meet with KGB chair Vladimir Kryuchkov, but he was "called away" at the last minute, and I met instead with his deputy, who was cordial and professional.

I wasn't surprised by the last-minute change and didn't read anything into it at the time. Little did I know the KGB leadership was in the throes of plotting a coup and that Kryuchkov was busy trying to build support for it. Nevertheless, we spent a few days in Russia and were accompanied everywhere by several of the KGB's most senior officers. They seemed relaxed and showed no visible sign of tension about the political situation in Moscow. However, I did pick up on the restiveness of the citizenry and their seeming lack of fear of the KGB credential that was flashed on occasion during our travel.

It is interesting to note that at least one of these officers was a very senior intelligence official who was deeply involved in running the Ames and Hanssen spy cases. Although I didn't know that at the time, during our visit he no doubt concealed a knowing smirk about how much damage had been and continued to be done by these traitors within the CIA and the FBI. I feel I had the last laugh, though, as it was this man's KGB, perhaps the most resolute actor in the Cold War, that weeks later hastened the inevitable collapse of the Soviet Union.

U.S. intelligence sources in Moscow learned of the coup plot ahead of time, allowing Washington to give Gorbachev three warnings, one delivered to him directly by President George H. W. Bush during the summer of 1991. However, Gorbachev remained sanguine and confident. KGB chief Kryuchkov launched his coup attempt over three days in August 1991, seeking to wrest power from Gorbachev and squelch his reform platform. But the coup was thwarted by a civil uprising and ended up emboldening reformists and a restive populace, thus weakening the Communist Party and ultimately destabilizing the Soviet Union. Days after the affair was brought to a close, the statue of Dzerzhinsky was felled by an angry crowd. Pictures of the desecrated figure became some of the most iconic images of the end of the Cold War.[15]

The failed putsch led by Kryuchkov sounded the death knell for the Soviet Union. It is fitting perhaps that in my role as a senior CIA official I was there as a witness to the last hours of Dzerzhinsky's edifice. It is deeply ironic that though Kryuchkov was sent to prison along with the other coup plotters, save one, the KGB itself was one of the only surviving entities in Russia.[16] And in fact, the surviving plotters were all eventually amnestied. Although it was reorganized and renamed, the KGB is one of the few enduring institutions in Russia.

Following the failed coup, FBI agent-turned Soviet mole Robert Hanssen's KGB handlers did everything they could to reassure him that they—the KGB—were still operational. Hanssen's KGB handlers wrote him in October, "There have been many important developments in our country lately. So many that we'd like to reassure you once again. Like we said: we've done all in order that none of those events ever affects your security and our ability to maintain the operation with you."[17]

Although Hanssen eventually went silent for most of the decade, the KGB was true to its word. It kept operating unabashedly as communism crumbled and a new Russia emerged. And once Hanssen did recontact them in 1999, he was able to resume standing communications and the use of dead drops—hiding places in public spaces such as the base of lampposts, under stairways, or behind fences, where one person drops off the information and another person collects it at a later time—with his Russian contacts without a hitch.

Today's SVR and GRU are the latest incarnations of this enduring legacy of a Russian spy apparatus that has outlasted many rulers and systems of government. It is not insignificant that today Putin personally is trying to restore the legacy of the hard-line KGB leaders, including Dzerzhinsky and Beria. Indeed, his strongman image and nostalgia about the greatness of Stalinist and Soviet Russia do much to reveal his personal ambitions and intentions for Russia.

LESSON TWO

Intelligence is a critical lever of foreign policy.

There is nothing more necessary than good intelligence to
frustrate a designing enemy, and nothing that requires
greater pains to obtain.

—GEORGE WASHINGTON, letter to Robert Hunter Morris, January 1, 1756

2

Shaping and Reshaping the CIA

Only when the United States eventually came to see the Soviet threat as truly formidable and existential was our government able to make the huge cultural shift needed to create the CIA. Until the World War II era there was no institutional belief that the United States might need an intelligence capability beyond what was needed for military engagements. Even after the CIA was created, it took significant time for the FBI and the nascent CIA to develop counterintelligence expertise. There are important parallels between this period of time and today, when the traditional mandate of intelligence has been blurred and its function and reliability called into question.

In contrast to the long tradition of Russian intelligence, the CIA did not even exist until 1947. As the Iron Curtain began to descend on Europe, President Harry Truman quickly set out a policy to address emergent political realities and allow the United States to assume its leadership role on the global stage through the Truman Doctrine. Among other things, the 1947 National Security Act created the CIA as a civilian agency whose two principal missions were to spy and to engage in covert action to block our adversaries.[1] The CIA built off the remnants of William "Wild Bill" Donovan's Office of Strategic Services (OSS), which was the clandestine and paramilitary arm of the U.S. government during World War II. The CIA was designed to be a counterweight to the Soviet military and foreign intelligence agencies, the GRU and the NKVD, which had been actively involved for years in spying and encouraging insurgency against Western interests.

To counter Soviet aggression in Europe after Stalin successfully set up pro-Moscow regimes in Romania, Bulgaria, and Poland, Truman supported the Greek government in suppressing communist rebels there. He also bolstered Turkey and Iran in rejecting greater Soviet influence in their countries. Most important, Truman relied heavily on the CIA to block the Communist Party of Italy from coming to power in the 1948 Italian elections. It is possible that if the Communist Party had prevailed in that election, Italy would have moved into Moscow's orbit, providing the Soviets with an excellent platform for further penetrations into Europe. The covert action playbook used in the Italian elections—a combination of financial support for opposition parties and interest groups, as well as the mobilization of a national propaganda campaign—became for years the CIA blueprint on how to run political campaigns on foreign territory.[2]

In 1950 former army general Walter Bedell Smith, President Dwight Eisenhower's chief of staff during World War II, was put in charge of the CIA. He was a strong figure who also had the benefit of Truman's trust to keep a firm hand on the CIA. Allen Dulles, widely acknowledged in Washington as the most experienced, knowledgeable, and well-connected WWII spy veteran, secured the post of deputy director of the Plans Directorate (now National Clandestine Service) to take charge of all of the agency's worldwide spying and covert operations.[3] As the agency's first spymaster, Dulles arguably had the best assignment in CIA, and one I inherited many years later.

Dulles had joined the OSS during World War II and worked as chief of station in Bern, Switzerland, then a hotbed of clandestine operational activity by Allies and Germans alike. Dulles gained a reputation as a flamboyant operator who liked to move in high-class, politically powerful circles, where he was renowned for his gift as a raconteur. Mostly this style worked in his favor, but sometimes it clouded his judgment. According to long-standing agency lore, as a young diplomat and de facto resident intelligence officer in Switzerland during World War I, Dulles purportedly blew an opportunity to meet Bolshevik leader Vladimir Lenin in Switzerland before Lenin returned to Petrograd (St. Petersburg) to foment the 1917 revolution. The version that I heard most often was that Dulles turned down Lenin's call because he was "entertaining" two blond Swedish tennis players. Former CIA director Dick Helms notes that the most reliable version came directly from Dulles, who told Helms he was playing tennis with an attractive female partner and didn't want to be interrupted by a relatively unknown Russian.[4] That misjudgment might have altered history.

During Dulles's time, the Operations Directorate was sharply divided between those who felt the true role of the agency was espionage (Office of Special Operations, or OSO) and those who pushed for political and paramilitary covert action (Office of Policy Coordination, or OPC, which reported to the State Department, not the CIA, until 1950). One side favored the patient cultivation of sources and the other, the decisive use of covert action. The rivalry was so intense that in long-standing agency lore the OPC station in Thailand once kidnapped an OSO communicator to keep OSO from reporting an OPC screw-up. Consolidating them under the Operations Directorate was an inspired and effective solution that gave them common cause and put the two approaches at the service of one another but did not eliminate the tension. When I joined the agency in the late 1960s, the espionage group came to dominate the directorate and its culture, but with the country on a constant war footing today the pendulum has swung in favor of paramilitary intelligence. I suspect such oscillation will continue in response to world events and the proclivities of agency and White House leadership.

Along with Allen Dulles, the Operations Directorate's original leadership consisted of a group of talented and entrepreneurial veterans of the OSS. The CIA's "founding fathers"—Frank Wisner Sr., Desmond Fitzgerald, Tracy Barnes, Kermit "Kim" Roosevelt, James Angleton, Richard Helms, and Richard Bissell (who was not former OSS but was nonetheless a key member of this cohort)—were among the many who built the CIA and its operational programs. A key binding ingredient among them was their unbridled "can do" spirit that shaped the OSS ethos of running bold and high-risk operations during WWII. This ethos became the cornerstone of the CIA culture. The agency's founding generation was coming off the bloodiest war in history, with tens of millions of deaths and casualties. Their appetite for risk and quick action was forged in the crucible of WWII. The world was more accustomed then to military and intelligence forces taking heavy casualties in confrontations against the enemy.

These experienced operators constructed the unique culture and craft of intelligence. Many of them were anglophiles, had Ivy League educations, and came from the upper echelon of East Coast society. They were also emboldened by their successes in WWII and deeply motivated by their mission. This confidence led to an ésprit de corps that was determined, creative, and somewhat uninhibited. There was no task too intractable and no risk too perilous. They were young—most of these officers were in their thirties and early forties—with only a couple of years of experience in learning and plying the tradecraft skills of espionage and covert action and no experience in running a large and complex intelligence agency. Still, they managed to turn the CIA into the most effective and sophisticated intelligence organization in U.S. history.

Their success was facilitated by the fact that they and their spouses were very much part of the "Georgetown Set"—the Washington elite of the 1950s and 1960s—which included the likes of Secretary of State Dean Acheson, *Washington Post* publisher Philip Graham, and a renowned mix of journalists and foreign policy experts like Stewart Alsop, Joseph Alsop, Walter Rostow, James Reston, Paul Nitze, Clark Clifford, Averell Harriman, George Kennan, and David Bruce. The benefits of this cozy elite relationship among media personalities, policy wonks, and intelligence operatives created a unique environment for policy debates and streamlined negotiations and decision-making. It is in this environment that the CIA was created and its leadership selected. And because of their relative youth, these early leaders were to stay in positions of power and play key roles in CIA for the next twenty-five years.

When I arrived at the agency in 1967, the Georgetown Set was still running strong, but as with similar power groupings in history, it was not sustainable and had ended by the early 1970s. Over the years the chasm between Georgetown and Langley grew wider, and there is nothing that has resembled the Georgetown Set since then, especially as far as the CIA is concerned. Long before I arrived at the CIA's seventh floor (policy-level offices), the CIA was no longer networked deeply among the political elite in Washington. While the CIA directors are included on important guest lists for their inside knowledge and their novelty factor, they are rarely part of the elite Washington DC political network. Moreover, it is particularly difficult to imagine a similar Georgetown Set in today's polarized and dysfunctional Washington political environment. We are all the worse off for this void.[5]

Because I held the post, I often wondered how Dulles, part of this Georgetown Set, spent his time as operations director and how different the job might have been back then. Communications were unquestionably more rudimentary and slower paced, so more of the operational decision-making by necessity had to take place in the field, far away from the cumbersome Washington coordination process. Also, the chain of command and organizational structure was much smaller and tighter, both inside and outside the agency. I'm probably fantasizing that Dulles was tied less to his desk than I was. When I had Dulles's job, the world I knew seemed to be a whirlwind of meetings and nonstop decisions on everything from minor personnel disputes to the use of force. My best guess is that the substance of the position didn't change much over the years, but the process and pace have become more laden with bureaucracy. However, without doubt, both then and now it is the most consequential job in the Western spy world.

Nonetheless, I have a hunch many of these early leaders and their operations would have a hard time adapting in today's intelligence world, with its rigorous regulations and limitations. Moreover, they would have had grave difficulties in facing the lessened appetite for regime change using covert action. In today's world we seem to be much more inclined to rely on overt military solutions, as in the case of Iraq, Afghanistan, Syria, and Libya. Still, even without a homogenous cohort like the Georgetown Set and a more convoluted state of world affairs than the post–WWII order, it will take a similar political will to recalibrate the way we must.

An Evolving CIA

To understand how we have come to such a critical moment for intelligence services, it is helpful to look at how the role and actions of the CIA evolved. While it took the United States a while to discern the threat from the Soviet Union, once we did we were almost single-mindedly focused on it. The CIA got off to a running start. From an espionage point of view, during the 1950s the United States needed to clear the deck of legacy spies in our midst, which we were able to do by the end of that decade. And the agency played to its strengths, having the many OSS veterans in its ranks engaging in a series of covert actions in Iran and Guatemala that were highly effective in containing the Soviet Union. These initial successes had the unfortunate effect of muddling our perception of some of the limitations to engaging in covert action, and at the beginning of the 1960s the CIA dove head-long into the Bay of Pigs fiasco without hesitation. Fortunately, before long we were able to recover and prevail in the Cuban Missile Crisis, in large part thanks to Soviet intelligence assets who had started to come our way. With that, the agency began the formidable exercise of forging tradecraft and intelligence asset management capabilities.

Throughout the 1960s, 1970s, and 1980s our intelligence actions against the Soviets could be described as those of dueling banjos. We had traitors among us, and they had defectors who came to us. We recruited extraordinary assets and lost many of the most valuable ones. We had highly successful intelligence covert actions and a few spectacular failures. While activities in Europe along the Iron Curtain were central to our focus, as were actions behind the curtain itself, every action in Africa, the Middle East, Asia, and Latin America was couched in the binary terms of an existential zero-sum game against the Soviets. In fact, throughout the Cold War our struggle against the Soviets, as well as our containment policy, was central to everything we did. It was during this time that we began to struggle with the nuances and art of counterintelligence, especially with regard to enemies within our midst. Some of the most important and emblematic cases of this cloak-and-dagger battle will be explored in the coming pages, which will relate a clear prescription on how best to understand and counter Russia's current intelligence assault. Indeed, to Putin it is still an existential zero-sum game, and he will deploy the needed resources to meet his ends.

When the Berlin Wall fell in November 1989, it marked a symbolic end to the Soviet system. For a brief period it seemed that the power and influence of the United States would go virtually unchallenged. Our intelligence focus was quickly redirected away from the former Soviet Union and toward emergent transnational issues like counternarcotics and counterterrorism.

Soon most of us in the CIA pivoted to a new sort of innovation in tactical intelligence collection—targeting and analysis in the spheres of narcotics, nuclear proliferation, terrorism, and digital/cyber security. It was a time of refocusing and soul searching about our mission.

In 1990 I served as one of the first heads of the Counter Narcotics Center (CNC), created by then-CIA director William Webster to focus largely on this type of tactical targeting and analysis. These were the first days of linkage analysis and big data. I spent a good deal of my CNC time working to break up the Colombian cartels and rooting out their leadership, especially the notorious drug trafficker Pablo Escobar, who was eventually killed in 1993.

These years were a very difficult time for the agency, and several factors combined to relax its stance against a seemingly defeated opponent. While the CIA played a significant role in winning the Cold War, morale sagged as it came to an end and its overriding sense of mission dissipated. The agency's budgets and personnel were drastically cut, and the revelation of the treason of Aldrich Ames hit the agency hard, leaving a great deal of recrimination, bitterness, and self-doubt. This was amplified by a persistent and oversized congressional and media assault on the agency. Everyone seemed to simultaneously lose perspective on the spying business and the reality that having traitors inside intelligence organizations goes with the territory and is virtually unavoidable, best defensive efforts notwithstanding. These circumstances dovetailed into a flagging sense of mission, especially when it came to Russia, which led to a strategic disadvantage in the future.

The U.S.-Russia "intelligence game" took on an extra layer of complexity with the fall of the Soviet Union. A flood of information, resources, and people poured over to the West. The iron veil of secrecy fell, upending long-standing truths. We would learn quickly of traitors in our midst—not only Aldrich Ames but other Russian spies within the FBI and CIA, including Earl Edwin Pitts and Harold James Nicholson, respectively.

While these former Soviet volunteers represented a treasure trove of intelligence for us, our focus had shifted away from Russia, and these intelligence opportunities were either not fully exploited for their strategic value or turned away. We didn't develop the wealth of potential sources who came our way and thus missed a golden opportunity to construct a bulwark of intelligence against a resurgent powerful adversary. But U.S. policy makers failed to foresee and prepare for Russia's inevitable regeneration. This strategic shortfall is felt more acutely today as we try to make sense of what Special Counsel Robert Mueller called Russia's "sweeping and systematic" interference in the 2016 election and to reposition our intelligence posture more effectively against Russia. It's hard to say how many more assets we could have had in place had we handled this differently and how we might be better poised to counter Putin's cyber assaults on our political process and defense industry, as well as his aggressive incursions abroad.

In this context I recall a conversation with Robert Gates, when he was CIA director under President George W. Bush, that resonates still today when contemplating Russia. We were sitting across from one another in the agency's senior executive dining room. I was serving as chief of the Latin American Division at the time, and we had a lively discussion about the fall of the Soviet Union and the likelihood that the KGB would inevitably return to power and influence. We shared the view that it could come as soon as the next five years because of Russia's lack of a democratic history or deep parliamentary roots. We agreed this would be the formidable challenge that future Russian leaders would have to overcome to make Russia into a genuine democracy. Sadly, while it took a few years longer than that for Putin to fashion himself into an autocrat and for the KGB/FSB to solidify its key position in the bureaucracy once again, the Russian democratic experiment failed. While I don't know if Gates ever wavered in his view, for my part there were moments early on when I thought a democratic, new Russia might prevail. But those moments didn't last long, and today we must live with the results of this failure.

Both inside and outside the CIA there was a loss of a sense of urgency and a corresponding sense of purpose. Both the Clinton and then the Bush administration and the Congresses during each lacked the appetite for the policy focus and budget required to address "big power" adversaries under the prevailing American hegemonic paradigm. They were more driven and interested in pursuing stateless and rogue-state asymmetrical threats—terrorism, drugs, and counterproliferation.

I observed firsthand the irresistible draw of these targets when I was named the associate deputy director of operations (ADDO) and not long thereafter the acting deputy director of the Operations Directorate, in 1995.

A New Age of Espionage

It is not insignificant that Comrade J's revelations were only just beginning to make their way through American policy and intelligence circles when the 9/11 terrorist attacks occurred. From that moment on, the CIA would have the lead intelligence role in combating terrorism, and the overall mission would be to destroy al-Qaeda and then ISIS. This is where the political leadership and the American people wanted to place their national security bet. Any prospect of a significant refocus on Russia was lost in the havoc. The fighting largely would be a combined effort of the CIA and our armed forces on the battlefield abroad, and that effort has resulted in relying more heavily on tactical intelligence collection and paramilitary action.

Sitting in New York City, working in private sector intelligence, I missed the full import of the October 2002 congressional authorization for President Bush to use military force, as he "deemed necessary," if Saddam Hussein didn't come to terms with us on his alleged weapons of mass destruction (WMDs). The joint resolution, however, also went on to say that it "supported and encouraged diplomatic efforts" to resolve the situation.[6] I wrongly assumed Congress was giving the president this approval to strengthen his hand in putting pressure on Saddam Hussein and that the UN inspectors would be allowed to complete their mission to find any WMDs before force would be used. That turned out not to be the case. The Bush administration moved immediately into war preparation mode. The consequences of this action have had a gigantic and detrimental impact on our foreign policy and our national security ever since, including the reduced emphasis on Russian (and Chinese) targets.

The wars that followed 9/11, in Afghanistan and then Iraq, resulted in the loss of more than four thousand U.S. troops and immeasurable casualties, as well as hundreds of thousands Iraqi dead, millions of refugees, and the conflagration of Syria and instability elsewhere. The paramilitary requirements needed to support a protracted struggle in Afghanistan and Iraq, as well as Libya and Syria, significantly altered the mission, culture, and mind-set of the CIA, including its recruiting, training, assignments, and leadership. That was an almost inevitable outcome of confronting two wars for so long.

Meanwhile, Russia remained doggedly focused on reversing the greatest losses it suffered at the end of the Cold War—its territorial influence and the opportunities to undermine the institutions that challenge it, most importantly NATO and the Western democracies. It kept as its centerpiece a strategic focus on the United States as a target, as it had throughout the Cold War.

Our intelligence investment in Russian targets is still not as robust proportionally as Russia's is against us, and it is not at the level it ought to be. Russia's resources, strategic focus, and tactics have remained unabated since the end of the Cold War. And Russian determination to subvert key American and Western institutions has gained momentum through the power of technological advances.

Furthermore, polarization in our national politics is more acute than it has been in decades, which is constraining our ability to respond effectively to Russian aggression. We should not allow policy positions to be informed by party politics at either extreme when what we need is balanced, bipartisan approval for dealing with Putin's aggressive cyber operations against the United States. This polarization in Washington hampers U.S. capacity to effectively confront Russia in a new arena—internet-facilitated election interference. Russia has developed an innovative approach to a decades-old struggle, and our intelligence services need solid, bipartisan policy support to adapt and counter it.

Now that we have evidence of Russian penetrations and attempted penetrations in U.S. political, military, business, technical, media, and financial circles, we must recalibrate our strategic response to Russia and our intelligence posture to support it. Our current strategic shortfall will not be quickly remedied. As was the case at the beginning of the Cold War, today we are behind in grasping the depth of the Russian intelligence penetration. This is not to suggest that nothing has been done about Russia; on the contrary there are major programs within the U.S. government and transnational institutions aimed at combating malign Russian activities. What is important, though, is to recognize that the threat posed by Russian actions has been subjugated by a plethora of other threats. It is essential to refocus our attention on Russia and other "big power" adversaries like China as our most threatening rivals and respond strongly, which is now feasible as we reduce our military involvement in Afghanistan and the Middle East.

LESSON THREE

The ambition and ingenuity of Russian intelligence operations are unrelenting.

The heart and soul of the Soviet intelligence was subversion.
Not intelligence collection, but subversion: active
measures to weaken the West.

—Retired Soviet general and spymaster OLEG KALUGIN

3

A Study in Russian Spycraft

Active Interference

It is clear that Russia interfered in the 2016 U.S presidential election in order to "provoke and amplify political and social discord in the United States."[1] The tactics Russia has employed to do so included disinformation, cyber hacking, influence campaigns, and aggressive efforts to establish ties with U.S. political players. The attack on the U.S. election was a multifaceted effort designed to maintain a plausible measure of deniability. It played on existing societal fissures, and we must take it seriously.

As early as the summer of 2014, Dutch intelligence cyber operatives successfully penetrated the Russian hacker group Cozy Bear and observed their cyber attacks, which were launched out of a university building next to Red Square in Moscow. The Dutch observed Cozy Bear hacking into the U.S. State Department and the White House. With access to their computer network and, more important, their security cameras, the Dutch observed members of the SVR physically directing Cozy Bear's activities in perpetrating these attacks. On both occasions the Dutch alerted their U.S. intelligence counterparts, who were able to deploy sophisticated countermeasures and disrupt what was characterized at the time as the most sophisticated and aggressive cyber attack to date on the U.S. government.

Then in 2015 the Democratic National Committee (DNC), the Democratic Congressional Campaign Committee, and the presidential campaign of Hillary Clinton were attacked by both Cozy Bear and its GRU correlate, Fancy Bear. As we now know, the success of that attack has had severe and wide-ranging consequences.[2] In 2016 the data retrieved from the DNC hack were released by the GRU-created sites DCLeaks and Guccifer 2.0, and later by WikiLeaks, at critical moments during the U.S. presidential campaign, notably on the first day of the Democratic National Convention.[3]

Also, according to the indictment issued by Special Counsel Robert Mueller, Russia's Internet Research Agency (IRA) directed an influence campaign toward the United States. The IRA is a purportedly independent research group working out of St. Petersburg and run by Yevgeny V. Prigozhin, a close ally of President Vladimir Putin often called "Putin's Cook." These Russian state proxies ran the 2016 influence campaign, known as Project Lakhta, together with an internal department at IRA known as the "Translator" department. Project Lakhta allegedly used stolen American identities to create social media accounts, promote rallies, and purchase ads on social media.

IRA operatives even posed as American activists when they traveled to the United States to conduct field research. The IRA is essentially an internet "troll factory," where divisive and provocative material is created and then posted and shared thousands and thousands of times via automated computer programs (called "bots") across all major social media platforms. The IRA created 470 Facebook sites and 129 event pages designed to impersonate American political organizations or initiatives. These bots made the inflammatory posts exponentially more effective by ensuring that they were seen by as many people as possible. In the end approximately 80,000 divisive political posts on Facebook were shared millions of times and reinforced by 2,752 Twitter accounts and more than 1,000 YouTube videos. The Facebook posts alone are estimated to have reached at least 29 million U.S. persons and "may have reached an estimated 126 million people."[4] The posts sought to exacerbate existing societal tensions and sometimes amplified content that originated from Americans themselves, including hashtags such as #HillaryDown after Hillary Clinton fell ill on September 11, 2016, or #WarAgainstDemocrats on Election Day. They were mainly against Hillary Clinton and in support of Donald Trump and, to a lesser extent, candidates Bernie Sanders and Jill Stein. Three thousand political ads were placed on Facebook by Russia or its prox-ies right before the election and promoted through 180 different Ins-tagram accounts.[5]

The operation went beyond deploying divisive social media mes-sages. From media reports, Special Counsel Mueller's indictment of Russian operatives on July 13, 2018, and the first section of the Senate Intelligence Committee's report on the 2016 Russian election inter-ference, we know that GRU officers probed and penetrated election infrastructure at the state and local levels in all fifty U.S. states, begin-ning in at least 2014 and carrying into at least 2017. The agents gained access to election websites, voter registration systems, and voter look-up systems through spear phishing emails. Importantly, the indictment concluded that these measures did not affect voter tallies or election results. The Senate report concludes that these efforts were most likely reconnaissance efforts for possible future interference.

In October 2018 the Counterintelligence and Export Control Sec-tion of the Justice Department's National Security Division indicted Elena Khusyaynova for attempted interference in the 2018 election. From that indictment and other reports we know that Russia's social media campaign strategy is continuing to evolve and is well funded. Notably, bot accounts are becoming more difficult to detect, as they are being managed by a combination of coding and human intervention, which makes them seem more like real people, and the Russians are quickly learning how to effectively orchestrate social networks' algo-rithms.[6] They are also adapting quickly to evolving detection strategies. Confronted with social networks' stepped-up efforts to thwart Rus-sian misuse of their platforms, Russians have begun to enlist locals to set up accounts and buy existing accounts from locals to appear more authentic and escape detection.[7] Furthermore, press reports indicate that Russian troll social media accounts are becoming more subtle and effective at impersonating real candidates and advocacy groups.[8] Rus-sia's intelligence services are simultaneously disseminating disinforma-tion on the COVID-19 pandemic via legitimate-seeming websites with no clear links to Russia, and that information is picked up and ampli-fied, sometimes unwittingly, by sites that traffic in conspiracy theories.[9]

What is perhaps even more alarming is that according to these same sources, other strategic rivals of the United States—likely including China, Iran, and North Korea—are also seeking to engage in their own interference campaigns in our elections.

These efforts by Cozy Bear, Fancy Bear, and the IRA follow a Russian pattern of using Russian government intelligence agencies, third-party entities such as the IRA, and state-funded media such as the RT network and the newspaper *Kommersant* to advance foreign policy objectives. We know that they were mutually reinforcing in their efforts to sow confusion, exacerbate partisanship, and propagate distrust of media and democratic institutions.

The engagement of *aktivniye meropriyatiya*, or active measures, was a foundational tactic used by the KGB and its satellite intelligence arms to influence events. Active measures often took the form of influence campaigns employing disinformation and propaganda—fake documentaries, forgeries of U.S. government documents, promulgation of conspiracies, deliberate smear campaigns, and publication and dissemination of classified information, as well as the manipulation of it. The campaigns often involved entrapping, blackmailing, bribing, and intimidating people in positions of power. They were designed to obliquely, perniciously, and incrementally undermine the West, its freedoms, its system of government, its institutions, and its values during the Cold War.

Today these tactics are part and parcel of a Russian strategy that has been described as new generation warfare or hybrid war, and they represent a grave risk to our national security.[10] The "new" part of this strategy is the technological platforms that make many of Russia's efforts considerably more effective. But despite all the bombast and rebranding, this is not actually a new strategy. The underlying techniques have not changed since the beginning of the Cold War.

Russia had ample opportunity to hone its post–Cold War active measures approach by perfecting it for nearly two decades. Before targeting the U.S. elections, it deployed influence campaigns in Azerbaijan, Bulgaria, Estonia, Georgia, Hungary, Latvia, Lithuania, Montenegro, Serbia, Slovakia, and most especially Ukraine.

New Berlin

If Berlin and the Berlin Wall were considered the front line in the Cold War between Russia and the West, then today the crosshairs have moved farther east, to Kyiv, the capital of Ukraine. In December 2018 I traveled to Kyiv to help promote the publication of the Ukrainian edition of my book *Good Hunting*, which had gained traction there because its emphasis on the Cold War CIA-KGB covert action struggle is highly relevant to Russia's present-day intelligence efforts to undermine Ukraine's democracy and territorial sovereignty. Little did I know that Ukraine would take center stage in American politics in 2019.

As part of my book tour, and to collect new data for this book, I had several private, high-profile meetings with top policy and intelligence officials in the national security arena. These included the interior minister, the director of the Ukrainian equivalent of our National Security Council, high-ranking members of military intelligence, and Patriarch Filaret of the Ukrainian Orthodox Church. What emerged from these discussions was a distilled understanding of the extent to which Ukraine has become Russia's proving ground for aggressive military and covert political action—the front line in a new Cold War struggle with Russia. The common takeaway from each of these meetings was that U.S. military and intelligence support was badly needed to hold the line and that Ukrainians would "fight to the last man" to defend the country's sovereignty.

Although my trip was not political, it garnered considerable media attention, which spiked when it was leaked to the press that I had met with Patriarch Filaret, who awarded me the Ukrainian Orthodox Church's Saint Andrew Medal for my work at the CIA in defense of Western democracy. The leak falsely credited me with providing support for the ongoing schism between the Russian and Ukrainian Orthodox Churches, and the story was picked up and broadcast throughout Moscow and Kyiv. The Russians were pushing the bogus narrative that the CIA was behind the schism and that authorities in Kyiv wanted to portray themselves as partners with the CIA. My protestations that I was simply there on a book tour were drowned out in the uproar, which my agency friends found far more humorous than I did.

Everyone was reeling from the Russian capture of three Ukrainian ships in the Kerch Strait in a brazen attempt to gain control of the Sea of Azov. Of course this was just the most recent in a string of Russia's efforts to recover ideological and territorial influence over its border states. The most jarring example was of course the Russian annexation of Crimea and invasion of eastern Ukraine in 2014. But even before that there was a decade-long campaign of election interference, support for fringe political entities, and debilitating cyber attacks.

I came away from the trip with a much-heightened concern about Russian designs on Ukraine and the certainty that the Russians would use all their intelligence resources to gain the upper hand. The concern has more recently been sharpened with Ukraine's election of President Volodymyr Zelensky, whom insiders see as inexperienced and who could possibly make unnecessary concessions to Russia, including its de facto annexation of Crimea. U.S. intelligence officers have reportedly informed Congress that Russia conducted a disinformation campaign to deflect blame for meddling in U.S. elections in 2016, seeking to pin the accusations on Ukraine as the culprit instead of Russia.[11]

We know now that Russia began disseminating disinformation intended to undermine U.S.-Ukrainian relations through a network of high-profile Russians and Ukrainians as far back as 2017. Furthermore, Putin claimed in a February 2017 press conference that the Ukrainian government had been assisting Hillary Clinton's 2016 presidential campaign, in part through funding from friendly oligarchs.[12]

Dominance over Ukraine has for centuries been a top priority for Russian leaders, who understand that without Ukraine, Russia remains a far less powerful state.[13] If Russia's efforts to legitimize its de facto annexation of Crimea and strengthen its influence in Ukrainian politics are successful, the United States will be facing a much stronger adversary, one whose area of effective control expands along our NATO allies' borders. Consequently, Ukraine's political, military, and economic independence has enormous geopolitical significance for the ongoing struggle between Russia and the West.

Integral to its strategy is the effort to undermine Ukraine's democracy by using covert action initiatives, including "fake news," meant to exacerbate cleavages within Western political, religious, and social centers, as well as to subvert public confidence in cornerstone democratic institutions like a free press, elections, and diplomatic alliances. Russia is coupling these covert action efforts with robust intelligence collection activities to undermine this democratic government, and we need to be mindful of these intentions in our dealings with Russia.

In overseeing these covert actions, Putin seems not to recognize the progress the Ukrainian military and intelligence services have made with the support of Western allies in recent years. Ukraine forces have evolved to the point where they can "punch above their weight." The Trump administration's decision to introduce lethal support to U.S. military aid to Ukraine, especially the Javelin antitank weapons system, evokes parallels with the Milan antitank missile system that was introduced into the war in Afghanistan against the Russians in the mid-1980s. While its forces might not be able to repel a full-fledged Russian invasion, Ukraine, like the Afghans, could inflict considerable damage on the Russians and sustain a destructive campaign of resistance for many months, especially with logistical support from Western allies. This is an example showing that it is essential for the United States and European Union to continue to provide steadfast political, economic, and appropriate military support to Ukraine and to match Putin's escalations.

But Putin runs a great risk of underestimating the resolve of the Ukrainians to remain a free and independent people. Every place I traveled during my book tour, the same pledge was forcefully repeated: "We will never give in. We will fight to the last man."

Importantly, this also was the predominant sentiment expressed by the powerful Ukrainian Orthodox Church and Patriarch Filaret, who has emerged as the moral leader for the Ukrainian people in their struggle against Russia. In this deeply religious nation, the Ukrainian Orthodox Church is tremendously important, and its 2019 split from the Russian Orthodox Church has become a hot-button issue with Putin. This is a tough pill for Putin to swallow, and it may well result in more forceful efforts to subjugate Ukraine to his will, especially given his appetite for high-risk adventures. Disinformation will very much be part of this effort. Russia would be unwise to underestimate Ukrainian nationalism.

Dezinformatsiya

Disinformation is not just the dissemination of false stories; it is the creation of several often conflicting counternarratives, all aimed to create cleavages and undermine facts, as illustrated in recent Russian-orchestrated *dezinformatsiya* campaigns in Ukraine, Poland, Hungary, the United Kingdom, Germany, France, and the United States. Our first understanding of the robust and continuing Soviet intelligence strategy and its use of active measures of disinformation via the propagation of "fake news" came from several high-profile defections early in the 1960s.

In the spring of 1964 a Czechoslovakian documentary team discovered four barnacled and time-worn chests at the bottom of Devil's Lake in Šumava National Park, not far from the country's western border. Inside was a collection of Nazi treasures, including documents of historical significance, such as a catalog of wartime Nazi sympathizers. The discovery was met with international accolades, and it galvanized those seeking to pursue the prosecution of Nazi war criminals. However, the documentary that chronicled the chests' recovery was very poorly received in West Germany, where nearly everyone was eager to move beyond the postwar period and cement stronger and more equal ties with their Western counterparts. What no one knew at the time was that it was all a deception—the chests and their contents had been faked. One of the divers who happened to "discover" the first of the boxes was Ladislav Bittman, who in fact worked for Czechoslovakia's intelligence service. Operation Neptune, as the orchestrated deception was dubbed, was an elaborately designed and successful disinformation campaign to isolate the nascent West German government from the rest of the West. The international press ate it up. At its core it was "fake news" and a predecessor of Russian activities to come. "Fake news" provides an often credible, alternative account of the world and endeavors to form cleavages within a target population, to discredit the press and more generally create doubt that truth is a discernible thing. In this case the entire story was fabricated, but in many cases the story has partial truths, which may make it even harder to debunk.

Bittman defected to the West shortly after witnessing the brutal Soviet crackdown on the Prague Spring, a 1968 uprising that revealed the depth and breadth of disillusionment simmering behind the Iron Curtain. He characterized the Soviet disinformation strategy or active measures as "PR in reverse" and a "slow game" in which a trickle of nefarious and disconcerting stories would prompt people to begin to doubt the U.S. system and its Western values.[14] While working for the Czechoslovak Secret Service, Bittman disseminated fabricated U.S. conspiracy plots, many targeting the developing world. For example, diplomats' signatures, taken from U.S. officials' Christmas cards, were sent to the Czechoslovak embassy in Washington, where they were used to produce fake letters, telegrams, and memoranda as proof of these invented plots.

While some disinformation campaigns aim to propagate falsehoods, other efforts may involve weaponizing information—sometimes true and sometimes not—for destructive purposes. The best example of this is the leaking of privileged or classified information and often intermingling it with false or misleading information. One of Bittman's greatest successes as an agent focused on disrupting CIA worldwide operations by publishing a book called *Who's Who in the CIA*. Pulling information from Czechoslovak and East German archives, the book purportedly listed all known (roughly three thousand) CIA officers worldwide. While some of those listed were indeed the names of CIA officers, many others were the names of American diplomats, public officials, journalists, and judges who had no affiliation with the CIA whatsoever. The confusion and damage caused by this act of disinformation was widespread. This tactic would be repeated on several notable occasions, one of them with tragic consequences for the agency.

In 1969 CIA officer Philip Agee was asked to resign because of his unsteady behavior, attributed to heavy drinking, increasing debt, and other personal troubles. Agee had served in Ecuador, Uruguay, and

Mexico and during his last tour had fallen in love with a left-wing Brazilian dissident named Angela Camargo Seixas. Shortly thereafter, in 1973, according to former KGB official and noted spymaster Oleg Kalugin, Agee walked into the KGB's Mexico City *rezidentura* offering to provide them with sensitive U.S. intelligence.[15] However, the KGB thought he was a provocation and rebuffed him. Agee then approached the Cubans and traveled to Havana, where he worked hand in hand with its intelligence agency, the DGI, to publish *Inside the Company: CIA Diary* in 1975. Detailing CIA operations around the globe, Agee had provided the identities of 250 CIA officials operating abroad, as well as the identities of some CIA agents and sources, which wreaked havoc on the agency.

With the help of the DGI and with information provided by the KGB, Agee started a newsletter called *Covert Action Information Bulletin* and a magazine called *CounterSpy*, which was devoted to exposing CIA officers and operations worldwide. Agee published two other books about CIA activities in Western Europe and Africa. He is believed to have compromised hundreds of CIA employees.

It is hard not to see parallels with the information released via Russian intelligence's online moniker Guccifer 2.0 on DCLeaks and WikiLeaks in 2016, which likely used the classic Russian tactic of mixing genuine information and communications with conspiracy theories propagated on those same sites. In so doing, Russian intelligence was able to selectively use materials stolen from Hillary Clinton and her senior advisors to disrupt her presidential campaign and, by extension, the U.S. democratic process writ large. It also caused ongoing havoc in the Western press, which, much like intelligence agencies, is confronted with the burden of making sense of a tsunami of information without the proper time, resources, or traditional norms to vet and validate that information.

It was impossible for the United States to build a case against Agee, as it did not have definitive evidence that it was either willing or able to present in court that he was a spy and because disclosing employee identities was not a crime at the time. Agee became persona non grata in most parts of the West.[16] In 1982 the U.S. Congress passed the "Anti-

Agee" Bill, or the Intelligence Identities Protection Act, which crim-
inalized the disclosure of the identities of CIA officers.[17]

Among the revelations from *CounterSpy* and *Covert Action Information Bulletin* in 1975 was the identification of Richard "Dick" Welch
as a CIA officer in Peru. I had worked for Welch personally when I
started in the Latin America Division. My responsibility was to report
to work before dawn every day to review the cable traffic coming in
from all Latin American field stations, prioritize the issues, and flag
the important ones for review by Welch, who ran the foreign intelligence (espionage) operations, and by the head of the covert action
operations when they came into the office. The first word that comes
to mind when I think of Dick is "gentleman." He had grace in thought
and manners that immediately inspired confidence and trust. He was
someone you could look up to and after whom you could model your
own style of dealing with people. While he didn't wear his character
on his sleeve, above all he was a brave and totally committed officer.

In the summer of 1975, when Welch was assigned as CIA station
chief in Athens, he was targeted by leftist extremists. Greece had experienced a violent coup in 1967, resulting in a military dictatorship, put
in place with considerable force and lasting until 1974. The extremists on the left blamed the CIA for assisting the military and set out
to even the score. Since Welch's name had been compromised earlier,
the November 17 terrorist group was able to identify him and track
his movements. On the night of December 23, 1975, they waited for
Welch to return from a Christmas party with his wife and driver. When
the driver pulled into the driveway, where the terrorists had taken out
the garage light, Welch was accosted and executed with a Colt .45 in
front of his wife. This cowardly deed reverberated throughout the
CIA, fueling rage and disgust. For years the CIA hunted for the killer,
and finally in 2002 the shooter was apprehended and sentenced to life
in prison for other terrorist attacks, the statute of limitations having
expired for Welch's murder.

What the stories of Bittman and Agee illustrate is that Russia is well
versed in developing multiple counternarratives filled with a combination of half-truths, false moral equivalencies or "whataboutisms," big

lies, distractions, and information purges. These efforts can have a specific operational goal, as was the case with the U.S. election interference in 2016, or a general aim of sowing confusion and discontent. One
of the best examples of the latter was the anti-Trump "Not My President" rallies organized in major U.S. cities by the Internet Research
Agency trolls following President Trump's electoral victory. These are
the same Russian trolls that in large part supported Donald Trump's
candidacy before the election. Another example of disinformation
is that after news of the DNC hack was announced on June 14, 2016,
GRU officers created the Guccifer 2.0 persona, which falsely claimed
to be a lone Romanian hacker, to undermine the allegations of Russian responsibility for the intrusion.[18]

These same techniques were used after the Russian military forces
illegally occupying Ukraine shot down Malaysia Airlines Flight 17
using a technique that Yale historian Timothy Snyder calls "implau-
sible deniability." In the aftermath Russian news agencies promoted
several conflicting, illogical, and untenable stories that tried to shift
blame and sufficiently muddy the narrative: that it was a Ukrainian
missile or aircraft that brought down Flight 17 in an attack meant to
target President Putin, that it was an error made in Ukrainian flight
training exercises, and that there were witness accounts of Ukrainian
fighter pilots in the area. These stories were successful in creating sufficient noise to instill doubt about the true narrative that Russian soldiers shot down the plane.[19] Putin's offer in Helsinki in the summer
of 2018 to form a joint inquiry with the United States to investigate
what transpired in the 2016 U.S. presidential election is yet another
Russian effort to provide an alternative narrative to what we know
is the truth.

Looking back, we can see that the 2016 covert activities related to the
U.S. election were clearly part of a long-established Russian playbook
but with a clear technological advantage. The tactics and techniques
used by Bittman endure today, but the difference now is the power of
modern communication technology and the internet. Today's "fake
news" conundrum seems so intractable because Facebook, Instagram,
Twitter, Google, and the proliferation of alternative news sources give

Russia and others who wish to promulgate disinformation an enormous distribution platform that is exponentially more powerful and therefore more damaging than what existed during the Cold War. The ultimate goal remains the same: to undermine trust in and the stability of democratic society.

Fundamentally, the role of disinformation is not only to provide one or many alternative accounts of the facts. It is also an effort to subvert the truth itself, to make truth so inaccessible and unreliable that efforts at trying to seek out truth are in vain. Putin's goal to undermine Western democratic institutions has not changed from that of his communist forebears, and his determination is just as strong. Our resolve to counter him should exceed his resolve to weaken us.

Mokrye Dela, or "Wet Work"

There are few constraints on the scope of possible action by Russian intelligence operatives. On the extreme spectrum of covert action, the KGB, the NKVD, and Cheka were no strangers to political assassination. While seemingly uncommon, it is still used today. In 2006 Russia passed a law permitting extrajudicial killings abroad by Russian armed forces and special service operatives targeting individuals accused of "extremism," including individuals "causing mass disturbances, committing hooliganism or acts of vandalism," and "slandering the individual occupying the post of president of the Russian Federation."[20] In 2018 Russian intelligence agents poisoned former GRU spy for the British Sergei Skripal in Salisbury, England, using the powerful nerve agent Novichok, likely as a warning to would-be traitors seeking safe harbor in Western countries. This was not an isolated incident. A Russian assassin captured in Ukraine in 2016 targeted six people—killing one—for helping Georgia (unsuccessfully) try to fend off a 2008 Russian attack. Former FSB officer Alexander Litvinenko was poisoned with radioactive polonium-210 in 2006 in the United Kingdom, and there is reporting that Russian special forces killed former Chechen separatist president Zelimkhan Yandarbiev with a car bomb in Qatar in 2004. There have also been several highly suspicious, in-country assassinations: Russian opposition politician Boris Nemtsov in February 2015; human rights activist and lawyer Stanislav Markelov and independent journalist Anastasia Baburova in 2009; and journalist and human rights activist Anna Politkovskaya, murdered in her stairwell in 2006. Russian opposition leader Alexey Navalny was poisoned with Novichok in 2020 in what is believed to be a failed assassination attempt by the Kremlin.

Throughout history, assassination has often been employed by Russian authorities to eliminate political rivals, foreign heads of state, troublesome secessionists and nationalists, and of course defectors. Most emblematically, Leon Trotsky, Communist Party leader and ally of Lenin, was assassinated in Mexico in 1940 by NKVD agents on orders from Stalin. Several attempts on Yugoslavia's communist leader, Marshal Josip Broz Tito, were also made. The Soviets openly acknowledged the existence of a department known as SMERSH (an acronym signifying "Death to Spies") until 1946. KGB assassin Nikolai Khokhlov defected to the CIA in 1954 with colorful accounts of "bullets coated in cyanide and fired from an ingenious pistol concealed in a packet of cigarettes," intended for use against a Ukrainian nationalist leader. Khokhlov later survived a retributive poisoning by thallium, which calls to mind the polonium-210 that would be used against Alexander Litvinenko in England in 2006.[21] Khokhlov's defection was followed by that of another KGB agent, Bogdan Stashinsky, who confessed to killing two prominent Ukrainian nationalists in exile, Lev Rebet and Stepan Bandera, with an atomizer gun that released prussic acid (hydrogen cyanide) to kill targets without leaving a trace.[22]

According to an official Soviet account, *mokrye dela*, or "wet work" (a glib reference to the spilling of blood), was put on hold or generally slowed in the late 1950s. However, future events would contradict this assertion. The KGB became obsessed with targeting defectors, as would be proven when Bulgarian dissident Georgi Markov was assassinated in September 1978 by a Bulgarian agent on Waterloo Bridge in London with a KGB-designed "umbrella gun" that fired a pellet laced with ricin. Another Bulgarian dissident, Vladimir Kostov, had survived an identical attack in Paris a month earlier.[23]

Beyond its sphere of influence, the KGB had a violent and ambitious political action contingency program that had Western targets.

In 1969 another KGB agent, Yuri Bezmenov, defected from his post in India as a Soviet press officer working as a senior manager for the newly minted and innocuous-sounding Research and Counter-Propaganda Department in the Russian embassy in New Delhi. What he actually did was pursue active measures such as blackmailing and intimidating local government officials, inciting mass demonstrations, and creating front organizations to support subversive and radical groups abroad. But most shockingly, Bezmenov was also tasked with creating lists of people to marginalize through smear campaigns or worse. A literal hit list was developed in the event of a communist revolution or, in Soviet terms, "liberation." In his memoir, *Love Letter to America*, Bezmenov claimed he witnessed how such a list was effectively used when the Hanoi communists captured the southern city of Hue in Vietnam and reportedly killed several pro-Western intelligentsia in the space of one evening.

Bezmenov's story shows that Russian operatives have decades of experience collecting intelligence on and attempting to subvert government officials and other important stakeholders in foreign countries. Most of the efforts described by Bezmenov were essentially contingency planning, which means that the Soviet Union endeavored to be prepared for any eventuality. We would be naïve to think that Russia has not sought to do the same in the United States.

Also in the early 1970s agents of the British security service, MI5, observed that Soviet trade delegate Oleg Lyalin, a suspected KGB officer, was having an affair with his secretary, Irina Teplyakova. This affair was exactly the kind of vulnerability MI5 was looking to exploit, and it moved quickly and convinced Lyalin to provide information on Soviet spying activities within Britain. This sort of approach is always risky because one is essentially forcing a spy's hand in cooperating, and any information obtained would have to be treated with great circumspection.[24] When Lyalin was arrested for drunk driving in London, he understood that he would soon be recalled to Moscow for certain reprimand, so he and Teplyakova decided to defect.

In his debriefings Lyalin passed to MI5 and MI6 everything he knew about KGB operations in London and Europe. As a result, the United

Kingdom expelled 105 Soviet officials in what was a tremendous public success for MI5 and a boon for Western intelligence. Lyalin was the first KGB operative to defect publicly to the United Kingdom since World War II. Less commonly known is Lyalin's specific role in the KGB.

Lyalin was assigned to Department V. In the local KGB rezidentura, Department V agents were charged with planning sabotage, including the repression of minority dissidents, widespread penetration of dissident movements and emigrant communities abroad, as well as the stoking of insurgencies. They planned to use assassinations, kidnappings, and terrorism as tactics in these activities. Lyalin had been tasked with identifying important British political and public figures who could become targets of assassination in a confrontation with the West.

Most important, Lyalin revealed that in the case of a future crisis, the Soviets were planning to immobilize critical Western infrastructure by using Soviet operatives, mercenaries, and dissident groups. He outlined sabotage contingency plans that had been designed for Bonn, London, Paris, Rome, and Washington. Lyalin's efforts were part of a greater effort to thoroughly scope Western landscapes for infrastructure targets, weapons cache sites, and airborne and maritime landing sites for sabotage. This operation extended from North America and Europe to Turkey and Israel and even Japan and Hong Kong.[25] Russia is continuing these same efforts today. The U.S. Department of Homeland Security and FBI issued a joint alert in March 2018 that "Russian government cyber actors" were targeting critical U.S. assets across key industries, including energy, nuclear, water, aviation, and critical manufacturing.[26] We can also be sure that they have laid in agents to carry out these operations.

We now know from recovered Soviet intelligence archives like the Mitrokhin Archive and accounts from Soviet officials like retired KGB general Oleg Kalugin that many Department V special actions were either unsuccessful or deemed too risky in the end.[27] Irrespective of their lack of success, their intent was instructive. New insight into Department V exposed the ambition and inclination for violence embedded in Soviet strategy, as well as the willingness to use covert violence. This same inscrutable determination endures today. What is worrisome is that the Politburo had to rule by consensus, which likely allowed for some of the most unbridled and destructive plots to be tempered or squelched, whereas today Putin has almost unchallenged control. We are dependent upon the stability and judgment of one man who has now been in control for almost two decades.

It is crucial and instructive to note that Putin sees all things from the perspective of a former intelligence agent. Putin's approach to dealing with political adversaries and foreign and domestic rivals draws straight from the playbook of Soviet active measures and special actions, as demonstrated by his willingness to quash domestic opposition and meddle in Western elections. One need only look to how detractors have been treated, whether they be political rivals like Mikhail Khodorkovsky or Boris Berezovsky, dissidents such as Alexei Navalny or Boris Nemtsov, whistleblower Sergei Magnitsky, human rights activist Stanislav Markelov, independent journalists such as Anastasia Baburova, Natalia Estemirova, and Anna Politkovskaya, and of course Alexander Litvinenko and Sergei Skripal. The luckier ones are in prison or live in exile. Lethal measures—wet work—have been part of the Russian playbook for a very long time and remain in the twenty-first-century toolkit.

Influence, Elicitation, and Entrapment

Of course there are more subtle ways the Russians conduct influence campaigns, and they continue to use them. Few people realize just how much intelligence spies can gain through elicitation and entrapment techniques. By asking seemingly innocent questions on important intelligence issues, spies are often able to create a valuable, complex mosaic of sensitive information consisting of seemingly minor unrelated tidbits of classified information from an assortment of contacts. No doubt the internet and social media have amplified the targeting abilities of those using this technique.

Entrapment too often starts with a temptation or the request for an innocuous-seeming favor, service, or meeting. The target will often be implicated before he or she is even aware of it. This approach is visible in the Russian intelligence effort to make inroads into the Trump campaign team during his run for president, whether by exploring potential development deals in Moscow, sending a representative to provide "dirt" on an opponent, or using an academic "cutout" to start a relationship with an aspirational foreign policy advisor.

But not all elicitations are financially or politically related, at least on the surface. A "honeytrap" is an effective ruse used by Russian foreign intelligence services to use sexual encounters to elicit privileged information or compel someone to do something, either through blackmail or pillow talk. The women used to do this bidding in the past were often called Swallows; men were called Casanovas or Romeos, so named by the infamous East German spymaster Markus Wolf, whose industrious use of attractive East German men to seduce single West German women allowed him access to every echelon of the postwar West German government.[28] Wolf also used women in traditional honeytrap operations. His Stasi intelligence service recruited a nearly endless supply of West German assets by reportedly setting up a bordello in Bonn and equipping it with cameras. In addition, he would send women all over Europe to try and seduce West German diplomats and intelligence officers. Targets were also lured through complex blackmail operations built on "debts, discontents or debauchery."[29]

The Soviets were highly adept at setting honeytraps for foreign diplomats in Moscow. In the 1950s and 1960s the French seemed particularly vulnerable to this method. Maurice Dejean, the French ambassador in Moscow from 1956 to 1962, fell for the charms of "Laura." While they were in bed together, a KGB agent posing as her husband burst in and violently threatened Dejean. He foolishly confided in a close Russian acquaintance, who was also an undercover KGB officer, and asked his assistance in placating the enraged husband. This episode made it easy for the acquaintance to occasionally ask Dejean about privileged information on French policy. Under Dejean's tenure, his attaché, Colonel Louis Gribaud, was also caught in a honeytrap and committed suicide rather than face disgrace.[30]

The very first clandestine CIA officer to be placed in Moscow also fell victim to this tactic. In 1955 Edward Ellis Smith, whose KGB pseudonym was "Little Guy," was sent with the intention of becoming the point of contact for a valuable Soviet mole, Pyotr Popov, when Popov was recalled to Moscow from his post in East Germany. Smith arrived under diplomatic cover as a State Department employee, albeit unknown to the State Department. Smith or "Ryzhiy" (Redhead), as the Soviets called him, was quite confident in his ability to attract women with his good looks. The Russians saw right through him and placed the very attractive "Valya" directly in his path, as a maid in the embassy. As they hoped, Smith "seduced" Valya, who used a camera with a special timer hidden in her purse to document their sexual encounters. The Russians approached him with the photos to try to turn him to do their bidding. Smith dithered, eventually refused, and reported the whole affair to the U.S. ambassador, Charles "Chip" Bohlen, including the fact that he was a CIA officer. Smith was sent home and fired. Bohlen was reportedly a good friend of President Eisenhower and relayed the incident to him while on the golf course. The president reportedly stormed away to call Secretary of State John Foster Dulles. All in all, it was not an auspicious start for the agency in Moscow.[31]

There is no small amount of luck and propitious timing that informs the relative success or failure of an intelligence effort. The fall of Harold Macmillan's government in Britain at the beginning of the 1960s is an excellent example of how we—as well as the Russians—cannot always imagine the implications of our initial endeavors.

In 1961 MI5 learned from Soviet spy Oleg Penkovskiy that the Soviet naval attaché Yevgeny Ivanov was in fact a GRU officer operating in London. Ivanov was attractive and charming and seemed to have a taste for London society life. MI5 thought that he might be turned or persuaded to defect. Ivanov became close friends with Stephen Ward, an osteopath and portraitist who rubbed shoulders with Britain's high society, including Randolph Churchill, Lord Astor, and Prince Philip. This was a strange situation because MI5 was trying to set up conditions to compromise Ivanov, and yet it was Ivanov who via Ward had uncanny exposure to Britain's elite at their most gregarious and perhaps least discerning state of mind.

Ward lived with the nineteen-year-old Christine Keeler, who danced as a showgirl and spent weekends hobnobbing at Ward's cottage on Lord

Astor's estate. It was there that Ivanov met Keeler, and it is believed that they started a liaison. Keeler also caught the eye of Britain's secretary of state for war, John Profumo, who attended one of Lord Astor's summer parties in the summer of 1961. The two had a brief affair while Keeler was reportedly also sleeping with Ivanov. Ward told MI5 of the affair between Profumo and Keeler, thus forcing Profumo to immediately put an end to it.[32] But rumors began to circulate in the tabloid press, and the public became entranced with the idea that the secretary of state for war and a Soviet spy had shared the same mistress at the same time.[33]

When the story started to break, the Soviets wisely recalled Ivanov to Moscow, where he could not be subject to scrutiny by the British government or the press. The media loved the scandal because it had loops within loops of intrigue. While it seems that Keeler had little sophistication in understanding national security secrets, it is possible—had she wanted to—that she could have collected a great deal of softer, albeit valuable, information about the political and economic developments in Britain and among its allies. As the headlines became more salacious, the scandal reached a fever pitch in June 1963, when Profumo was forced to resign after he lied to the House of Commons about his affair with Keeler.

Decades after the Profumo scandal, when I was paying a CIA courtesy call on Britain's director of military intelligence, the director's first action was to walk me over to a huge closet to show me where Profumo and Keeler had had a sexual liaison. He seemed genuinely proud to share this bit of history, even if it was ultimately viewed as a successful Russian action against the British.

The Profumo Affair was a crushing blow to the Macmillan government, serving as an indictment of the integrity of the entire conservative ruling class. The revelations surrounding Profumo occurred on the heels of other scandals: the exposure of the Portland Spy Ring, comprising three illegals and two of their collaborators living and spying unabashedly in Britain, and the exposure of British traitors George Blake and John Vassall. Even though Prime Minister Macmillan tried to tough it out, he too ended up stepping down, in October 1963, and his party lost the elections. There could not have been a better result for the Soviets, who generally sought opportunities to disrupt governments hostile to their cause and relished any opportunity to display the shortcomings of Western governments.

These cases should resonate when one considers events during the Trump administration. Given that President Trump came from outside the Washington political establishment, it is doubtful the Russians had meaningful preexisting assets operating within his campaign circle. It follows that once he had won the Republican nomination, Russia would be aggressive in its attempts to exploit relationships that were already in its orbit. This situation explains the apparent desperation and excessive effort by the Russians to penetrate the team.

Information Confrontation

Russia's use of active measures has been exponentially bolstered by social media and technological advances. In exploiting these new tools, Russia has come to understand well the asymmetrical capability of cyber attacks for both intelligence collection and covert action purposes. It thrives behind the veil of "plausible deniability" offered by them. Moreover, because of its fundamental and strategic weakness relative to the United States, Russia sees its cyber capability as a means by which it can establish equal footing in the real world with the United States. In so doing it relies heavily and often unconvincingly on such "plausible deniability." In the ongoing struggle between Russia and the United States, cyber is the new battlefield, and in that field of combat the GRU has become the most visible and aggressive actor among Russia's security services. However, there is strong evidence that both the SVR as well as state-funded yet independent actors like the IRA are important players in Russia's cyber force.

Intelligence services worldwide have been busy for years collecting and integrating open source data—by mining social media and networking sites, trying to exploit the emergent internet-of-things (the interconnection via the internet of computing devices embedded in everyday objects, enabling them to send and receive data), using artificial intelligence (AI) and machine learning, as well as crunching big data. Such data usage is now an integral part of any modern intelligence service. What this means is the scope of intelligence collection has widened and the amount of data to parse has exponentially multiplied. Digital intel has also ushered in a new age of vulnerability and the onset of cyber warfare.

Russia has moved full speed ahead into this technical intelligence action space, and it first directed its cyber active measures at Ukraine. Russia conducted a series of disinformation campaigns and cyber attacks against Ukraine to support its military incursion into the country, the culmination of a decade-long campaign to win this key strategic territory back into its sphere of influence.

Hours before the announcement of the result of Ukraine's 2014 elections, the pro-Russian, Kremlin-linked group CyberBerkut hacked the website of the Ukrainian Central Election Commission and announced that ultra-right presidential candidate Dmytro Yarosh had won. It was pure fiction; Petro Poroshenko had already won the presidency.[34] Other cyber attacks, including those carried out by the SVR's Cozy Bear, involved hacking, denial of service attacks, and malware attacks against key financial, energy, and government infrastructure in Ukraine in an effort to disrupt the country's general state of affairs. In December 2015 hackers cut electricity to 250,000 Ukrainians just before Christmas. This was one of the first examples of a cyber attack that caused real physical damage to critical infrastructure. In the fall of 2016 Ukraine's pension fund, the country's treasury, its seaport authority, its railway, its ministries of infrastructure, defense, and finance all came under attack, gravely affecting operations. Then in December 2016 another attack on Ukraine's power grid unleashed malware capable of independently sabotaging critical infrastructure without direct command-and-control by hackers. The most damaging cyber attack on record was the NotPetya assault on Ukraine in 2017, which deployed a form of malware known as ransomware through an accounting software that held critical files hostage in exchange for payment. The attack was debilitating to Ukraine and ended up affecting people in more than sixty countries.[35]

During this period, similar cyber attacks were carried out against Western allies in Europe and the United States to punish these countries for their support of Poroshenko and further advance strategic efforts to undermine Western democracies. Since at least 2015 a Russian hacking group referred to by many as Energetic Bear or Dragonfly has been conducting hacks aimed at both surveillance and contingency planning as well as sabotage against the U.S. energy grid and nuclear infrastructure, notably targeting power switches.[36]

What Russia has done in Ukraine is a cautionary for the Baltic states, the rest of eastern Europe, and ultimately all of Europe and the United States. So disconcerting are the attacks on Ukraine, according to reports in March 2018, that even DARPA, the R&D arm of the Defense Department, was investing resources and working projects in Ukraine in the domain of information security. This initiative is strategically important because Ukraine is one of the best possible testing grounds for countermeasures against cyber attacks, having been the target of unrelenting attacks from Russia since 2014. This is indeed one of the types of important defensive postures—in addition to sanctions—that the U.S. government needs to enhance in the wake of the Russian interference, which will need to be deployed elsewhere as well.[37]

In 2015 the CIA added a new directorate for digital innovation to harness information technology's ability to collect intelligence and conduct covert action against our adversaries. This was a major development for the CIA and an essential evolution in the intelligence business.

Operators today, both covert and paramilitary, have access to a level of technology that my colleagues and I could only have dreamed about. Rather than laboring with files and lock-and-pick kits for hotel break-ins, today's spies can fabricate a digital hotel master key in minutes. On the higher-tech level there are "kinetic energy harvesters" that when strapped to the knee generate power through walking, as well as handheld forensic imaging tools and on-the-go data centers. Drones are now equipped for all sorts of configurations and missions, from surveillance and target tracking with thermal imaging cameras to detonating IEDs using radio frequencies. The hi-tech game cuts both ways, however. An essential part of an operator's training is now to learn how to avoid being tracked by the signals emitted from so much of our everyday toolkit, starting with the ubiquitous smartphone.

U.S. and Russian intelligence agencies today have the extraordinary capacity to probe the sensitive details of each other's national security, financial, and private sector infrastructure. What we see today in the public domain is only the tip of the iceberg. In the shadow of the 2016 election hacking, it has become ever clearer that how we collect, process, manage, and secure our information, both within the U.S. government as well as in the private sector, will determine our national security and our ability to compete, especially against competitors like Russia and China.

We are quickly approaching a world where "mutually assured cyber destruction" will apply across a broad spectrum of nations, which may serve as a deterrent for all the major players. The most likely and worrisome exceptions to this development are North Korea and Iran, which, along with nonstate actors like ISIS, might underestimate or disregard our response to a damaging attack on the United States and thus undertake a high-risk assault with disastrous consequences for them and others.

Currently, though, our cyber challenges flow from the competing interests of our greatest geopolitical competitors—Russia and China. These complex and opaque interplays can be expected to grow in importance in Washington over the next few years as we struggle to manage our resurgent "big power" relationships with our increasingly aggressive competitors. Unlike the Cold War, these conflicts will be devoid of communist ideology. They will instead be rooted in nationalism and the self-interest of nation-states. Russia is seemingly unbridled in its use of cyber operations as a way to disrupt and distract its enemies on an ongoing basis. It is a relatively inexpensive means of wreaking real and debilitating havoc on one's adversary. At present, efforts to thwart this assault are hugely insufficient.

If we look at Russian spycraft in its totality and through the arc of history, a stark and disconcerting picture emerges: Russia is actively seeking to subvert the Western order and is still playing from its Cold War playbook. Our response to this assault will determine how successful the Russians will be.

LESSON FOUR

Putin sees the world through the eyes of a Cold War spymaster.

There is no such thing as a former KGB man.

—Russian president VLADIMIR PUTIN

4

A Spymaster President

If Russian foreign policy today is a combination of active measures, disinformation, influence and patronage campaigns, and overt acts of aggression, it is because Putin cut his teeth in the dark shadows of the Cold War as a KGB officer and then sharpened his skills while running the FSB.[1] Putin's perception of power dynamics and human nature is inextricably linked to his tenure in the intelligence world, starting with his experience in East Germany at the end of the Cold War. He has been trained to identify and create leverage against adversaries and then to control those levers to advance Russian interests against the West.

Despite the many proxy wars and shifting allegiances that marked the Cold War in the developing world, the front lines always remained the NATO–Warsaw Pact confrontation, with East and West Germany the center of the bull's eye. The literal line between East and West was made real by the Berlin Wall in 1961. East German spymaster Markus Wolf worked tirelessly along this "invisible front" in the Cold War.

Wolf, regarded by some as perhaps the most skillful and successful spymaster of the Cold War, was the head of the East German First Intelligence Directorate (HVA) for more than thirty-four years and a pioneer in modern spycraft. Wolf is infamous for his unbridled drive, inventiveness, strategic patience, and impolitic cruelty. Because his family was Jewish and had communist affiliations, Wolf fled Hitler's Germany, first to France and then to Moscow, after obtaining political asylum there. That the Soviet Union saved his family from the Holocaust was a prime motivator for Wolf throughout his life. After the war he was profoundly committed to German communism and antifascism and determined not to repeat the German atrocities of the past. It was perhaps this zeal that made him so driven in his espionage on the one hand and blind to its perversity on the other. Wolf looked back at his career as one with a noble purpose that prevented a hot war for more than thirty years. However, his tactics, and the merciless application of his spycraft, are his actual legacy.[2]

Vladimir Putin spent five years under Wolf's sphere of influence as a KGB political intelligence officer in Dresden, ending with the fall of the Berlin Wall in 1989. Just as many in Russia were embracing the optimism of *perestroika* and *glasnost*, Putin was isolated in the dystopian shadow of Wolf. As the Berlin Wall fell, Putin was reportedly burning documents in a basement in Dresden and resenting the silence from Moscow and the impotence it represented. After the wall fell, Putin was forced to watch the complete retreat from all Warsaw Pact countries, the debacle of the KGB failed coup, and the loss of influence over Soviet satellite states—especially Georgia, Kyrgyzstan, and Ukraine— that turned toward Europe and NATO. The resulting economic collapse and profound sense of anxiety over Russia's future and place in the world stayed with him and influenced his political choices twenty years later.

Putin's fifteen years of service in the KGB—five in Dresden—honed his political skill and gave him the experience he needed to adroitly manipulate people and situations as he rose politically, first in St. Petersburg and then in Moscow.

I've been intrigued for several years by the speed and effectiveness with which Putin rose to the highest level of the complex Russian political system and consolidated his grip on its byzantine bureaucracy. His meteoric ascent wasn't a matter of pure luck. It would not have happened if Putin weren't an innately cunning and effective operator. Born in 1952 into a family of modest means, Putin grew up on the streets of Leningrad (St. Petersburg), learning judo first for survival and later for dominance. He sought out a career in intelligence and distinguished himself enough to obtain the much-coveted posting of foreign intelligence officer in 1985.[3] In 1990 Putin returned to Russia as the Soviet system and, more important for him, the symbols of Russian greatness crumbled. He has often stated publicly that the collapse of the Soviet Union, and its attendant loss of power, was the greatest tragedy of his generation. Putin's key driving force is to restore "Mother Russia" after the humiliation and disarray that followed the end of the Cold War. All his actions must be seen in the context of this single theme and his dogged determination to reverse it at all costs.

After he left the KGB, Putin was taken under the wing of St. Petersburg mayor Anatoly Sobchak, who mentored him during his early political development. Putin developed a reputation as a loyal and competent technocrat with an astute understanding of how Russia's oligarchy navigated the post–Cold War period and amassed considerable wealth in the process. Putin kept close account of vulnerabilities, illegal acts, areas for leverage, areas for *kompromat*. He then landed a position in Moscow on President Boris Yeltsin's staff, where he ingratiated himself to key power brokers and was soon recognized as an effective, dependable "company guy" who wouldn't rock the boat and who, like Yeltsin, was beholden to Russia's emergent oligarchy. Yeltsin took a liking to him and in July 1998 appointed him director of the FSB, which is Russia's counterpart to the FBI but operates with far less legal restraint than the U.S. bureau. Putin's tenure in the FSB allowed him to master his skills in profiling, targeting, and finding and exploiting adversaries' vulnerabilities, and he eventually established a system of governance answerable mainly to him. It may be that his experience with the virtually unchecked powers of the FSB, rather than the KGB, had the most lasting influence on him politically and explains his aggressive actions against foreign governments in the West.

In August 1999 Putin was named acting prime minster after the flailing Yeltsin had reshuffled his cabinet for the fourth time in less than two years. Putin took a commanding and tough approach to the civil war in Chechnya, a cunning and dramatic move that earned him high praise across Russia. On January 1, 2000, Yeltsin surprised the outside world by resigning and designating Putin acting president and prime minister six months ahead of presidential elections. In doing so, Yeltsin shored up Putin's succession and assured immunity for himself and his assets.

It took Putin nine years to rise from mid-level KGB officer to leader of Russia. As he cemented his own power and veered away from the democratic constructs put in place after the collapse of the Soviet Union, Putin developed an intransigent certitude that only he could restore Russia to its former greatness. The longer he stays in power, the more convinced he becomes of the merits of his stance. To secure his position, Putin unseated many of the oligarchs of the 1990s and replaced them and their attendant wealth with his own group of loyalists. He cultivated a tight inner circle primarily made up of former KGB and FSB colleagues, known as *siloviki*. This circle has fed his ego for years, and he now has an almost messianic view of himself as the savior of Russia.

In reality, he is playing a strong hand with inherently weak cards. Russia depends on oil and gas income to keep its corrupt and sclerotic economy afloat, and a decade of oil price volatility and weakness have undermined Russia's economic strength. The country's economic problems are a major factor in Putin's heightened aggressive posture, as they pose the greatest challenge to his autocracy and make Russia's need to reassert itself on the geopolitical stage ever more pressing.

His foreign policy actions—like his use of force to back Bashar al-Assad's regime in Syria and his pursuit of strategic partnerships with Iran and the Gulf states—should be viewed through this lens. He is in one sense ensuring that Russia maintains access to a strategic path to the Mediterranean and a defining stake in negotiating oil prices, as well as a powerful seat at the table in Middle East politics. In addition, he is seeking to maintain outsized strategic influence over Europe's energy markets and to exacerbate its refugee crisis—both concrete means of influencing and destabilizing European politics. He doesn't have time to rebalance the global scale, so he is racing to create areas of foreign policy leverage and to cultivate instability with his adversaries to tip the strategic hand in his favor. His actions in Syria also check what he sees as a Western penchant to bring about the end to dictatorships in the Middle East that Americans deemed unsavory— like those in Libya and Egypt.[4]

In pursuing his goal to restore Russian greatness, Putin will call upon strategies lifted almost verbatim from Russia's intelligence playbook. Consequently, we can expect that he will do whatever it takes, including using Russian intelligence and active measures, to keep himself in power and assert Russian power abroad. As Russia reemerges under Putin's leadership, and as the global balance of power shifts toward another great power struggle, we can be sure that Putin's intelligence services are using all available tactics, old and new, to conduct covert action operations and to penetrate U.S. and other Western governments. We should consider doing the same if we are to recalibrate our relationship with Russia from a position of strength.

Russia's brief brush with democracy was painful, unsuccessful, and humiliating, and Putin saw the Western approach to Russia during this time as condescending and malicious. He sees Western support for democratization, rule of law, and pluralistic values as being in direct opposition to his agenda. Russia's reemergence on the international scene has been concomitant with Putin's reconsolidation of power under an autocratic system, and he sees the presence of Western media and NGOs—especially religious organizations and human rights groups—as Western meddling in Russian affairs. Putin also sees American and European institution-building and the expansion of military alliances into Russia's traditional sphere of influence—including democracy-building in Russia under the aegis of then-U.S. secretary of state Hillary Clinton in 2011 and 2012—as an assault and a possible abrogation of the traditional Moscow Rules. He has publicly cited the antidoping investigation into Russian athletes during the 2012 Winter Olympic Games in Sochi as a U.S. effort to undermine Russia. He also (wrongly) saw a nefarious American hand in the publication of the Panama Papers, which were millions of anonymously leaked documents related to more than two hundred thousand offshore entities created by the Panamanian law firm Mossack Fonseca. In many cases these entities helped wealthy individuals and public officials perpetrate fraud, circumvent payment of taxes, and avoid international sanctions. Many Russians close to Putin were implicated in the affair.

Putin has thus redoubled efforts to drive a wedge between members of Western military and diplomatic alliances, most importantly NATO and the EU, and to undermine the democratic process in the West. So it is not surprising that Putin has put significant resources into disinformation efforts in his desire to subvert the soft power and public confidence in the democratic systems in the United States and Europe. Still, his actions in the 2016 U.S. election represent a significant new tack. When Russia directed its efforts against U.S. domestic politics, they were more robust than anyone could fathom at the time.

The intelligence community's finding that Putin's interference in the 2016 presidential election sought to boost the candidacy of a political newcomer (whose policy trajectory was unknown) over a seasoned practitioner with well-established foreign policy priorities shows how much risk Putin is willing to take.[5] Russian officials, like their counterparts around the world, tend to value stable and predictable adversaries because they provide the best opportunity for avoiding major foreign policy missteps or direct confrontations. Most intelligence actions are taken with an important and specific strategic or tactical goal in mind. But sometimes actions are taken recklessly, as a game to be played, rather than as an essential lever of foreign policy. The mere fact that Putin approved active measures against the U.S. election system to help bring a particular presidential candidate to power suggests he is far less strategic and far more dangerous than I had thought. It shows an unhealthy appetite for high risk in a world leader and limited ability to fathom the full and long-term consequences of covert actions. The question that emerges is the undergirding motivation for Putin's action: Is Russia taking risks for tactical sport or as a misguided strategic escalation of confrontation with the West?

One example of this type of gamesmanship—albeit on a much smaller scale—has stayed with me for many years and is a reminder of how feckless covert action can be. On my initial assignment abroad, in Chile during the early 1970s, my first residence in Santiago was on calle Gertrudis Echenique, only a few blocks from the Russian embassy. Shortly after arriving at the station, I commented to a colleague that the neighborhood seemed to have an unusually large number of stray cats. He laughed, pointing out that the CIA station had run a "great" disinformation operation in my neighborhood against the Russians a few months before I arrived. The station had placed an advertisement in the local press announcing that the Russian embassy would give a small number of escudos (the local currency) to anyone who brought a stray cat to the embassy. Dozens of people took the ad seriously and brought cats to the embassy. When they didn't receive the anticipated recompense, they just left the stray cats out front. These cats quickly populated the neighborhood.

This was just the type of mindless covert action that serves no useful purpose other than harassment and invariably provokes countermeasures. Intelligence is not merely a game to be played; it is an essential lever in foreign policy. Neither we nor the Russians ought to engage in covert action unless it has a strategic and meaningful purpose. Something seemingly frivolous can turn out to have a more lasting or consequential effect by provoking genuine and sustained hostility from the adversary.

Is it possible that today Russia has anchored much of its intelligence strategy to a long succession of "stray feline" operations, especially in cyberspace, in hopes that chaos and disinformation will prevail before successful countermeasures are applied? Considering Russian election interference from this optic might explain why Putin was willing to abrogate the Moscow Rules. The successive actions of both the SVR and the GRU in the cyber sphere appeared to be merely disruptive and tactically effective, rather than strategically important.

It is also possible, in this scenario, that the Russians themselves didn't have a clear perception of how disruptive their actions would be and how outraged Americans would become when the election interference came to light. Russia's active measures might have had a "boiling frog" effect on both Russia and the United States, the situation in which the frog doesn't realize it is in jeopardy until it is too late to jump out of the pot. Likewise, as Russia's active measures progressed without any significant countermeasures from the United States and without being held to account by any effective means, those active measures became more and more unbridled, until they passed a major threshold, a point of no return.

Add to this that the GRU, the military and more tactically minded intelligence agency in Russia, apparently led the assault, which may have contributed to this myopic perspective. As a primarily military entity, it may not have had a full appreciation for the political impli-

cations of its actions. It may not have been fully apprised of the KGB/
SVR understanding with CIA and others about the important red line
articulated in the Moscow Rules. Even if it was fully aware of that line,
perhaps it was simply more aggressive and willing to act because of its
military culture.

From this vantage point, Putin's election interference efforts, while
dramatic, ultimately undermined even Russia's short-term goals, such
as sanctions relief. Russian intelligence officers no doubt felt as clever
as the U.S. Santiago station had, but its efforts have galvanized a portion of the American public and much of Europe against accommo-
dation to Russia.

If Russia is deliberately abrogating the Moscow Rules, that would be
far more worrisome. An even worse possibility is to see recent events as
an effort by Putin and Russia to undermine democracy and the global
order. From this perspective, Russia has fired the first shots across the
bow by using active measures to subvert democracy by turning democratic norms and institutions against democracy itself.

Some have called the Russian election interference an indication
that Putin has adopted a new hybrid theory of warfare known as the
Gerasimov Doctrine, named after General Valery Gerasimov, who
believed that events like the Arab Spring and the Color Revolutions
in eastern Europe were effectively perpetrated by Western intelligence
agencies. While his was a flawed analysis and one that seemingly under-
pins Russia's waging of a quasi second cold war, the prevailing ambiguity behind Russia's motivations is exactly why we need spies within
the heart of the Kremlin to help determine exactly what the Russian
leadership is really thinking.[6]

If we are to effectively respond to this intelligence assault and possibly establish grounds for a new relationship with Putin, we must see
him soberly for what he has done, what he is capable of, and who he
is—an intelligence operative and spymaster at heart who relies heavily
on the tradecraft and toolbox of his intelligence agencies to advance
his foreign policy goal of reasserting Russian power abroad.

LESSON FIVE

As long as there is human frailty, people can be persuaded to spy for Russia.

Human nature is not black and white but black and grey.

—GRAHAM GREENE, *The Lost Childhood*

When sorrows come, they come not as single spies, but in battalions!

—SHAKESPEARE, *Hamlet*

5

Spies among Us

The Real "Americans"

There are several types of intelligence operatives or assets working for Russia. Some are sent from Russia, some reach out to or are recruited by Russia, and many are at first unwitting, while others are forever devoted to Russia. The first of these are Russian "illegals" or intelligence operatives with "non-official cover" (NOC) status and are not the kinds generally reflected in Hollywood films. Their profiles are often rather prosaic and underwhelming. Their taskings are long, even boring much of the time, and they are often unsuccessful. What is most important to realize is that they do indeed still exist today.

On July 16, 2018, federal prosecutors charged twenty-nine-year-old Mariia Butina with conspiracy and acting as a foreign agent for Russia. In December 2018 she pleaded guilty to the charges and was sentenced to eighteen months in prison. She was released on October 25, 2019, and deported to Russia. Unconventionally, Butina engaged in both covert political action and espionage. She allegedly sought to develop back-channel connections between Moscow and Washington with the help of American political operatives and at the same time collected targeting information on potential U.S. sources within the orbit of the Trump campaign. She sent such data back to Moscow. She was "handled" by senior Russian official Alexander Torshin and received financial backing from Russian oligarch Konstantin Nikolaev. Using the cover of a graduate student at American University, she anchored most of her political work around gun rights and cultivated a relationship with the NRA, which she then leveraged in her initial attempts to make contact with the Trump campaign.[1] The case of Butina is somewhat perplexing because of her unorthodox dual-use activities, her use of what seemed to be her real identity without official cover, and her funding through an intermediary. Although she does not seem to have been a formally trained intelligence agent, it is difficult to know definitively much about Butina other than the fact that she was an innovative "illegal" element in the ongoing intelligence operation carried out against the United States during the 2016 election.

Butina in many other ways joins the rank-and-file of Russian "illegals" or "NOCs," the undeclared foreign agents with non-official cover who have walked among us. In 2015 three individuals were charged as part of an alleged "spy ring [that] attempted to collect economic intelligence and recruit New York City residents as intelligence sources." Two of the individuals, Igor Sporyshev and Victor Podobnyy, reportedly operated under diplomatic cover while working out of the Russian Federation's permanent mission to the United Nations in New York City. But the other, Evgeny Buryakov, was working under a commercial cover as an executive at VneshEconomBank (VEB), Russia's state-owned national development bank. In the course of investigating these undercover SVR agents, FBI agents were able to obtain remarkable audio recordings of conversations between Sporyshev and Podobnyy from within the SVR office in New York City. In the recordings they discuss the lengths of their postings, their covers, and even the mundane nature of their jobs. Still, the recordings offered incredible insight into the day-to-day operations of the SVR agents in New York and provided irrefutable evidence that these individuals were tasked with continuing the job that Tretyakov or Comrade J had been tasked with more than fifteen years prior: to recruit spies who could provide privileged access to the political, military, economic, technical, and financial sectors of American society. In keeping with this strategy, one of the individuals whom they targeted was a future junior foreign policy advisor on the Trump campaign, Carter Page.[2]

Like something from the popular television series *The Americans*, only two years prior, in June 2010, thanks in large part to an SVR deputy officer for the U.S. section of its S Directorate and information provided by U.S. spy Aleksandr Poteyev, ten Russian nationals were arrested on charges of conspiracy to "act in the United States as agents of a foreign government, specifically the Russian Federation." Some were operating as "covert SVR agents who assume[d] false identities, . . . living in the United States on long-term, 'deep-cover' assignments," while others, like Anna Chapman, used their real identities but operated as undeclared Russian foreign agents. These individuals were dispatched to live in the United States as "illegals," and some had been in the United States for more than twenty years, many with children born in the United States.[3] These agents were tasked with developing entrenched connections to their communities and assigned to "recruit sources who are in, or are able to infiltrate, United States policy-making circles," with the hopes of collecting important intelligence for the Russian government or handling sources with this access. The spies exchanged information via old-fashioned dead drop and brush passes and received encrypted, radio-ciphered messages, radiograms, and shortwave radio messages in addition to electronic communications. Perhaps most interestingly, in at least two cases they used mobile roaming virtual private networks (VPNs) to exchange important files from public locations. In the end, however, the spies were identified in large part through sloppy tradecraft—meetings with other members of the spy ring, Russian diplomats, or known intelligence officers. The ten spies arrested in 2010 returned to Russia as part of a swap that included Sergei Skripal, the former Russian spy later poisoned in Britain, in March 2018.[4]

One of the spies from the 2010 ring arrests, Mikhail Vasenkov, known as Juan Lazaro, took his identity from a three-year-old child who had died of respiratory failure in Uruguay in 1947. In 1979 Vasenkov immigrated to Peru, where he became a naturalized citizen and met Vicky Pelaez, a leftist Peruvian journalist, whom he married in 1983. The two moved to the United States in the mid-1980s. She openly worked as a leftist Spanish-language journalist and he was ostensibly an anthropologist, but in reality, first and foremost, they were working for Russian intelligence.

The Russians began using this tactic as far back as the 1920s. For quite a long period throughout the Cold War, U.S. counterintelligence posture made it difficult for Russians to plant their agents within our midst. This is not to say they didn't try or that they weren't successful. But the development of these entrenched and intricate networks was quite challenging. Dismantling these rings, then as now, not only alerts us to the counterintelligence challenges afforded by a democratic and open society but also to the significant investment and risk that Russia is willing to take, as well as the strategic horizon that they envision.

An Officer of the Soviet Intelligence Service

How Russians establish their alter egos within the United States is a long and complex process. Deployed illegals' taskings have ambitious long-term stakes for the Russian state, and these individuals are willing to sacrifice their lives for the cause.

In 1927, more than half a century before anyone had ever heard of Mariia Butina or Anna Chapman, Eugene Maki left the United States to return to his father's homeland of Estonia. In 1952 someone who called himself Maki returned to the United States, but his name was actually Karel Häyhänen, a lieutenant colonel in the Soviet state security service and an "illegal" spy who had co-opted Maki's identity. In 1940 Häyhänen crossed the border into Finland under his newly assumed identity, married, applied for a U.S. passport, and immigrated to the United States in 1952. He lived in the United States without incident until one day, in 1957, he appeared at the steps of the U.S. embassy in Paris and basically said, "I'm an officer in the Soviet intelligence service. For the past five years, I have been operating in the United States. Now I need your help." Häyhänen had run afoul of his boss after botching a number of intelligence operations due to excessive drinking and had been recalled to Moscow. Instead, he chose to defect, and he provided valuable insight into Soviet illegal spycraft and handling. Not one member of the 2010 spy ring gave us the same mea culpa, with all its salient and revealing information, though we gave them little opportunity to do so.

Häyhänen provided fascinating details to investigators. He had rarely communicated directly with his contacts. Codenamed Vik, he signaled his arrival in the United States by placing a red thumbtack in the sign for horse cart rentals next to the historic Tavern on the Green restaurant in Central Park. Had he suspected that he was under surveillance, he was to place a white thumbtack instead. Most information was exchanged through dead drops. He revealed that pens, pencils, batteries, and hollowed-out coins were also used to transport sensitive information.[5]

Häyhänen's main task was to operate a radio and transmit back to Russia information on U.S. nuclear and submarine technologies. Häyhänen gave information that led the United States to believe that the Soviets were cultivating a robust "illegals" program. He identified the heads of the operation as Vitali Pavlov and Aleksandr Korotkov, two intelligence officials operating "under official diplomatic cover." Pavlov was one of the KGB's top officers during this era and an avid proponent of Soviet covert action before World War II.[6] This 1950s tradecraft parallels almost perfectly what we know about how more recent illegals were handled by Russian officials under official diplomatic cover, like Russian ambassador Sergei Kislyak, or individuals with legitimate roles in Russian institutions, like Russian Central Bank director Alexander Torshin and VEB chair Sergei N. Gorkov.

Information provided by Häyhänen helped authorities identify several Soviet assets and intelligence agents. Most important among these was his superior, whom Häyhänen knew only as "Mark," the owner of a photo studio in Brooklyn. "Mark" was located, arrested, and interrogated in 1957, but he gave up absolutely no information as to his espionage activities, nor did he reveal his true identity. After weeks of interrogation, the only thing he admitted was his name, Rudolf Ivanovich Abel.[7] This was not his real name—the real Rudolf Abel was a friend and colleague of his in the Russian clandestine service. It was a signal to Moscow that he had been captured and that he would be following a set protocol. He was convicted of three counts of espionage and sentenced to thirty years in a U.S. federal penitentiary. After protracted negotiations, captured CIA U-2 pilot Gary Powers was swapped for the KGB colonel Abel in February 1962 on the Glienicke Bridge in Berlin, along with American graduate student Frederic Pryor, who had been held for six months by the East Germans.[8]

Eventually we would learn that Abel's real name was William August Fisher. Fisher was born in Britain, moved to Russia after World War I, was recruited into the Soviet intelligence service out of school, and was immediately dispatched to the illegals service. He worked as an illegal in the United Kingdom and Scandinavia before World War II.

Much like the members of the 2010 spy ring, Fisher was sent to the United States and tasked with developing a robust espionage network without any ties to the legal Soviet presence. Fisher was instructed to take on existing spies as well as recruit new ones. The Rosenbergs and the Krogers (also known as Morris and Lona Cohen) were members of Fisher's network. Because the Rosenbergs never confessed and the Krogers escaped (to later spy for the Soviets in the United Kingdom as part of the Portland Spy Ring), his presence remained undetected. By all accounts he was professional, diligent, and successful for the nine years he spent in the United States before his arrest.[9]

If Fisher was evidence that Soviet illegals were from formidable stock, Häyhänen was the incarnation of the consummate spy blunder: unprofessional, an alcoholic, and prone to noticeable rows with his Finnish wife. His sheer incompetence reportedly enraged Fisher, who never trusted him and who made his complaints known to Moscow. Matters came to a head when Häyhänen stole $5,000 that he and Fisher had buried in upstate New York for the wife of a Soviet spy, Morton Sobell, who had been sentenced to thirty years in prison as part of the Rosenbergs' case. The Fisher/Abel case left the intelligence world reeling. Because Fisher refused to talk and because Häyhänen was essentially ignorant of the identity of both Fisher's handlers and local intelligence assets, it was very difficult to assess the true level of Soviet illegals' penetration into the United States. U.S. intelligence didn't know it at the time, but while Fisher may not have been the lone deep cover spy in the United States, there seemingly were no legions of Fishers living across America.[10]

What was clear, however, was that there was a concerted and formidable effort on the part of the Soviets to garner U.S. intelligence wherever and whenever they could. This effort has not changed and is still pursued with vigor today. What the Abel case revealed, like the 2010 spy ring and the case of Mariia Butina, is the strategic patience of Russian intelligence and the lengths to which they will go to gather intelligence about our national security posture. Its focus has not changed since the end of the Cold War and neither have its tactics.

NSA: The Not (Yet) Secure Agency

There certainly are numerous Russian intelligence operatives who are dispatched to the United States to serve in Russian installations with the mission to penetrate U.S. targets. Many of these officials are relatively easy to identify. Far more numerous and difficult to identify are Americans who can be recruited to spy at Russia's behest. One of the lower-hanging fruits for recruitment comes from the rapid expansion of the intelligence trade into the cyber sphere. Although many see big data, satellites, drones, and cyber espionage as the playing field of the future, much of our successful technical collection begins with human spies, even in the cyber age. The same tradecraft of assessment, vetting, targeting, and collecting applies in cyberspace just as it does in the "real world," and it is conducted by real people. The Russians know this full well and are actively seeking to recruit people to assist in technological spying.

In May 2013 Edward Snowden walked out of an NSA facility in Hawaii with a USB drive holding some of our country's greatest cyber strategies, though he was not yet acting in the service of the Russians. This information—through deft Russian maneuvering—would end up in Russia's hands. The damage he wrought cannot be overstated. What he shared with the Russians provided them with a nearly endless supply of information essential for effective cyber espionage. The Russians are almost certainly still mining his data and using it today. Since then at least two other NSA contractors have been implicated in severe national security breaches. In 2015 an unnamed NSA contractor's personal computer was hacked (with help from the SVR-linked Kaspersky security software), exposing key code and U.S. offensive hacking techniques and defense methods. In 2016 Booz Allen contractor Hal Martin was arrested for removing more than 50 terabytes' worth of data from the NSA over two decades, though proof that he provided information to the Russians, if it exists, was never made public. Nonetheless, all of these breaches have severe implications not only for how to protect against further leaks but how protected—or unprotected—we are from aggressive cyber attacks by a foreign state or nonstate actor.[11]

The Russians have found particular success in attracting sources from within the National Security Agency (NSA). From its creation in 1952, the NSA was charged with creating ciphers, encoding techniques, and protecting communication lines used by the entire U.S. military and intelligence community. The NSA also sought to intercept and decipher the communications of foreign governments. In a striking parallel to today's antiterrorism focus, in its fervor to make quick progress the NSA committed a serious error in assigning primacy to technical competency above all else. Without assessing the full security suitability of its contractors, the NSA created huge vulnerabilities in its programs that led to terrible intelligence losses. The United States suffered two strategically important breaches in quick succession, thus exposing the capabilities of a nascent and hugely important aspect of U.S. intelligence-gathering activities.[12]

First, William Martin and Bernon Mitchell—two highly intelligent mathematicians who objected to American nuclear policies—defected to the Soviet Union in 1960 and made a public statement revealing information about U.S. spying activities, on both enemies and allies.[13] Martin and Mitchell provided key details about U.S. technical capabilities, including the locations of sensors that the NSA used to intercept Soviet transmissions, NSA codes and code-breaking techniques, and the fact that the U.S. could not yet break Soviet codes. The NSA concluded at the time that "beyond any doubt, no other event has had, or is likely to have in the future, a greater impact on the Agency's security program."[14] This remained true until Snowden leaked documents revealing the United States' and its allies' technical surveillance programs. However, Soviet archives now suggest that the pair could not provide the desired sensitive information about American cryptographic techniques and were of little intelligence value beyond the revelations contained in their initial debriefings.[15]

The second major breach for the NSA was perpetrated by Korean War hero Jack Dunlap.[16] While working as the chauffeur and courier for the NSA chief of staff, he provided the GRU with countless sensitive documents, which included CIA estimates of Soviet forces in Europe, design plans for cipher machines, NSA manuals, and possibly information allowing the KGB and GRU to identify traitors in their organizations. During a routine polygraph, Dunlap raised suspicions about some other criminal activity he had engaged in to help grant him access to sensitive material. This occurred about the same time that a spy for the CIA alerted the United States about Dunlap's activities. Faced with grim prospects, Dunlap committed suicide.[17]

This rapid series of revelations prompted the NSA to substantially reform its operations—by changing secret codes and encoding techniques and technology—and amend much of its security and recruitment protocol. But the damage done by these breaches was far worse than individual embarrassments and lost information. The Soviets had gained insight into the whole of American intelligence gathering—its architecture, its technological capability, its aspirations, and its limitations. These were the first shots fired in a new type of informational technology war that has evolved into the cyber wars we know today. The recent breaches place us in largely the same position now as then.

Like his defector predecessors in the NSA, Snowden will likely suffer the same fate they did. Whether he wittingly set out to empower the Russians or not, he has been deftly manipulated into becoming an agent of influence for the Russian state. And just like his forerunners, he is exhausting his pertinence and utility. He and others who wish to emulate him should note that while many of them sought to return home, none of them could, and most of them died miserable and in obscurity.

During the Cold War, just as now, the NSA traitors' poor suitability to their tasks was perhaps overlooked largely because of their technical or linguistic ability. This oversight is emblematic of an emerging problem within the intelligence community—the need for intelligence analysts and officers with linguistic skills *and* proficiency in understanding and utilizing complex technical data or cultural nuance. We find ourselves in an ever-more complex counterintelligence predicament in which it is difficult to assess an individual's true loyalties or hierarchy of loyalties, whether to the family, tribe, ethnic group, religion, ideology, or country of origin. These individuals can be quite vulnerable to compromise or manipulation by foreign intelligence services. One need only look at the case of Jerry Chun Shing Lee, a former CIA case officer who was arrested in January 2018. As a naturalized American citizen originally from China, he was allegedly targeted by and then eventually persuaded by the Chinese intelligence services to give up everything he knew about the CIA's intelligence operations in China.

Not of Ideologues but of Scoundrels

Intelligence operatives like Jerry Chun Shing Lee who can be compelled to spy for our adversaries are often drawn in not for ideological purposes but for more venal motives. At points before and after World War II the Russians enjoyed a bursting spring of spies in the West who were drawn to the communist cause. But as the reality of Stalin's Russia clashed with the "utopian dream" and as running espionage operations on U.S. soil became increasingly difficult when American counterespionage capability matured, the Russians had to look elsewhere. The Soviets pivoted toward targeting individuals whose motivations were less ideologically driven and more focused on self-interest or compromise. They sought targets who needed money to keep a mistress, to settle a debt, or to feed a gambling addiction or who might accept help fostering a revenge narrative or stroking for a fragile ego. They also sought individuals who might be susceptible to blackmail.

The Soviets also benefited from a number of "walk-ins"—individuals drawn not by principle or valor but less vaunted motivations. This inglorious cohort of traitors tended to have an oversized sense of self-importance and entitlement undergirded by a feeling of underappreciation or marginalization in their current circumstances. The Soviets were skilled at cultivating and handling these sources, taking traitors looking for one-off trades in exchange for a lump sum and transforming them into reliable intelligence assets by appealing to their delusions of grandeur and providing them with significant financial inducement.

The first notable scoundrel spy, Robert Lee Johnson, spied for the Soviets on and off from 1954 to 1962. His Soviet handlers did not think much of him at first because he was a drunk and a gambler and was married to a mentally unstable Austrian former prostitute named Hedwig Pipek, or "Hedy," with whom he fought constantly. Embittered that the U.S. Army had failed to see his true career potential, he sought political asylum in East Germany while serving as a sergeant in Berlin. The KGB convinced him to return immediately to his post in West Berlin as an "agent-in-place," first in Berlin, then in the United States, and eventually in Paris, where he was stationed at the Armed Forces Courier Center, which handled the most important military and diplomatic documents for NATO and the United States in Europe.

Through an ambitious and protracted effort, Johnson was able to gain access to the central vault.[18] Over the course of two years Johnson provided the KGB with information of the highest value: U.S. cryptographic systems, codes, and ciphers; the numbers and locations of U.S. nuclear warhead deployment across Europe; NATO's plans for its defense of Western Europe; and assessments on perceived Soviet strengths and weaknesses. Johnson singlehandedly provided the Soviets with a canny strategic advantage over the West. Khrushchev was reportedly so pleased with Johnson that the KGB sent him on a holiday to Monte Carlo and awarded him the rank of major in the Red Army.

When Johnson was transferred back to the United States in 1964, he was exposed by KGB defector Yuri Nosenko. He was sentenced to twenty-five years in prison, but in 1972 Johnson met his end at the hand of his estranged son, who visited Johnson at the Lewisburg federal penitentiary in Pennsylvania and without a word stabbed his father in the heart.[19]

Johnson's legacy of treachery reminds us that one individual, even a deeply flawed one, can do enormous damage. Among a handful of American intelligence traitors, there were two who would work for the Soviets to devastating effect against our most sensitive national security interests. One was Aldrich Ames, a CIA case officer.[20] The other was Robert Philip Hanssen, an FBI counterintelligence agent.[21] These cases are well known to those who follow the intelligence business.[22]

What strikes me from the cases of Ames and Hanssen is how fundamentally unexceptional these men were. They were pedestrian people who worked within our national security apparatus and, while ill suited for the work, were not flagrantly unfit.

Ames and Hanssen both came to the intelligence business through their fathers' influence. Carlton Ames worked at the CIA for years, unimpressively by all accounts, on counterintelligence matters. Howard Hanssen was a Chicago police officer and a harsh disciplinarian who was psychologically abusive (or worse) and went out of his way to denigrate his son directly and in public. Hanssen's "father issues" perhaps created a seedbed for betrayal of authority figures and institutions. Although Hanssen would publicly praise his father and his anticommunist intelligence work within the Chicago Police Department, some ascribe a revenge motive to Hanssen's spying, that its ultimate goal was to undermine his father's professional legacy. In his own letters to the KGB, Hanssen claimed that he had wanted to be another Kim Philby from the early age of fourteen.

Ames's experience with Russian operations and his Russian-language capability kept him at the table of many very sensitive operations, but he was generally viewed as a mediocre operations officer throughout his career.[23] Like his father, his skill in recruiting agents was virtually nil. He not only lacked the good social aptitude needed for recruiting, but his seemingly arrogant pseudointellectual approach to life and operations rubbed many of his colleagues the wrong way. He was intellectually lazy in his work, performing well only when he liked the task, while everything else was given short shrift. Ames's drinking was a well-known issue among many of his colleagues and superiors. His career did progress, but far more slowly than it should have according to his own perceptions of his real worth. In retrospect, it is surprising that he reached the mid-level of the CIA structure, even more so that he was positioned in the middle of the most sensitive Russian agent operations run by CIA's Soviet Division.

Hanssen first wrote to the GRU in 1979. Although he had been working for the FBI for only about three years, he already felt marginalized and underappreciated. Some suggest that financial strain and professional resentment led him to betray his country. In fact, Hanssen thought himself intellectually superior to most people in general and his coworkers specifically, and his air of condescension made him a target for badgering and ridicule in the office.

Despite his rather abrasive and humorless personality, Hanssen had an acumen with computers and took an active role in integrating computer systems into the FBI's arsenal of counterintelligence work. Unfortunately for American intelligence, this role provided him with excellent access to very sensitive data, including technical operations and the identities of many of the FBI's and CIA's most sensitive sources.

Outwardly, Hanssen was a brusque but seemingly upstanding member of his community. In truth he was made of a very curious mix of devotional religiosity and sexual deviance, evoking a troubled and tortured individual. He was a member of Opus Dei, a small and staunchly conservative organization within the Catholic Church, but he regularly clandestinely video-recorded his sexual activity with his wife, unbeknown to her, which he then transmitted to a friend. He frequented strip clubs and engaged in a supposedly nonsexual relationship with one of the strippers, Priscilla Sue Galey.

From a counterintelligence perspective, both Hanssen and Ames had traits that might have predisposed them to duplicity. Neither was socially adept, both overtly demonstrated their contempt for others, and both were strained financially. Each considered himself intellectually superior to others and underappreciated in their work, but both were considered mediocre and neither of their careers had progressed as they had hoped. Still, because of Ames's Russian experience and language capability and Hanssen's technical fluency, both men had access to incredibly sensitive intelligence and would work for the Soviets for an extended period—Ames for nine years, Hanssen on and off for twenty-two. They sent scores of people to their death and undermined several important American intelligence efforts.

On a personal note, I met Ames shortly after I joined the agency. I ended up working adjacent to him for some months before entering the operational training at the "Farm." His job was to review field cables to headquarters and highlight key data on Russia while I reviewed traffic from Eastern European stations. Our interchanges were fairly convivial; almost all of them concerned the spying business. On this subject he was a good conversationalist and steeped in intelligence lore. Unlike me, he had been raised in a CIA family and was an avid reader of spy novels. He particularly enjoyed Eric Ambler books and gave me one of his favorites, *A Coffin for Dimitrios*. Our paths diverged, and I lost contact with Ames. But we would cross paths again fifteen years later in Rome, when I was assigned there as chief of station. Ames was working under my supervision as chief of the Hard Targets Branch, working on operations against the Soviets, the Eastern Europeans, the Chinese, and the North Koreans. Ames's performance was consistent with his lackluster track record in previous foreign assignments. Before I departed Washington, I had been advised that his recurrent drinking problem had again surfaced early in his assignment to Rome, but after another rebuke and detox program, he reportedly had his drinking relatively under control. His seeming restraint probably was due to his wife, who was leaning hard on him to stay sober. His drinking binges reportedly occurred when she was not with him, either while he was out of town or she was traveling.

Shortly after I arrived in Rome, I had a one-on-one session with Ames and warned him that if he fell off the wagon, he would be sent home, and I asked the deputy chief to keep an eye on him. This probably surprised and disappointed Ames, who wrongly assumed our friendly relationship many years earlier would cut him some slack. It was soon clear to him that we weren't going to pick up where we had left off. Perhaps because of this, he kept his distance from me, apart from a few social encounters early on. We also had a confrontational exchange over a Bulgarian walk-in (codenamed Motorboat) whom Ames was reluctant to polygraph. I had to push him to get it done. I would learn later that he made sure the test was invalid.   Motorboat didn't show for the next meeting because Ames had advised the Soviets about his potential defection and they had him yanked back to Sofia. We would find out years later that he was dealt with harshly.

Treachery didn't stop with Ames and Hanssen. Much intelligence about other compromises came to the surface in the immediate aftermath of the collapse of the Soviet Union as scores of KGB/GRU defectors provided information to Western intelligence agencies while looking for money or better prospects outside of the new Russia.[24]

An Endless Well

During this period of transition in Russia, the number of people who volunteered to spy for the SVR—the new moniker for the KGB—spiked. And the landscape was expanding. The end of the Cold War left countries scrambling for grounding, and that included new intelligence. Over the ensuing two decades, high-profile cases would emerge involving individuals willing to spy for Cuba, China, North Korea, Israel, Venezuela, Iraq, Syria, Hizballah, Iran, and others.[25] Most painfully, though, this list also included the most senior CIA officer up to that point ever to be arrested for espionage, albeit not the one whose activities were the most damaging.

When I was acting deputy director for operations in 1995, I made a trip to the Farm to meet with the new trainees. Because of my imposing physical stature and stern look, I have become accustomed to the seat next to me at dinner or on the train being the last one filled. I have learned that I must take the initiative to speak to people rather than waiting for them to approach or speak to me. In my capacity as head of CIA worldwide operations, I met with countless people whom I would struggle to recall today. However, I have a distinct memory of Harold James Nicholson, who was an instructor, walking up to me without a care in the world and, though we had never met before, making conversation as if we were the oldest of friends. He was breezy and at ease, and our exchange left me feeling as if there was something rather eccentric and enigmatic about him. It wasn't a negative or positive feeling specifically, rather just a unique and enduring one.

Nicholson, like Ames, had a pronounced streak of laziness in his work habits. Marty Roeber, a top Latin American analyst and deputy chief of the Latin America Division, also recalls meeting Nicholson at the Farm when Roeber was taking the chief of station course in preparation for an assignment abroad. Nicholson advised Roeber "to coast through it and don't bother to strain yourself." To top it off, he suggested that when Roeber got to the field, "let others do the work and enjoy the prerogatives of being chief for a few years"—hardly music to the ears of any hard-charging officer. Roeber was incredulous and marked it up as Nicholson being a misfit assigned to the Farm, where he would unfortunately be a terrible role model for any aspiring officer who came across his path. But this underperforming mind-set matches up very well with other traitors' work ethic.[26]

Like Hanssen and Ames, Nicholson's father, a U.S. Air Force master sergeant, worked for the government. Also, like them, Nicholson had a very high opinion of himself. He joined the CIA in 1980 and rose rapidly in the ranks, serving as a case officer in Manila, Bangkok, and Tokyo, before being sent to Bucharest as chief of station and then to Kuala Lumpur as deputy chief of station. However, in 1992, while in Romania, he suffered a messy divorce. He was granted custody of his children and struggled during his next assignment in Malaysia, feeling increasingly crushed by his financial obligations. He applied for an extension of his assignment but was refused. This rejection incensed him and, coupled with his financial stress, led him to offer his services to the Russians.

His next assignment was at the Farm, and he used his access to devastating effect. From 1994 to 1996, he passed the identities of nearly all incoming CIA case officers to the Russians. It was during this time that I had my brief encounter with him. Of course I had no notion that he was a traitor. But in retrospect I wonder if his peculiar demeanor toward me was in fact a mischievous nod to the wanton disdain that he held for the CIA and its leadership. In late 1995 a series of polygraphs indicated that Nicholson might be lying on some key questions. In the post-Ames era, this set off a very substantive investigation that quickly showed extravagant spending and inexplicable deposits following international travel. Surveillance teams observed Nicholson meeting with his Russian handler and depositing his ill-gotten gains. Nicholson was arrested in November 1996 and was sentenced to nearly twenty-four years in prison. But prison would neither chasten nor cow Nicholson. In fact, it perhaps made him even more brazen and callous.

In 2006, carefully instructed by his father, Nicholson's son Nathan walked into the Russian consulate in San Francisco with a letter of introduction from his father and a photo of the father-son pair from the visiting room of his father's prison. Over the next two years, at clandestine meetings in Mexico City, Lima, and Nicosia, Nathan shuttled written communications between his father and the Russians, which amounted to details of debriefings on how Nicholson was caught, who polygraphed him, who interrogated him, and his assessment of errors he or they made in tradecraft, as well as a series of other secrets that Nicholson thought valuable. Clearly the Russians wanted to know how Nicholson was caught, if they had made errors in tradecraft, and whether there was a traitor in their midst who had helped the CIA catch him. Nicholson also conveyed his health information, proposed an escape plan, and gave the Russians information about his other son, Jeremiah, who worked on electronic warfare at Tyndall Air Force Base, essentially suggesting that they approach Jeremiah to spy. In return, Nathan received about $37,000.

For most of his activities, Nathan was under FBI surveillance, and in 2009 both he and his father were indicted. Because Nathan had clearly been manipulated by his father, he received a sentence of one hundred days of community service in addition to the seventy-two days he had served in jail. His father received an additional eight years in prison.[27] I don't have anything good to say about traitors to America, and I reserve special opprobrium for men like Nicholson who draw their families into their ignominy.

What we need to take away from these lessons is that, given Russia's relentless targeting of the United States, we can be sure that they are constantly seeking to recruit or to offer hospitable terms to those offering sensitive information about the United States. While these traitors will be rare, some are certainly aiming to seek out Russia today despite its autocratic leadership. Furthermore, given the significant expansion of people working in the national security sphere since 2001, it is almost a certainty that there are other spies like them within our government today. The question is whether Putin has a strategic edge because of these spies.

LESSON SIX

It takes a spy to catch a spy.

As everyone who is involved in counterintelligence work understood, your greatest victories are your worst defeats.

—SANDY GRIMES, CIA counterintelligence specialist and spymaster

6

A Spymaster's Rules in Counterintelligence

- -

A Quiet Task

Recalibrating our intelligence resources toward Russia is a matter of urgency. Russia has been unrelenting in its pursuit of intelligence gains against the United States since the end of the Cold War, and our attention has largely been elsewhere. It is important to grasp the full scope of Russian active measures that have been used against us in order to achieve such a recalibration, especially given the ambitious and dexterous playbook of active measures they have developed in the cyber age. Further, Russia's deployment of intelligence operatives and recruitment efforts has likely been successful, so there is a pressing need to understand thoroughly the extent of Russian penetrations into our government. This understanding will come most effectively by reinforcing the often forgotten but critical arm of intelligence work: counterintelligence (CI).

The counterintelligence mandate is a difficult and time-consuming one. One thinks of the traditional purview of espionage as successfully cultivating and then running intelligence sources and conducting covert actions, but among the chief objectives of the counterintelligence mandate is detecting weaknesses within our own system, sometimes in response to a breach but primarily in exercising tradecraft discipline. This involves the constant vetting of case officers, sources, analysts, and technicians in our own agencies as well as monitoring our foreign intelligence adversaries. An open, democratic society makes the task more difficult because people have rights to privacy and freedom of association and movement, and any investigative effort must be underpinned by a legitimate legal authority.

Special Counsel Robert Mueller's investigation into Russian interference in the 2016 presidential campaign and several long-standing counterintelligence investigations at the FBI show that the Russian intelligence net was cast over an impressively large number of individuals associated with Donald Trump's campaign. Attempts to penetrate the campaign leveraged business connections, offers of assistance, invitations for in-person meetings with President Putin and other senior Russian government officials, and policy proposals to repair and strengthen U.S.-Russian relations, all demonstrating a substantial effort by the Russians to find sources and potential agents of influence. This level of activity is not surprising during changes in administrations, especially when a Washington outsider is elected and Russia has to start near ground zero to develop access to key players in the new administration. What is new is that we were able to observe much of it through the lens of a major public investigation (appendix).[1]

Russia's push to develop Trump campaign sources should have been expected and probably was expected among intelligence professionals. It is what most major governments do in the spy business—look for witting and unwitting sources of political, military, technical, and government intelligence. Furthermore, this Russian intelligence effort is very much in line with the most emblematic and ambitious methods of operation of the KGB and GRU and something Russian intelligence has been doing since the Russian Revolution. While it should not surprise us, it should remind us how necessary it is to galvanize our efforts to uncover them. As we look at this operational activity, we need to keep on the forefront of our minds that this effort will continue for the foreseeable future. We know that the Russians cast the net wide, but what remains to be understood is what spies they were able to recruit in it.

Lost in the flurry of known activity is likely a great deal of unknown activity. We must assume that Russian efforts were not limited to those targeting the Trump campaign. The tenacity of the Russians leading up to and during the 2016 election is evidence of their desire to develop high-level government contacts and a wide portfolio of assets across the American economic and political landscape. Russian interference activity was aggressive and targeted, but we know very little about how these strategies were designed and calibrated, suggesting a more sophisticated intelligence capability than just that exposed by the Mueller Report. The greatest evidence of this is that the report made no mention of Russia's foreign intelligence service, the SVR, only the GRU and other entities with no official affiliation to the Russian government. Finally, as of this writing there were twelve still-secret ongoing cases referred to other prosecutors, which, if consistent with the Mueller Report, will likely highlight Russia's additional aggressive behavior.[2]

To take this idea further, it is important to contemplate the possibility, no matter how unlikely, that Putin's policy decisions may be rooted in well-informed intelligence coming from sources in the White House, the State Department, the Defense Department, or the U.S. intelligence community, as has often been the case in the past. These discoveries have always come as a shock, and yet we continue to make them and must see them as an inevitable part of this business.

Understanding the full scope of Russian penetrations can be learned only through intensive counterintelligence investigations conducted by U.S. law enforcement and intelligence services. In the investigations that informed the Mueller Report, there were FBI agents within the Special Counsel's Office whose mission was to share counterintelligence for ongoing investigations. These investigations follow the evidence and begin with an understanding that there might be a problem. Then there is deep exploration into how the facts relate to the potential problem. There are electronic trails of communication, financial records, documents, surveillance, interviews, and, most important, the recruitment of our own sources within the Russian intelligence system, a process handled by American intelligence services and their allies and carried out to support the ongoing investigation. So far, the work on the "Russia investigation" has evolved into at least seventeen different sets of charges of varying nature, some directly related to Russian interference and many others linked to other affirmed or alleged activity uncovered in the course of the analysis, including attempted interference by or specious influence campaigns arising from other countries, including Turkey, Saudi Arabia, UAE, and Israel. And yet we still do not understand where this all will lead.

One of the most interesting historical cases underscoring the point that we never know the outcome of a counterintelligence investigation in advance is that of Ethel and Julius Rosenberg, the central characters of the most storied Soviet spy trial of the Cold War. The discovery of their actions arose from an investigation into an entirely different Russian spy network, one led by Klaus Fuchs, a German-born British nuclear scientist. Information on Fuchs's actions was discovered in a Gestapo file recovered after the end of World War II, as well as from a decoded Venona cable. We had had the cable in our possession since 1945, but we were able to single out Fuchs only after we knew the questions we were trying to answer: How did the Russians come to detonate a nuclear bomb in 1949? Did they use American scientific technology to do so? Understanding the nature of the threat quickly led U.S. investigators to Fuchs, who pinpointed Harry Gold, a courier delivering material to and from Soviet consul Anatoly Yatskov and several Soviet spies, including Fuchs. Gold led investigators to David Greenglass, a machinist at Los Alamos whose brother-in-law was Julius Rosenberg. Ultimately, it was discovered that Julius Rosenberg was steering a significant effort to recruit scientists working at key positions across the U.S. government and private industry.[3]

The United States possessed intelligence that could have led investigators to the Rosenbergs as early as 1945, but the Rosenberg trial did not start until 1951. Once interest in Russian penetrations reached a critical mass, the pointed investigation took less than two years, which is relatively quick. Many CI investigations go on for many years. News of another spy in the U.S. atomic project, Oscar Seborer, who passed critical intelligence to the Soviets on the workings of the bomb's trigger, did not come to light in the public domain until 2019, though the FBI had been aware of him for seventy years.[4]

Our impatience to understand everything concerning the recent investigation into Russian interference in the U.S. election overlooks the time and depth of inquiry required to gain a full picture of what is transpiring. Counterintelligence is often a slow and thankless task.

It bears repeating as we anticipate future elections that Russia will continue to deploy significant resources to collect intelligence on our political, military, economic, technical, and financial sectors and seek to recruit, cultivate, and manage human sources from within these sectors. They scrutinize all of the presidential candidates with the aim of securing access to sources of information within each candidate's orbit.

Political Circus

The conclusions in the Mueller Report will reverberate for many years and unfortunately are likely to remain politicized. However, if we focus on the report's most important findings, we see that Russia systematically and repeatedly engaged in actions to interfere in our internal affairs and that we must endeavor to address these actions with Russia or protect our nation from the next assault, which reports suggest has been under way for some time.[5]

Russian intelligence activities against the United States have been perpetrated relentlessly from 1917 until today. The Mueller Report provides a classic example of how Russian intelligence agencies have worked in our country for many years. What is new is the now-omnipresent use of cyber tools for spying and covert activities. That Russian intelligence weaponized cyber technology was a surprise and change in tactics, but that the Russians continue to aggressively collect intelligence on its U.S. targets is a certainty. What isn't certain is to what degree they will weaponize cyber tech in the future, but it will be Putin's policy decision.

Perhaps most ironically, when partisan bickering interferes with initiatives to mount an effective defense against Russia's interference, it helps fulfill the most ambitious of Russia's presumed objectives: namely, to sow doubt about the integrity of our elections, our institutions, and our democracy.

Mole Hunt

One of the best examples of how a counterintelligence investigation is conducted is how we determined the reason behind the staggering number of intelligence losses at the height of the Cold War.

This is not a perfect parallel to today's challenges. The following account tells of resolving a number of penetrations, whereas at present we are facing a multipronged intelligence effort by Russia and other hostile states. But this account does give insight into the work, challenges, vagaries, and peripeties of a counterintelligence investigation.

Awareness of the greatest counterintelligence problem in CIA history started in the summer of 1985, when the agency began to lose contact with our most important Soviet sources stationed abroad: a KGB counterintelligence agent in Lagos did not return from his leave, and then a GRU officer in Lisbon also failed to return from leave. Later, in November, a Washington DC–based KGB scientific and technical officer who was working with us traveled back to the Soviet Union as part of the "honor guard" escorting Vitali Yurchenko, a Soviet defector who had opted to reverse his defection. We would never see him again. Also in November a KGB illegals support officer in Bonn traveled to a KGB conference in East Germany and disappeared.[6] Although it would take us a while to find out, all of these sources had been arrested, tried, and executed for their espionage on our behalf.[7]

In February 1986 a highly sensitive CIA technical operation known as Absorb was blown when the KGB "discovered" a shipping container stocked with plutonium-seeking sensors meant to identify and monitor nuclear warhead sites in the Soviet Union. Also, at the beginning of 1986 five of our sources who were living in Russia were rounded up, and CIA Moscow station officer Mike Sellers was declared persona non grata (PNGed) following his attempt to meet with a source.[8] All save one of these sources would be tried and executed.[9]

Still more losses were to come. In December 1986 a KGB political officer who had worked with the FBI in San Francisco was arrested and sentenced to fifteen years in a labor camp. In February 1987 a KGB political intelligence officer who had worked for the CIA in Indonesia in the 1970s was arrested, tried, and executed.[10] The near-simultaneous loss of eleven agents was tragic and disorienting.

Although the CIA would not learn of it until 1988, we lost another high-value source in July 1986, when Major General Dmitri Polyakov, a retired GRU officer who had faithfully worked with the CIA for more than eighteen years in Moscow, Burma, and India, was arrested. Polyakov had been unexpectedly recalled to Moscow in May 1980 for a military attaché meeting, which both he and the CIA assumed was a routine matter. Alarmed at first that Polyakov did not return from that meeting, the CIA was relieved to discover that he regularly published articles in a Soviet sports magazine called *Okhota* and guessed that he had retired. Concerns grew again in 1986, when Polyakov's son was unexpectedly recalled from India and Polyakov's articles stopped appearing. In fact, Polyakov had been initially exposed by Robert Hanssen, who was a GRU source in 1979, a fact that prompted Polyakov's recall and forced his retirement. Nothing else happened to him at the time, likely because, according to Burton Gerber, a former senior CIA Soviet expert and spymaster, the GRU would not have wanted the KGB to know that a GRU general had been a longtime spy for the Americans.[11] However, after his arrest in July 1986, Polyakov was summarily tried and executed on March 15, 1988.

This situation was made all the more confounding because we had only just come to terms with the significant losses caused by Soviet spy Edward Lee Howard. As a freshly trained CIA case officer, Howard had nearly been assigned to the Moscow station but was let go after failing a predeployment polygraph in 1983. Bitter and disgruntled, he made contact with the Soviets and revealed to them the existence of an underground cable tap (known as CKTAW) on traffic pertaining to Soviet R&D in the defense field outside of Moscow and, more devastatingly, that we had Adolf Tolkachev, an extraordinary aeronautical engineer working in the heart of the Soviet military establishment, as a source. Soviet defector/re-defector Vitaliy Yurchenko had put us on to Howard, and he fled to the Soviet Union before we could catch him.[12]

What we didn't know at the time was that in 1985 both CIA intelligence officer Aldrich Ames and FBI counterintelligence officer Robert Hanssen had begun spying for the KGB. Hanssen had first spied for the GRU for three years starting in 1978 (when he betrayed Polyakov) before cutting ties with them. Then in 1985 Hanssen wrote anonymously to the KGB offering his services. As for Ames, once he resolved to approach the Russians, he used his position as a member of the CIA's Soviet Division as a pretext for organizing a meeting with a Soviet arms control specialist, Sergei Chuvakhin. But on the fated day Chuvakhin never came to the meeting. After downing several vodkas that left a cloud of alcohol working on his mind, Ames made the short walk to the Soviet embassy and left a package at the front desk for the KGB resident officer. A month later Chuvakhin invited him for a drink at the Soviet embassy, to be followed by lunch. This should have been a huge red flag to both the FBI and the CIA. Such a meeting never happens unless the KGB wants something.

When he arrived at the embassy, Ames was quickly ushered into a secure room, where he then met with KGB counterintelligence officer Victor Cherkashin, who would handle Ames. Chuvakhin would be their go-between. The Russians maneuvered Ames very effectively, playing him like an operational fiddle, stroking his ego and deep-seated need for respect. It is amazing, given Ames's training and experience, that he was so easily recruited to give over far more than he had initially intended. In what came to be known as the "big dump," Ames gave the Russians the identities of nearly every Soviet source we had. Eleven of our most valued Russian agents were executed, and dozens of lower-level operations were compromised, along with several highly valuable technical operations.[13]

Deep within the agency the mole hunt team labored to identify the source of the epidemic of losses that plagued Soviet operations. It would take until 1994 to arrest Ames and until 2001 to identify Hanssen.

First, probes were run in Russia and Africa to determine whether the KGB had tapped into our communication lines. Those probes came up clean. Still, as a result, a stricter compartmentalization of sensitive cases was put in place and a super-encipherment system created. The CIA's Counterintelligence and Security Office staff and the FBI opened formal investigations in 1986. But the scope of the investigations was vast, spanning decades of intelligence and unknown numbers of people in the CIA and the FBI who could have obtained access to information that could have compromised all these sources.[14]

What's more, the Soviets did their part to confuse the CIA. In January 1986 a CIA case officer in Bonn received the first of six letters, from an individual referred to as Mister X, stating that there was a breach in the CIA communications component in Washington. After much ado, it was determined that Mister X was a deception operation meant to draw attention away from Ames and Hanssen. In March 1986 Moscow station officer Erik Sites was arrested while trying to meet a source known as Eastbound, who was later determined to be a dangle who was further disrupting operations and resources in Moscow.

From December 1986 into 1987, nearly a year's worth of staff hours and resources was diverted from regular operations to try and assess whether U.S. Marine sergeant Clayton Lonetree was at the root of the agency losses. Lonetree was posted as a guard to the U.S. embassy in Moscow in 1984 and was lured by a honeytrap to work for the KGB. He was transferred to Vienna in March 1986 and in December 1986 confessed to the senior official there that he had let the KGB into the U.S. embassy in Moscow. In the end it was determined that neither Lonetree nor an embassy break-in were the source of the major leaks under investigation. Lonetree was convicted, sentenced to thirty-five years in prison, and released in 1996.[15]

By 1988 the deluge of intelligence losses seemed to have been stemmed and the sense of urgency had abated. Then in June of that year the Moscow chief of station, Jack Downing, was on a train to Leningrad when a passenger passed him a note stating that he was a KGB counterintelligence officer and he desired to defect. Over the next year Aleksandr Zhomov passed documents to Downing, including a highly specious KGB log of all Moscow station activities from 1984 to 1986, suggesting that many of the arrests of our sources were due to poor tradecraft and not from a spy in our ranks. This was plausible since the KGB had enormous resources with which to surveil the city and since Western embassies were under constant observation, as were their employees. Most maids and personal staff served as KGB informants, and places where Westerners were known to visit had surveillance teams assigned to the vicinity. But blaming errors on SIS and CIA tradecraft and playing up the effectiveness of Soviet surveillance was a well-known KGB tactic to protect Soviet sources. In July 1990, when he was given his exfiltration instructions, Zhomov did not defect and was determined to be another high-level dangle sent to muddy our trail in the search for traitors. While this sidetracked the agency, it reinvigorated our concern that the spy or spies among us might still be active.[16]

The effort languished until 1991, when the head of the Counterintelligence Center (CIC), Jim Olson, and his deputy, Paul Redmond, put together a team made up of several Soviet and counterintelligence experts, including Sandy Grimes, Jeanne Vertefeuille, Dan Payne, and two special agents from the FBI, Jim Holt and Jim Milburn. As this new task force got to work, they focused mainly on the prospect of a human penetration of the CIA. They created a list of "160 Agency employees who, at first glance, had at least access to information about one or more of the sources who had been compromised."[17]

To give focus to the investigation, the task force, along with some key members of the CI leadership, ranked the five or six candidates who they felt merited further scrutiny. Although this method of targeting can be seen as casual, haphazard, and overly intuitive, after consolidating the results through a weighting system by rank, it is telling that Ames figured at the top of the list, though several other candidates emerged as possible targets as well. The effort proceeded on many fronts: a fresh analysis of all compromised cases, a security review of all 160 employees on the list, and a psychological review of the top candidates. In addition, there were debriefings of defectors and sources, a review of any reporting on CIA penetrations since the 1970s, and the targeting of KGB officers who might have knowledge of human penetrations. The investigators looked at their travel, aliases, and awards or promotions to see if ever there was any crossover with our study of our own targets. This latter effort would yield fruit when it was revealed that a KGB officer traveled to Bogotá at the same time Ames did.[18]

The team also informally interviewed CIA employees who had held key positions in 1985, a year of multiple agent losses. Diana Worthen, a CIA veteran, came forward to provide the team with a fact that would prove critical. When Worthen had served in Mexico City with Ames, she befriended his wife, Rosario Ames, and gained firsthand knowledge that Ames and his wife were living paycheck to paycheck. This weakened the prevailing hypothesis that Ames's recently observed prosperity came from Rosario's wealthy family and further compelled the team to focus on him. Ultimately, the CIA team was able to create a convincing chronology showing that Ames made large deposits following several meetings with Sergei Chuvakhin, the Soviet diplomat in Washington he was supposedly trying to recruit in 1985.[19]

The final piece of the puzzle fell into place in 1993, when a sensitive Russian source reported that there was a spy within the CIA codenamed "Kolokol" and that he had met his handler in Bogotá and Rome in the late 1980s.[20] With such data, the FBI was able to open a full investigation into Ames in order to collect the hard evidence that would be needed to hold up in court. The FBI put heavy surveillance on Ames, wired his home and CIA office, penetrated his computer, and grabbed his trash. They even went so far as to rent a house on the next street to use as a safe house for these various operations. Time passed slowly, but in the end the trash grab paid off. Falling back on his innate operational laziness, Ames had failed to destroy a yellow Post-it that contained a draft "ops note" to his KGB handlers proposing their next operational meeting and how to signal a response.[21] With this information, the FBI had enough incriminating data to obtain an arrest warrant. On February 21, 1994, nearly nine years after he walked into the Soviet embassy, Ames was summoned to CIA headquarters. Within a few blocks of his residence, Ames was apprehended, and shortly thereafter his wife was arrested.

The announcement of Ames's betrayal stunned and devastated the agency. However, since I had been asked by the counterintelligence unit months before about the possibility of Ames being a spy (and I had replied in the affirmative), I was not shocked when he was arrested. Nonetheless, the fact that I had known him so long and up close produced a deep sense of anger and resentment about his betrayal.

The investigative team and the top officials at the CIA first took his discovery and arrest as a great success. But as Soviet expert Sandy Grimes noted, "as everyone who is involved in counterintelligence work understood, your greatest victories are your worst defeats." The CIA was taken aback by the sudden and screeching criticism of the agency for having a spy within its institution. The tone was set quickly, and the agency just couldn't steer the ship away from the highly negative congressional and media criticism. I found particularly hurtful a bit-ing cartoon showing a CIA figure in cloak and dagger pulling open his cape to reveal the name "Ames" on his chest. The entire episode was painful for everyone at the CIA, and even internally it has taken years for people to fully appreciate how important a feat it was to catch Ames and, looking toward the future, to accept that spies always exist within even the best intelligence services.

In fact, the real success in the Ames case went unheralded. The dedicated CIA counterintelligence group's dogged, rigorous, and indefatigable effort received virtually no recognition. The focus was on finding people to punish for the Ames breach, and regrettably, many people's careers were marginalized or cut short as a result. By contrast, the KGB rewarded and gave medals to the officers who uncovered treachery within their system. It is a different way of looking at counterintelligence successes and failures. After all, the Ames cases revealed just how successful the agency had been in recruiting many highly placed spies inside the KGB/GRU national security structure before Ames's betrayal of them.

It is important to realize that the stakes for espionage remain as high today as they were during the Cold War. And we should not assume that Ames's treachery is the type of episode assigned to the past.

There Will Always Be Spies

A counterintelligence investigation is never truly finished. I recall CIA officers wearing "Never Again" buttons after Ames's betrayal, even though I knew we had another traitor in our national security arena. I was aware of at least a dozen CIA officials who were being evaluated as possible spies. After Ames's arrest, as the counterintelligence professionals plowed through his debriefing and the analysis of the agent losses, it became clear that Ames's betrayal of our sources didn't explain a few of the other key compromises.

High on that list was the matter of Gennadi Vasilenko. Vasilenko was a KGB counterintelligence officer who was posted to Washington DC in the early 1980s. He had long been the elusive target of CIA case officer Jack Platt, who had given him the codename Monolight but had never succeeded in recruiting him. Platt went so far as to travel to Guyana to cultivate Vasilenko but to no avail. Still, in January 1986 Vasilenko was on a visit to Cuba and was arrested, repatriated to Moscow, and interrogated for months in Lefortovo prison before being released for lack of evidence. The KGB obviously thought the CIA had been successful. It is unlikely Ames could have betrayed the CIA's interest in Vasilenko, because he was in Rome during the time of his attempted recruitment and would not have had access to information concerning that operation.

The second case concerned Felix Bloch, a State Department diplomat who had come under suspicion when he was observed passing a bag to a suspected Soviet illegal named Pierre, who was under investigation by the French domestic intelligence service. (It was thought that Bloch's relationship with a Viennese woman to whom he paid thousands of dollars for sadomasochism and bondage sessions made him susceptible to blackmail.) The French shared their concerns with the CIA, which then passed the intel on to the FBI in the spring of 1989. However, within five weeks of the FBI starting an investigation, Bloch received a cryptic phone call informing him that Pierre was ill and that a contagious disease was the likely reason. And Pierre disappeared.

The team had to conclude that there was another traitor, and the assumption was that he or she had to be working for the agency. In retrospect, the investigation should have been expanded to include the FBI, where Robert Hanssen, the real spy, worked.

When I was appointed associate deputy director of operations in 1994, I was briefed on the continuing "post-Ames" spy problem. I had to insist on reviewing the list of prime candidates the investigation team had assembled, though they rightfully wanted to keep the information close to the vest. I knew several people on the list, but my instinct suggested that they didn't fit the psychological profile that I thought the traitor would likely have. I couldn't vouch for the others on the list and encouraged the team to press ahead. One of the most frustrating regrets in my career was departing in late 1996 for my final overseas posting without having identified the spy.

Hanssen never divulged his name to his handlers, and that decision served as a protective shield for many years. He also took great pains to control the dead-drop locations for caching secret documents and picking up his money. Intelligence services normally select the dead-drop locations, not the asset. He also made sure to pass on to the KGB the names of any FBI and CIA source who might be able to identify him as spy. This led to several key sources being compromised and executed, simply for his self-protection.

With the advantage of hindsight, it's surprising that Hanssen hadn't surfaced sooner on the FBI's radar as a possible spy within the American intelligence community. Just as the CIA had had trouble coming to terms with having a traitor like Ames not only within its ranks but in an extremely sensitive position, so was the case with the FBI, which missed several red flags. First, years earlier Hanssen's brother-in-law Mark Wauch had reported to his FBI superior his suspicions about Hanssen and his access to large sums of unexplained cash. This allegation was not acted upon. Second, when another FBI traitor, Earl Edwin Pitts, was apprehended and interrogated, he speculated that Hanssen might also be a spy. This was passed over, too. Third, in 1993 Hanssen caused quite an uproar when he came into his superior's office and brazenly boasted that he had successfully hacked into his computer, as he held in his hand a highly sensitive, recently drafted memo. He received accolades for his unorthodox technique in highlighting the vulnerability of the counterintelligence network infrastructure, but in hindsight Hanssen likely took a risky proactive countermeasure to have an explanation for why he may have hacked into the FBI's computer system. Fourth, code-breaking software was found on the computer that he used from his post as FBI liaison in the Office of Foreign Missions at the State Department. Fifth, as a self-preservation step, Hanssen ran his name and his addresses through FBI databases on several occasions to see if he was being investigated, which is not only against official protocol but also very rare.

The FBI seemingly ignored Hanssen's anomalous behavior and did not investigate him. In fact, Hanssen was never even polygraphed. Hindsight is 20/20, and security protocols are often developed in response to major breaches to guard against future ones. It was not until after the discovery of Hanssen's spying that polygraphs became standard procedure for FBI counterintelligence agents, which is an essential protocol for a rigorous counterintelligence posture. (Although necessary, it isn't sufficient: Ames "passed" two polygraphs during the time he was working for the KGB.)

The greatest irony in the Hanssen case was that in August 1987 he was tasked with assessing whether there was a Soviet intelligence penetration of the FBI following the loss of two Soviet sources for the CIA who had been based in the United States.

The Hanssen case finally broke when a former KGB officer came forward with the actual KGB file on Hanssen in hand.[22] Apparently this KGB officer had taken possession of it when the Gorbachev government fell, thinking that it would be a good bargaining chip if he got crosswise with the new KGB. While it didn't identify Hanssen by name, the file contained a voice telephone tape of Hanssen talking to a KGB officer. One of his fellow FBI officers immediately recognized his voice. Also in the file was a trash bag in which Hanssen had presumably placed secret documents for a dead drop. The trash bag still had Hanssen's fingerprints on it. To nail down the evidence even more, the FBI downloaded data from Hanssen's Palm Pilot device, which contained extensive amounts of compromising information. This sequence was dramatized in the 2007 movie *Breach*, which tells a modified-for-Hollywood version of the case.[23]

I had been out of the agency for about two years when I finally learned about Hanssen's arrest. My overwhelming reaction was one of great relief on two levels—the spy had been caught and thank God I didn't know him personally, as had been the case with Ames. Once again the arrest had me thinking about what type of mind can compartmentalize itself so well that it can hold strong religious and patriotic views and still be a traitor, responsible for the death of some of the CIA's best agents. On the Mother's Day that followed his arrest, I attended mass with my wife and children. The homily was uninspiring, and I started to think again about the Hanssen conundrum. As anyone who has attended a Catholic mass knows, there are several times during the mass when the parishioners stand. My mind was wandering to the Hanssen case. I wasn't paying attention to what the priest was saying, so when I felt others moving to stand, I proudly stood tall (six feet, five inches) in the middle of the church. I noticed my wife laughing uncontrollably farther down the pew, while two of my adult daughters, who also were laughing, motioned to me to sit down. Stupidly, I asked what was going on, and they responded in unison: the priest had asked all the mothers to stand up for a round of applause. I couldn't have been more conspicuous standing in the midst of a storm of cackles. As I sat down red-faced, I cursed Hanssen again under my breath.

At the end of the Cold War, before Ames and Hanssen, there was former CIA case officer Edward Lee Howard. After them, there was former FBI officer Earl Edwin Pitts and former CIA deputy chief of station Harold James Nicholson, among many others. Having spent the greater part of the last few years studying the Cold War and its key spy cases, I have become increasingly concerned, as others have, that there might have been another significant but unidentified "fourth mole" in the mid-1980s. The treachery of Edward Lee Howard, Aldrich Ames, and Robert Hanssen cannot account for the compromise of two important Western sources in the spring of 1985: Oleg Gordievsky and Sergei Bokhan.[24] Thirty years on, questions endure: Was there a fourth mole? Who else could have revealed the identities of these sources?

According to Victor Cherkashin, who handled the Ames and Hanssen cases for the KGB, there was certainly another or even many other unidentified Soviet spies in the U.S. intelligence community and the U.S. government.[25] While this is a troubling assertion, the same can be said about CIA sources whose identities I hope will never be revealed. This is part of the spy business and it always will be. But it doesn't mean we can afford to be complacent about it.

Given these enduring questions, it is prudent to assume that there are always spies operating in our midst and that we must regularly seek to discover them. We should not question today whether Russia has penetrated our government but determine where it has done so. The existence of double agents in our midst is a matter of fact in the spy business, and for this reason alone our counterintelligence program must remain alert to ferret out spies. The rank-and-file of the intelligence community needs to adjust its culture to accept the stark reality of the permanent presence of spies deep within its system. It must also take steps to continuously vet personnel and rigorously compartmentalize information so that no single traitor or set of traitors can wrap up our agent networks or reveal all our intelligence capabilities, leaving us no choice but to fly blind in evaluating the plans and intentions of our adversaries around the world.

Furthermore, considering the scope of the Russian effort to make contacts in the run-up to the 2016 presidential election, and given that both American and Russian intelligence services appear to have been largely successful in recruiting intelligence spies, it would be naïve to think that high-level sources haven't been recruited in recent years from within the diplomatic and political establishment in Washington. Since the end of the Cold War some three decades ago, Russia has not relented in its efforts to gather intelligence in the United States. It is a statistical certainty that there are spies working for Russia in the U.S. government.

LESSON SEVEN

Rigorous counterintelligence tradecraft should never succumb to destructive paranoia.

These with a thousand small deliberations
Protract the profit of their chilled delirium,
Excite the membrane, when the sense has cooled,
With pungent sauces, multiply variety
In a wilderness of mirrors. What will the spider do
Suspend its operations, will the weevil
Delay?

—From T. S. ELIOT'S poem "Gerontion"

7

Limits of Counterintelligence

The Rabbit Hole

Accepting the reality that there will always be spies in our midst can help create a healthy operational security posture and culture within the intelligence community. But in doing so we also run the risk of losing our way in a "wilderness of mirrors," as described in T. S. Eliot's poem "Gerontion."

This poem was much beloved by spymaster James Angleton of the Special Investigations Group (SIG), the CIA's counterintelligence operation. But while Angleton can rightly be credited with assuring the establishment of a robust counterintelligence function and uncovering several Soviet spies, he also was the generator of a quasi-paranoid and damaging spy hunt inside the CIA that had a profoundly deleterious impact on our worldwide operations against the Soviets for decades.

Angleton was an eccentric in a world crowded with eccentrics. He was a tough-minded heavyweight inside the CIA, buttressed by the unflappable support of Allen Dulles and then Richard Helms. Born in Idaho, he was raised in Italy and served in the OSS in London. He went to Yale, wrote poetry, and cultivated black orchids. As he rose in the ranks, he was eventually placed in charge of counterintelligence as soon as the function was created at the CIA in 1954, and he held the post until 1973, an amazing tenure in the spy world. Through his three decades at the CIA, Angleton was careful to cultivate an aura of mystery and authority. His office was usually darkened except for a desk lamp, which for visitors added to the mystique of working in the shadows.

At the start of the 1960s the CIA lost two very important spies, Pyotr

Popov and Oleg Penkovskiy, in very quick succession. This raised concerns that Western intelligence services might have embedded Soviet spies who had given up these two men. Soon after, troubling reports of not one but several deep penetrations came rapidly to the fore with the appearance of a valuable official from the Polish security service. Michael Goleniewski, former deputy chief of Polish military intelligence, defected to the West in the company of his East German mistress in January 1961. He provided a trove of consequential information to the United States, both before his defection and after, including the identities of not only hundreds of Polish and Soviet intelligence officers but also several very important Western spies, including an SIS spy for the Soviets, George Blake.[1]

With Angleton's legitimate concern about the growing problem of internal penetrations within the CIA, the timing could not have been more unfortunate for him to cross paths with Anatoliy Golitsyn, a KGB counterintelligence officer in Finland. Golitsyn had been a member of the KGB since 1945, and his main responsibility was to provide security for Soviets living overseas. He was a loner and critical of the lack of competence of his colleagues, many of whom perceived him as arrogant. With his prospects for advancement dwindling and his marriage failing, his posting to Finland provided him with an excellent opportunity to defect in December 1961.

Golitsyn provided information identifying several spies operating in the West, but it was the conclusive identification of Kim Philby and Heinz Felfe as traitors that shook Angleton profoundly and forever altered his perception of people and his ability to trust others. Golitsyn provided what he knew about the legendary Pyatyorka (Ring of Five), or Cambridge Five, who were all members of the British elite. The resulting investigation prompted Philby's defection to Moscow in January 1963. Corroboration of Philby's role as a member of the Cambridge Five was shocking in and of itself, but for Angleton it was personal, as the two had been close when Philby was stationed in Washington.

Philby's betrayal wasn't Angleton's only psychological blow by a purported ally. Heinz Felfe was a mole within the West German intelligence service (BND) whose successful use of intricate and far-reaching deception and diversionary operations—on Angleton's watch—kept his discovery at bay and compromised most Western intelligence operations in Berlin for more than ten years. The KGB recruited Felfe from German intelligence, and, through skillful manipulation and planning, managed to place him as deputy chief of section responsible for Soviet counterintelligence inside the nascent West German intelligence service. He held the post for six years and served as the West German counterpart to Angleton. The KGB also supplied a double agent feigning loyalty to the BND who would report false suspicions of KGB loyalty on individuals whom the KGB suspected of providing information to the BND. Felfe, tasked with investigating them, would leverage all resources available to the BND, including other Western intelligence resources. The discovery of these two spies changed Angleton.[2]

Golitsyn claimed that the Soviets were strategically seeking to penetrate every level of Western intelligence and already had many agents-in-place. If that hadn't been enough to stoke the fires of Angleton's counterintelligence instincts, Golitsyn reported that the KGB and GRU had deliberately dispatched fake spies and defectors as part of a vast disinformation campaign to undermine legitimate sources. To top it all off, Golitsyn said there was a Soviet spy, codenamed Sasha, working from deep within the CIA, which for Angleton was the most disconcerting of the revelations. They set Angleton on a dogged and unrelenting counterintelligence crusade across the agency. Angleton took on the search for Sasha with great determination—and destructive results.[3] Eventually Golitsyn was diagnosed by agency psychiatrists as a paranoiac, but even then Angleton was never persuaded that he might have hitched his cart to the wrong horse. Of all the 170 leads that Golitsyn gave the agency, beyond the useful information obtained in his initial debriefing, only two were ever corroborated.[4]

Perhaps there is no better example of this distortion than the Yuri Nosenko case. Nosenko, an officer in the KGB's Second Chief Directorate (internal intelligence), defected to the West in February 1964, shortly after President Kennedy's assassination. Nosenko had approached a U.S. diplomat in June 1962 while part of a Soviet delegation visiting Geneva and at the time agreed to work as an agent-in-place. He was an interesting and complicated walk-in. His father was close to Khrushchev and had been minister of shipbuilding when he died in 1956. Nosenko had enjoyed a relatively easy path, first working in naval intelligence for the GRU before he was called into the KGB's Second Chief Directorate, where his responsibilities included targeting and recruiting foreign tourists traveling to Russia. On a trip to Britain in 1957 he was deeply drawn to the higher standards of living in the West. Around the same time, he discovered that the KGB had a file on his late father, which he found deeply distressing. However, the catalyst for his overtures to the United States in 1962 was neither a high-minded sense of honor nor a desire to defect but rather the fact that a prostitute had stolen $900 worth of Swiss francs from him, a sum that the KGB was sure to notice had gone missing from its official accounts. Prior to the next KGB accounting, he offered his services to the United States in exchange for the lost sum and some asthma medication for his daughter.

Codenamed Foxtrot, Nosenko proved difficult to assess. Would he be a useful and reliable source? He showed up for some of his debriefings drunk, on the pretense of having stopped at several bars as a counter-surveillance method. Still, he provided very compelling information.[5]

When Nosenko made contact again in Geneva in January 1964, he wanted to defect because he believed that he was under suspicion by the KGB. The CIA tried to persuade him to remain in place, but Nosenko provided the CIA with information that would make it nearly impossible for them to turn him away.

Nosenko claimed that in his role at the Second Directorate he had met and vetted Lee Harvey Oswald when the future presidential assassin had defected to the Soviet Union. The KGB had assessed Oswald as "abnormal and unstable but not insane" and deemed him unsuitable for any sort of recruitment, though worthy of regular surveillance. Nosenko claimed that the KGB was pleased when Oswald returned to the United States and that they made sure his future attempts to return to the Soviet Union were thwarted. Over dinner years later Nosenko repeated to me with conviction this same description of Oswald. Nosenko reported that when Kennedy was assassinated, the KGB was highly concerned that the Soviet Union would be accused because of Oswald's prior presence in the Soviet Union. Furthermore, Nosenko was put in charge of an internal KGB investigation to determine whether any rogue KGB officers or agents might have taken it upon themselves to get involved with Oswald and his assassination plot. The KGB was acutely aware of the potential repercussions should any link to the KGB be determined.

Not surprisingly, Nosenko's claims were perplexing for the CIA. Here was a defector claiming that the KGB had absolutely nothing to do with the assassination of Kennedy or Lee Harvey Oswald. Was he telling the truth or was he an agent of deception? If Nosenko was lying, did it indicate that the KGB had played a role? Were they just hedging to ensure that the finger wasn't pointed at them? Angleton, tormented by Golitsyn's assertion that the CIA had been penetrated by a Soviet spy and that any KGB defections or recruitment could be a Soviet ruse, resolutely viewed Nosenko as a KGB plant.[6]

Several but not all members of the CIA's Soviet Division and the Office of Security shared Angleton's concerns, and, as an unfortunate result, a few months after Nosenko's defection he was transferred to the "Farm" and detained in harsh conditions for further questioning, which lasted nearly four years and included 292 interrogations. Nosenko never changed his story about Oswald and his intelligence leads, despite Angleton's suspicions, and eventually most came to object to how Nosenko was being treated.[7]

Nosenko was not the only casualty of what has been described as Angleton and Golitsyn's "folie à deux." The hunt for Sasha claimed many victims, including people I knew personally. The searchers rejected potentially valuable sources, and the effort hampered the promising careers of several CIA operations officers who fit Golitsyn's criteria for possible traitors. Angleton's probing and veil of suspicion over every Soviet source slowed the recruitment of Soviet spies for the remaining part of the decade. Eventually, nearly everyone fell under suspicion—including Angleton himself, creating an internal environment rife with suspicion and fear. In such a dark climate, Golitsyn's revelations and charges turned into suspicions and assumptions about other Western intelligence agencies, with painful repercussions. Angleton, prompted by Golitsyn, managed to raise suspicions about a KGB plant in the French security service and British intelligence. Unfounded accusations came to be known as an effect of "Golitsyn Syndrome"—the condition of seeing traitors where there were none.

With the benefit of hindsight, it now looks like there never was a Sasha, or at least not one who fit Golitsyn's description, with high-level access that would have backed up his claims.[8] Although it is likely that there were other penetrations of CIA, what many have lamented is that the search for the forever elusive Sasha arguably did nearly as much damage to the agency as any real traitor could have. The point may be exaggerated for effect, but it is an important and enduring lesson. We cannot let our concern about the risk of penetrations take us down the rabbit hole of paranoia that will infect the work force and impede our ability to aggressively collect. We need to be gimlet-eyed about counterintelligence problems but proceed in a balanced, lawful, methodical, and patient way to identify penetrations within the government.

Why did CIA director Richard Helms leave Angleton in the job as chief of counterintelligence for so many years, given his negative impact on Soviet operations and agency culture at large? Helms cultivated a well-defined image as a consummate operator who was grounded in the realities of the espionage world and the political pitfalls of covert action. He moved smoothly among the power elites in Washington (with the conspicuous exception of President Richard Nixon and his White House staff). Helms was the first CIA director I met in my long career and still looms largest among agency directors. At Helms's invitation, I had lunch with him in 1996, and this question about Angleton's tenure, which had troubled my positive impression of Helms for years, kept popping into my mind. It was on the tip of my tongue, but I felt certain it would put a damper on the rest of the lunch, and I let it drop. I regret it now since I still can't come to terms with it.

Fortunately for Nosenko, a new team was assigned to assess his claims, and he was moved to a more hospitable location, after which he passed his first polygraph in four years. He was exonerated of being a KGB plant, given a pension with back pay and a paid role as a CIA consultant, and relocated to an undisclosed location with a new identity.

Nosenko's exoneration remains a topic of debate among a few former CIA officers who still believe he was an agent of deception. I remain persuaded—by the evidence presented in a definitive, official CIA study and by my own dealings with him—that he was a legitimate defector. According to the CIA study, Nosenko identified 200 foreigners and 238 Americans who were of interest to the KGB.

He gave up nearly three hundred Soviet agents and their overseas contacts and nearly two hundred KGB officers. He revealed a treasure trove of information on Soviet tradecraft used to blackmail foreign diplomats and journalists. This is an unprecedented amount of information to disclose to protect a plot that neither then, nor now, had any other echoes.[9]

Like most CIA employees in the early 1970s, I never met Angleton personally. Most of the junior officers didn't even know what he looked like. Dave Phillips, former chief of the Latin America Division in the early 1970s, liked to tell the story about how one of his colleagues one day casually pointed out Angleton walking down the hall at headquarters. Thereafter, Phillips always stood a little taller and nodded in respect whenever he passed Angleton at work. When Phillips finally got a seat at the leadership table where all the division chiefs meet each morning with the deputy director of operations, he was stunned when he was finally introduced to Angleton and it was not the person he had been nodding at for years! The real Angleton pulled him aside in a rather conspiratorial manner after the meeting to welcome Phillips to the board and commented with great emphasis and mystery that he needed to get "The Briefing," which Phillips speculates was Angleton's theory about KGB penetrations of the CIA. And true to form, Angleton never gave Phillips "The Briefing."

Still, the intelligence and law enforcement commands have yet to integrate the most important lesson from the Angleton period: given the nature of our democracy and our freedom and rule of law, we are a more vulnerable target for espionage. Add this to the Russians' (and others') relentless desire to penetrate our intelligence services and other areas of our government, and it is a near certainty that there will always be spies in our midst. It is our job to uncover them without undermining ourselves.

How we thwart these spies and how we identify them without impinging on our own fundamental freedoms are essential questions we need to be mindful of going forward, especially given Vladimir Putin's determination to run cyber operations in the United States. No matter how we balance these issues, we will require a robust counterintelligence posture at all times, especially now.

It Takes a Spy

Given the assumption that espionage will continue in perpetuity, perhaps the greatest lesson we have learned over time, which KGB spymaster Victor Cherkashin echoes in his own memoirs, is that "spies catch spies" or, as it is often quoted in inside CIA, "it takes a spy to catch a spy."[10] Alger Hiss was exposed by Whittaker Chambers and Elizabeth Bentley, Kim Philby by Anatoliy Golitsyn, George Blake by Michael Goleniewski, Adolf Tolkachev by Edward Lee Howard, and Howard by Vitaliy Yurchenko. And many of our key assets in the 1980s were betrayed by Aldrich Ames and Robert Hanssen, who in turn were ultimately thwarted by other Russian spies. This is perhaps the most cogent argument for why we need to continue to cultivate human sources in the spy business. What would be most useful today would be a spy's insider view of what is really going on inside the GRU, the SVR, and the Kremlin vis-à-vis the United States.

Many of the details we have learned about the inner workings of the Internet Research Agency (IRA) in Russia and its effort to direct a carefully curated crew of trolls against the United States to interfere in the 2016 elections came to us from a young antipropaganda activist journalist named Lyudmila Savchuk. As part of her undercover investigation, Savchuk went to work for the IRA for two months. From her inside post, she provided details on the IRA's organization, tactics, technological capability, and strategic focus, making her one of the most important witnesses of the investigation.[11] According to press reports, much of what we know about the Kremlin's inner deliberations surrounding the 2016 election interference and Putin's command and control of the operation comes from an intelligence source with access to those deliberations.[12] In September 2019 reports emerged that that critical source had been exfiltrated two years prior, and we may no longer have access to that essential intelligence.[13]

In the intelligence world, an inside source is almost always the only way to get the backroom picture and definitive proof of treachery or subornation. If history is any judge, it is uncertain when we will get our next key policy-level Russian intelligence defector. Until then we will have to live with a level of ambiguity about the full scope of the interference in our political process. This fact alone makes the strongest case for strengthening our intelligence posture against the Russians to help develop the next generation of spies.

Next Generation Counterintelligence

The most important national security story to emerge from the Mueller investigation underscores the principal theme of this book—the Russians' unceasing efforts to undermine the United States and its democratic system. This is something the Russians have been doing against successive U.S. governments since the Russian Revolution in 1917, and their efforts persist even today, as amply demonstrated in the Mueller indictments.

It is equally clear that there are no credible signs that Putin will make a meaningful sea change in this policy any time soon. He is aggressively pursuing Cold War policies in Ukraine, Syria, Iran, Venezuela, and the states that border Russia, with a particular focus on reasserting Russian influence in Ukraine. He has courted longtime U.S. allies, for example, by selling advanced missile systems to Turkey, a NATO member, and signing large contracts with Saudi Arabia. Moreover, he is cozying up to China in a way very reminiscent of the old Sino-Soviet bloc policies, including converting dollar deposits to the yuan.

As can be seen in the detailed account of the many Russian intelligence cases put forth here, Russia's objectives and techniques (and short-sighted policies) are unchanged and will remain so for the foreseeable future. If we step back for a moment and look at these cases in a broader sense, we see that virtually all of them were compromised by spies within the Russian intelligence services.

That said, hopefully the sober conclusions of the Mueller investigation will help a consensus emerge in Congress—even if the report itself fades from most Americans' memories—that the United States must remain focused on maintaining CI efforts robust enough to defend us against Russia's continued onslaught. In that regard it will be important to recognize the limits to how quickly and broadly law enforcement and intelligence agencies can build up this effort using just traditional collection methods. It isn't enough to throw money at the problem. Recruiting human sources is a slow and selective process that only periodically produces an intelligence breakthrough. Great persistence and patience are required to break a CI case.

Unlike the intelligence tools available during the Cold War, we now live in the cyber age with ever-increasing and deeply penetrating potential CI capabilities, especially in the area of artificial intelligence and machine learning, which can amplify our investigative abilities against Russian spies and theirs against us. We need to harness these capabilities in a much more robust way. On the CI front it is not enough to develop capabilities to attack our enemies' cyber networks and protect our own national security infrastructure from attacks. We also need to harness cyber collection to the fullest to enhance our ability to hunt and catch spies, which the intelligence community is working diligently to accomplish.

Going forward, we must face the issue of how to balance critically important CI efforts and fundamentally precious privacy rights. It will be a conundrum requiring the wisdom of Solomon to solve.

1. Yalta Conference, 1945. Alger Hiss (center, dark gray jacket and bow tie) stands with Secretary of State Edward Stettinius (center left, double-breasted coat and hat). Franklin D. Roosevelt Presidential Library and Museum.

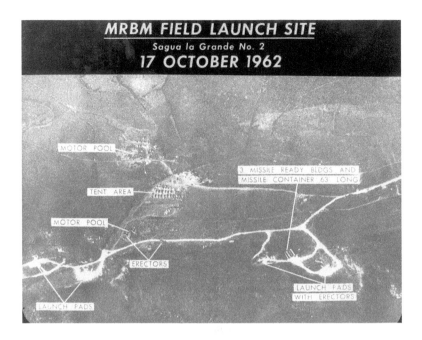

MRBM FIELD LAUNCH SITE
Sagua la Grande No. 2
17 OCTOBER 1962

MOTOR POOL

3 MISSILE READY BLDGS AND
MISSILE CONTAINER 63' LONG

TENT AREA

MOTOR POOL

ERECTORS

LAUNCH PADS
WITH ERECTORS

LAUNCH PADS

2. (*opposite top*) Oleg Penkovskiy, ca. 1961. Colonel Oleg Penkovskiy's military pass to the buildings of the General Staff and Ministry of Defense in Moscow (top). His military pass to the Intelligence Directorate of the Ministry of Defense (bottom). *CIA Analysis of the Warsaw Pact Forces: The Importance of Clandestine Reporting*, edited by Joan Bird and John Bird (Langley VA: CIA information Management Services, 2012).

3. (*opposite bottom*) Washington DC, 1969. James J. Angleton carrying the ashes of DCI Allen Dulles during Dulles's funeral service at Georgetown Presbyterian Church. Central Intelligence Agency.

4. (*above*) Cuba, October 17, 1962. An aerial view of medium-range ballistic missile field launch site number two at Sagua la Grande. Discovery of Soviet nuclear installations in Cuba triggered the U.S.-Soviet nuclear standoff known as the Cuban Missile Crisis. United States Air Force.

5. White House, Washington DC, May 24, 1984. President Ronald Reagan and First Lady Nancy Reagan with guests during a private dinner with Soviet Union defector Arkady Shevchenko (near left) on Truman Balcony. Ronald Reagan Presidential Library and Museum.

6. Russia, 1991: Jack Devine prepares to board a Soviet helicopter. Courtesy of the author.

7. Moscow, Russia, 1991: Jack Devine in front of KGB headquarters, known as Lubyanka. Courtesy of the author.

8. Moscow, Russia, 1991: Jack Devine inside KGB headquarters. Courtesy of the author.

9. (*opposite top*) Russia, July 7, 1986. Retired Soviet major general Dmitri Polyakov, the highest-ranking Soviet officer ever to have been recruited by the CIA, being arrested by unnamed KGB agents. His whereabouts were unknown until March 15, 1988, when official Soviet media outlet *Pravda* reported his execution for treason. *Russian Military Review Magazine*.

10. (*opposite bottom*) Arlington, Virginia, 1994. FBI agents arrest CIA officer-turned-KGB double agent Aldrich "Rick" Ames. Federal Bureau of Investigation.

11. (*above*) Moscow, Russia, undated. Sergei Tretyakov (facing camera) at the grave of Konon Molody, a Soviet KGB intelligence officer who in the 1950s stole nuclear secrets from the United States. Tretyakov, a high-ranking Russian KGB/SVR officer, was a double agent for the United States until he defected in 2000. Courtesy of the estate of Sergei Tretyakov.

12. Dresden, Germany, 1986. East German Ministry for State Security (Stasi) identification card for KGB agent Vladimir Putin. Putin received this ID card from the Stasi in his role as a KGB officer stationed in Dresden. The card gave Putin access to Stasi offices but is not an indication that Putin actually worked for the Stasi. Federal Commissioner for the Records of the State Security of the Former German Democratic Republic, bstu.de.

13. Helsinki, Finland, 2018. President Donald Trump shakes hands with President Vladimir Putin at a press conference following a bilateral meeting at the Helsinki Summit. Office of the President of the Russian Federation, http://www.kremlin.ru/events/president/news/58017/photos/54668.

LESSON EIGHT

As long as there is an autocratic government in Moscow,
there will be people willing to spy for the West.

I offer my services to you and I have some most
significant facts to share.

—GRU colonel OLEG VLADIMIROVICH PENKOVSKIY

8

Agents-in-Place

Born of Disillusionment

Russian agents of influence may have used the promise of derogatory information on an opponent to lure Trump campaign members to a meeting, but that meeting's real purpose was to discuss the eventual repeal of the Magnitsky Act should Trump be elected. The Magnitsky Act is a 2012 U.S. law that bars travel by and imposes financial sanctions on Russian officials suspected of human rights abuses. It is a very effective piece of legislation.

The Magnitsky Act is one of the tools—in addition to other sanctions—that the United States can use to target specific individuals who engage in particularly reprehensible actions at the behest of the Russian state. Since its passage in the United States, along with similar laws in Europe and Canada, the Magnitsky Act has significantly affected the ability of many in Putin's inner circle to travel, own property abroad, and use the international financial system.

The Magnitsky Act brings attention to the human rights violations of the Russian state. The legislation does this by recognizing substantiated claims by victims or their families, assigning responsibility to the identified perpetrators, and then penalizing those individuals. Putin despises this act, and it is of utmost importance to him that it be repealed. Exasperation with the Magnitsky Act and the hope of persuading a U.S. president to repeal it may have been among the motivations behind Russian interference in the 2016 election.

The individual who first sought to bring this accountability to the Russian state, who has championed efforts to design and pass legislation similar to the Magnitsky Act around the world, is U.S.-born investor Bill Browder. In the 1990s Browder became the largest foreign private portfolio investor in post-Soviet Russia, and his Russian holdings made him very rich. He began to observe specious share and capital transfers within the companies in which he was invested and, with the help of journalists and investigators, was able to document these corrupt transactions, which amounted to massive wealth transfers, often from Russian state assets to individuals within Russia's emergent elite class. For a brief time Browder was supported by newly elected Russian president Vladimir Putin in his purported efforts to root out corruption.

But as Putin came to consolidate power, especially after Mikhail Khodorkovsky was tried and imprisoned and other Russian oligarchs began to ingratiate themselves to Putin lest they suffer the same fate, Putin became less interested in clamping down on corruption. Browder's public investigations and "naming and shaming" campaigns became more and more of a nuisance. Eventually, in 2005, Browder was taken into FSB custody while trying to enter Russia, and he was later deported on national security grounds. He immediately liquidated his sizable investments there, paid a reported $230 million in capital gains tax, shuttered his businesses save a single administrative office, and never returned.

In June 2007 Russian police raided Browder's administrative office and his lawyer's office in Moscow. Shortly afterward, in a strange twist of events, Browder said that ownership of his company had been fraudulently transferred out of his name. He hired a Moscow-based legal team, which included Sergei Magnitsky, to investigate the transfer and assess what risks it might pose to him. Magnitsky reported that in December 2007 the new owner of the company had been granted a tax refund for the $230 million in taxes Browder had paid when he liquidated his assets in Russia. He also learned that criminal cases had been opened against Browder and his associates for theft of those funds from the Russian state. Browder and Magnitsky alerted Russian authorities to this misappropriation of Browder's company and Russian tax monies. Magnitsky also testified before the Russian State Investigative Committee, implicating members of the security service that had been involved in the raids on Browder's office and his lawyer's office.

Instead of investigating the case, in November 2008 Russian security services arrested Sergei Magnitsky. He was detained for a year, harshly treated, and repeatedly pressured to rescind his testimony and to confess that he stole the $230 million at Browder's instructions. Magnitsky refused. He remained incarcerated and was reportedly subjected to freezing temperatures and incessant exposure to light and sound and provided minimal nourishment, all of which were documented by Magnitsky and his lawyer. In November 2009 Magnitsky died after supposedly being refused medical treatment for acute pancreatitis and having been severely beaten. Magnitsky was tried postmortem, along with Browder, and convicted for the alleged theft of $230 million.

Angered by these events, Browder took it upon himself to seek revenge for Sergei Magnitsky's maltreatment and death. Over time he crafted a strategy to petition Western governments to ban travel and freeze the assets of the individuals who were involved in the human rights abuses against Magnitsky (and eventually other victims who had suffered similar abuse). In November 2012 the Magnitsky Act became federal law in the United States. Similar measures have passed in Britain, Canada, Estonia, Gibraltar, Lithuania, and Latvia—all places where rich Russians like to park their money.[1]

In Putin's July 2018 meeting with Trump in Helsinki, the Russian leader offered to form a joint investigation between Russia and the United States into the U.S. election meddling. The Russian leader offered to make the individuals named in the Mueller indictments available to U.S. authorities for questioning, and, in exchange, he had a list of individuals of notable concern to the Russian state whom they wanted to interview. Putin specifically named Bill Browder as one such individual. In fact, nearly every individual mentioned in the course of this proposition had made an indelible imprint in some way on the passage of the Magnitsky Act.[2] This went generally unnoticed by the media and public.

Browder first came to Russia as an opportunist hoping to score big in the "Wild West" of post-Soviet capitalism. He left Russia rich but outraged by the absence of any legitimate rule of law as it related to his business, as well as anxious to find a measure that would seek both absolution for his part in Magnitsky's fate and retribution for what had happened. What was extraordinary about Browder's experience and made his pursuit particularly effective was his intimate knowledge of the abuses Sergei Magnitsky was subjected to as well as his understanding of the specific power dynamics and the kinds of financial transactions underpinning the corruption within Russia today.

Browder's story is unique in many respects, but it is also a stereotypical Russian story. Systemic injustices and injuries to individuals create individuals who thirst for revenge, expiation, and restorative justice. These stories have played themselves out time and time again in Russia. Browder follows the path of many who strived and subsequently faced Russia's oppressive government over the past century. Many disillusioned Soviet officials of similar mind-sets volunteered to help Western intelligence during the Cold War. Their disdain for and despondency over the Russian system were results of the endemic injustice and corruption of that system. Their aid to the West greatly aided our struggle with it.

Self-Selecting Assets

What we need to contemplate now is how to develop sources willing to provide us with the most coveted intelligence. Throughout the Cold War, both Russian and Western intelligence services spent much of their time, energy, and resources trying to penetrate each other's services. There was a strong belief that the intelligence services were the best route to get to the essential question of what was on the minds of the key national security policy makers and their designs on the West. What was at stake for us was critical intelligence: information on Soviet intentions, capacity, and priorities, as well as its strategic strengths and weaknesses. From the beginning of the Cold War, the West suffered what can be described best as a shortfall in intelligence. Spying on the Soviet Union was harder than spying in the West. It was nearly impossible to penetrate the interior of the Soviet Union, and, even if one could, there was no real freedom of movement. Within

Russia the KGB had virtually limitless resources for surveillance and no legal constraints on following, wiretapping, spying, eliciting, entrapping, searching, or interrogating any person. The limited Soviet delegations abroad were closely watched by a massive counterintelligence force, making direct approaches difficult. This asymmetric operational environment remains largely unchanged today.

The most coveted and rare asset would best be described as the self-selecting insider who volunteers, offering to stay in their post and spy for the West. Most often these are volunteers prepared to assume great personal risk by working as agents-in-place. They were a logical result of a ruthless and autocratic regime that produced generations of enemies whom even its limitless counterintelligence assets couldn't track. Their motivations have been many and varied, but many were born out of historical grievances, great personal loss, or Soviet actions in response to key political moments.

Some came to us with profound historical family grievances against Stalin, grievances that were exacerbated by the Soviet system. Our first two Cold War encounters with this kind of spy came in the form of GRU major Pyotr Popov and GRU colonel Oleg Vladimirovich Penkovskiy. Popov was born to Russian peasants, and during his childhood he witnessed the confiscation of his family farm and the misery that ensued during the revolution. Penkovskiy's father died fighting with the White Army against the Bolsheviks when Penkovskiy was an infant, a fact that, once discovered, would negatively impact Penkovskiy's professional prospects, leaving him feeling embittered and betrayed.[3] Both Penkovskiy and Popov fought in World War II, were injured, and found their way to military training school before being transferred to the GRU.[4]

Others came to us following great personal losses at the hand of the Soviet regime. GRU asset Dmitri Polyakov, who spied as an agent-in-place for the United States for eighteen years, first approached a U.S. diplomat at the United Nations in 1961 with a willingness to share information with the United States after the untimely death of his son. Despite Polyakov's repeated pleas, his superiors had denied his son a transfer to the United States to undergo a potentially life-saving operation. Polyakov was twice posted to UN headquarters in New York in the 1950s and had previously been unsuccessfully propositioned by the FBI to work for the bureau. After his son's death, Polyakov proved to be a highly useful source, codenamed Top Hat, for the FBI, and he reported on Americans spying for the Soviet Union. The FBI turned Polyakov over to the CIA in 1965, at which point he was stationed in Rangoon, Burma (now Myanmar). The CIA jumped at his willingness to work as an agent-in-place, thereby offering an exceptional shot at a deep-level penetration.[5]

Others came to the CIA driven by complex combinations of circumstances, evolving ideological sensibilities, and personal interest. For Arkady Shevchenko, the highest-ranking Soviet official ever to defect to the West, his exposure to an array of international perspectives through his diplomatic work was directly correlated to his personal *glasnost* ("openness") and ultimate break from his country. Shevchenko first visited New York in the early 1960s, a time of social and civil rights changes being played out on the national stage, where he could witness the dynamics of an evolving America. By 1973 Shevchenko's diplomatic career in the Soviet foreign service was thriving, culminating in his appointment to the elite role of under-secretary-general of the United Nations in New York.

But much like Sergei Tretyakov, aka Comrade J, there was an uneasy tension between his duty to remain objective and unbiased in his service to all members of the international organization and the demands and restrictions placed on him as a Soviet national by his home government. Shevchenko described his life—in which he enjoyed the greatest privilege afforded by the Soviet system, including a country dacha, premier schooling for his children, and access to luxury goods—as a "golden cage." He felt the pressure of being under relentless scrutiny and surveillance by a cynical, corrupt, and oppressive leadership, which nevertheless provided great prospects for him and his children. Rather than galvanizing his sense of purpose, his exposure to the inner workings of the Politburo proved profoundly disturbing. In his memoir *Breaking with Moscow*, he wrote, "I sat at the same table with Brezhnev, Gromyko and other members of the Politburo. I saw . . . how their hypocrisy and corruption had penetrated the smallest aspects of their lives." Having ascribed himself the sobriquet of "Reluctant Spy," Shevchenko initially wished to defect but was persuaded to remain as an agent-in-place for two and half years.[6]

Perhaps the most emblematic case of an individual whose treachery was born out of the Soviet system is the case of Oleg Gordievsky, who seemed to have been bred for service in the KGB. His father was an NKVD officer, and his older brother Vasiliy was a KGB officer who encouraged him to join the KGB in 1963. The impetus for Oleg's disloyalty was not just the brutal suppression of the Prague Spring but specifically the Soviets' own intelligence operations during this time. In the spring of 1968 Oleg's brother Vasiliy was sent to Prague as one of many KGB illegal agents who posed as Western tourists, journalists, businessmen, and students charged with collecting intelligence from within the heart of the "counterrevolutionary" movement. They infiltrated unions, the press, universities, and political parties. Vasiliy and his cohort of illegals were involved in a host of (primarily failed) efforts to discredit leaders of the burgeoning Prague Spring, falsely linking its leaders to armed insurgency and counterrevolutionary conspiracies and trying to get some groups to accept money and arms from fabricated underground movements. They attempted to convince editors and journalists to publish provocative and inflammatory articles against the Soviet Union and engaged in efforts at character assassination and blackmail. Finally, they botched an effort to kidnap "counterrevolutionary" leaders.

The groundswell of liberalization emanating from all areas of Czechoslovak society was impervious to their efforts. Even the Czechoslovak secret service was considered unreliable if not supportive of the Prague Spring (and proved itself to be obstructionist during the crackdown). Adding fuel to the fire, there were factions within the KGB and the Politburo who cast the Prague Spring as a harbinger of a Western-backed coup or a NATO invasion. So the Soviets led military forces from Bulgaria, East Germany, Hungary, and Poland into Czechoslovakia in a full display of Soviet brutality and will to maintain power. It was swift, effective, and ruthless, and it planted the seeds of dissatisfaction in a number of Soviet spies to come.

Vasiliy, like many of his fellow Soviet illegals, was profoundly troubled by his involvement in Czechoslovakia and the brutality that followed. This experience contributed to Vasiliy becoming an inveterate alcoholic; he died of liver disease in 1972. Oleg was devastated.

On his second posting, to Denmark in 1974, Oleg, fueled by ideological disillusionment and deep personal loss, approached a British diplomat on the sidelines of a badminton court in Copenhagen and proposed his cooperation with the West. His collaboration would endure for more than a decade while Oleg was posted in Copenhagen, Moscow, and, most important, London. Oleg Gordievsky would be of enormous service to the West in the decades to come.[7]

Historical events like the Prague Spring brought to the West not only would-be dissidents but also some of our most ardent enemies, who came to us out of necessity. Whatever their personal reasons for coming, there is almost an inevitability to the stories of Gordievsky, Popov, Penkovskiy, Polyakov, and Shevchenko. When a state ruthlessly oppresses people, sometimes over generations, with a disregard for their individual dignity and personal aspirations, some of those people will find a way to fight back. These men did it by spying for the West. Russia's recent actions in Ukraine and Syria—modern-day cognates to Budapest, Prague, and Warsaw—may yet produce more spies for the CIA.

First Contact

However willing they might be to work with us, agents-in-place still must be able to first make covert contact with us, which is one of the riskiest endeavors they will engage in.

In the early 1960s, when people first started to come our way in significant numbers, the security environment in the Soviet Union was such that all foreigners were regularly surveilled and any interaction with a foreigner was regarded as suspicious. In fact, the prospect of recruiting any sources there was slim to none.

It was mere luck that brought the CIA a series of walk-ins—previously unidentified individuals offering information and services to the United States. Fortunately, many overtures were made outside of the Soviet

Union. A year into his first posting in Vienna in 1953, Popov approached the American vice-consul in Vienna, handing him a letter that offered information on new organizational charts of the Soviet armored division and asked for $120 in return. His letter told how he loathed the Soviet system, that he was tired of being part of the secret police, and, fortuitously for us, that he had a mistress whom he could not afford to keep without the CIA's help.[8]

Within the Soviet Union the situation was more difficult. Many overtures made by Soviets to foreigners were in fact designed to draw out CIA officials, forcing them to commit clandestine acts and allowing the KGB to apprehend them, question them briefly, and then expel them from the Soviet Union. This trick was used effectively by the KGB to undermine the agency, and the paranoia engendered by the restrictive and dangerous Soviet environment resulted in at least one tragic episode.

In November 1963 Alexander Cherepanov gave a visiting American couple a package filled with extremely sensitive materials from the Second Chief Directorate (the counterintelligence arm) of the KGB. Cherepanov's career had been stunted by professional disagreements and what was deemed his suspicious activity while serving in Yugoslavia. Cherepanov started bringing copies of sensitive material home, and he amassed a significant and valuable collection of papers with the intent of using the information as currency to exact revenge on his employers and possibly defect. The couple duly delivered the package to the U.S. embassy. However, the ambassador was away and the official left in charge overreacted. Suspecting a provocation, he decided to return the package to the KGB! CIA station chief Paul Garbler protested and managed to photocopy the papers before they were returned to the KGB.[9] While the fate of Cherepanov was initially unknown, returning the papers was essentially a death sentence if they were not a provocation. It should not have happened. If need be, the situation should have been adjudicated in Washington between the State Department and the CIA.

Cherepanov's papers revealed a great deal about the tactics used to surveil foreigners in Moscow, notably that the KGB used two tracers to track specific targets throughout Moscow: Neptune 80—a pheromone for female dogs in heat—was placed on the soles of the target's shoes and then could be tracked easily by dogs; and Metka, a "spy dust" that when sprinkled on clothing could be detected by an electronic device. The documents also disclosed surveillance plans and reports on all current U.S. embassy personnel, specifically, what was known about their current drinking and sexual proclivities. It is painful to imagine what else we might have learned had we been able to get more from Cherepanov. We learned from Nosenko that the KGB was quickly able to identify the source of the leak. Cherepanov fled and the KGB conducted a massive manhunt across the Soviet Union. He nearly escaped but was captured minutes from the border with Turkey. He was tried and executed in April 1964.[10]

Nevertheless, there were those who, for various reasons, took the risk to share compelling information with the United States, so a system had to be developed to vet these walk-ins. When a potential walk-in approached an American, all efforts would be made to identify the source, vet the source if possible, acknowledge receipt of his or her message, and set a follow-up meeting and protocol to communicate, all the while assuring operational security. Since there were almost no resources within Moscow, all of these actions would sometimes take a long time to accomplish when expediency was essential. On several occasions, with good fortune, the agency was able to make contact and run sources within Moscow.

Penkovskiy approached two American students visiting Moscow in August 1960 and pleaded with them to deliver an envelope to the American embassy. In a letter contained within a package, Penkovskiy had written, "I offer my services to you and I have some most significant facts to share."[11] As a gesture to prove both his bona fides and sincerity, Penkovskiy provided a list of all sixty of the incoming students of the Military Diplomatic Academy, the GRU's training school, diligently noted their likely future posts, and identified those who were being considered for illegal status. This information established that Penkovskiy was not a KGB provocation.

Penkovskiy's information could be readily vetted, as many of the candidates would be dispatched to military attaché offices abroad; these were staffed with GRU officers. Penkovskiy also promised to provide a list of every operational missile in the Soviet arsenal and requested instructions on how to deliver the information. He also left detailed directions on how to signal him and then how to leave the requested instructions at a dead drop. He indicated that he would start looking for the signal in three days' time.

Penkovskiy spent months making overtures to the Canadians, another American, and the British—all without alerting the GRU or the KGB— before establishing contact. This protracted delay demonstrates how very difficult it was for the CIA to operate in those days within Russia and how the absence of a timely response makes any operation riskier and more vulnerable to discovery. Finally, by luck and his own maneuverings, in the spring of 1961 Penkovskiy managed to travel to Britain as part of a scientific delegation. By then the SIS and the CIA knew who he was and had put in place an operation to debrief him.[12]

Stand Down

Fifteen years later it was the internal leadership at the CIA that was the barrier to making contact. After President Jimmy Carter's election in 1976, he appointed Admiral Stansfield Turner to head the CIA. Turner had had an impressive career in the U.S. Navy and had been a respected classmate of Carter's at the U.S. Naval Academy, but he was an outsider to the CIA's culture and operational world. Carter and Turner sought to move the CIA away from human-collected intelligence (HUMINT) toward a greater focus on technological intelligence. It was clear by the end of the decade that the intelligence war was becoming more technical and technological, requiring subject matter expertise in high-level specialties like physics, engineering, mathematics, economics, computer science, and cryptology. But HUMINT intelligence was still indispensable.

Where Carter and Turner went wrong was in their failure to understand that acquiring secrets, even those that were highly technical in nature, often requires human assets. It was still a human source–based intelligence game, with agents needed to gain lasting access both to technical data and to the plans and intentions of our adversaries, and that remains the case today. Even though our technological capabilities are considerably greater and we can process much more data, our practices of targeting, collection, and analysis remain reliant on humans. The key to penetrating adversarial technical capabilities, including cyber, often begins with a human source opening the door, often literally. Carter and Turner seemed to share an embedded distrust and ethical unease about spying.

The perceived value of human intelligence collection hit its nadir in the fall of 1977, when Turner fired 820 agency employees in one fell swoop, internally known as the "Halloween Massacre." I witnessed firsthand this profound and deeply demoralizing strategic error. This and some of Turner's other actions led to the early exit of many of the agency's experienced senior and mid-level officers, many with high-value skills, such as fluency in the Romanian language. He also instituted a hiring freeze that ultimately deprived the agency of a reserve bench of leaders for the decades to come. This situation was further complicated by Turner's reluctance to carry out risky clandestine and covert action operations. When I was running the operational side of the CIA and close to the end of my career, I could not help but wonder what the missing officers and new employees of those years could have contributed to the agency's leadership during a complex and tumultuous post–Cold War period.

In the Soviet Union especially, given the operating environment, Turner's reticence negatively impacted recruiting sources, as his approach relied mainly on either assets recruited out of country or volunteers. At the time the CIA had three highly sensitive assets who fit the former category.[13] Over the course of a few months in the summer of 1977 two of those sources, Aleksandr Ogorodnik and Anatoly Filatov, had been identified and caught by the KGB. Filatov was tried and executed by firing squad, and Ogorodnik's capture was coordinated to entrap CIA officer Martha Peterson, who was PNGed shortly after she tried to rendezvous with Ogorodnik in July 1977. When Ogorodnik was arrested, he offered to write a confession, and when given his CIA-furnished pen, he bit down on the barrel, which contained a cyanide capsule, and died. It was unknown at the time, but a spy from within CIA headquarters, Karl Koechner, had given Ogorodnik away.[14]

Following the loss of those two Soviet intelligence assets, a total "stand down" was ordered until the Soviet Division could "guarantee" that there would be no further breaches. This was an unrealistic requirement, and it effectively paralyzed the Moscow station for months. Even more maddening, a mysterious and most promising source made five unsuccessful attempts to contact the CIA just before and during this lockdown; the CIA nearly missed one of the most important assets of the Cold War.

Adolf Tolkachev, a middle-aged electronics engineer who was a cog in the Soviet bureaucracy in Moscow, undertook a discreet yet dogged campaign to gain the attention of the U.S. intelligence community by passing scribbled notes to individuals in or near cars with American diplomatic license plates. He offered his services in this manner on no less than five separate occasions over fifteen months from within the heart of Moscow—an admirable and dangerous feat. CIA leadership feared at first that he was a Soviet provocation, and in any case they were prevented from responding because of the stand-down order. At enormous personal risk, in his last letter he provided a detailed account of himself, including his full name, job description, and family details. Finally, we were able to make contact with him.[15]

With the exception of Cherepanov, these are all successful accounts of how willing assets were able to make contact with us. But they show how a difficult operational security environment, a lack of robust espionage infrastructure, and misguided CIA policies can make their task infinitely more difficult.

What worries me now is that it is virtually impossible to be an embassy walk-in today (which is not to suggest that it was an easy feat at U.S. embassies in the past, especially the most heavily guarded, such as our embassy in Moscow). How can one even begin to contemplate "walking in" to an embassy in the age of modern terrorism and ubiquitous CCTV in many of the world's capitals? Embassies and consulates abroad are rightfully impenetrable fortresses guarded to the hilt and monitored constantly by foreign intelligence services. It takes persistence and creativity to identify and establish discreet contact with CIA officials outside the embassy environment. Knowing how important the recruitment of human assets is to both our intelligence collection and our counterintelligence imperatives, we must take great care to correctly target the people who might be susceptible to working with us and to create opportunities so that potential agents can make contact with us. As the Carter/Turner era demonstrated, political will at the highest policy level is essential to carrying out these activities.

Handlers and Tradecraft

The stories of Popov and Penkovskiy were the bread and butter of my CIA training at the "Farm," where I trained at the beginning of 1969 in the art of recruiting agents, vetting walk-ins, surveilling targets, debriefing agents, and preparing and validating reports about clandestine meetings. I vividly recall sitting in class during the seminar on key Russian cases and listening to spymaster George Kisevalter, who was pacing back and forth across the stage as he spoke tearfully and in detail about his handling of these highly sensitive sources.

Kisevalter was and remains a unique personality in CIA lore. Born to Russian immigrants fleeing the Bolshevik Revolution, he was extraordinarily adept in gaining the confidence of his assets through his good humor, deep cultural and historical understanding of Russia, prolific linguistic aptitude, and his unassuming nature. Part of Kisevalter's success developed from his unique profile as both an American and a Russian. Because his personal identity was entrenched in both cultures and languages, he had the tools to create bonds of complicity and trust that other operators were unable to establish.

Kisevalter was brought in to handle Popov, whom he met, debriefed, and clandestinely gave operational guidance to for five years. Over many a boozy night with sturgeon and vodka while incongruously poring over issues of the *Farm Journal*, which he always requested, Popov supplied Kisevalter with crucially important information on Soviet military capacity, Soviet submarines, and guided missile systems. In an enormous stroke of luck, Popov was transferred to Karlshorst in East Berlin, which was the headquarters of the Illegals Section for Eastern Europe. Popov was then able to identify more than 650 GRU officers and provide many key leads to their corresponding illegals.[16]

Penkovskiy required a different approach. By the time he met with the CIA and SIS in London, he had his mind and heart set on destroying the Soviet system. He had devised an elaborate albeit untenable plan whereby the United States would provide him with miniature nuclear explosives that he could place in trash cans around Moscow and whose detonation would bring an end to the Soviet era. To him, this plan would place him in an imaginary pantheon of heroes. Penkovskiy yearned for personal recognition by figures of authority. (He insisted on meeting the queen or Lord Mountbatten but eventually settled for Dick White, the head of British intelligence.) Fortunately, Kisevalter was masterful in redirecting Penkovskiy and convincing him to focus his energies on gathering information from within the heart of Soviet military intelligence.

On his first visit to London, Penkovskiy provided the CIA/SIS team with the entire roster of Soviet intelligence personnel in London, furnished key information on Soviet surface-to-air antiaircraft missiles (SA-2) and Soviet medium range ballistic missiles (MRBMs), and informed on the tragic fate of a Soviet illegal in Paris who had gone missing. Penkovskiy also gave information on the current state of Soviet affairs: food shortages across the empire, cutbacks in military pay, a general crisis in Soviet military morale, and the Soviets' intention to remain aggressive in the Berlin Crisis. Most important, Penkovskiy informed the United States and Britain that not one of the Soviet intercontinental ballistic missiles (ICBMs) was yet operational.[17]

Penkovskiy had an extraordinary "exuberance for life" that he applied with fervor to his task of espionage. He showed himself to be very adept in using the Minox miniature cameras the British provided him to make copies of GRU documents back in Russia, as well as in learning a secret coding protocol that would allow him to decipher radio transmissions from the West containing specific messages for him.[18]

Aside from dinners with his British and American handlers and the occasional female companion, Penkovskiy's main remuneration comprised full colonel salaries (and uniforms) from both the United States and Britain that were kept in escrow for him in the West for when he would eventually defect with his family. Penkovskiy requested—and received—a number of items primarily intended for party officials with whom he wished to ingratiate himself. These spoils were hardly just compensation for the risks Penkovskiy took or the value of the information he procured, but his central motivation was the sense of importance of his mission.

Over the course of his short service to the West, he provided more than 110 cassettes of film with images of highly sensitive documents, including papers on top Soviet leaders' strategic thinking. He also provided insight on what he knew of current Soviet plans concerning Berlin and Cuba, assessments of the Kennedy government, the personal histories of leading Soviet generals, and the identities of at least 341 GRU officers in Moscow, 192 GRU officers and agents abroad, and 75 KGB officers and agents in London and Paris. In aggregate, Penkovskiy provided the West with a meaningful strategic intelligence advantage over the Soviet Union.

Penkovskiy was given a burst transmitter that could send a three-hundred-word message more than a thousand yards in under a second so that he could signal his contacts should timely information come available. He was instructed to activate the device near the American embassy if he needed to contact his handlers. Penkovskiy was also furnished with a protocol to alert the West should there be an imminent Soviet nuclear attack: this involved marking a lamppost with chalk, making a telephone call, and, depending on the reception message he received, either breathing three times into the phone or hanging up and remarking the lamp post and dropping information at a particular dead drop to be used only once.

Because of his diplomatic status, Penkovskiy had a legitimate reason to attend the American ambassador's diplomatic functions. While Penkovskiy had the pretext, he still couldn't be seen speaking to or handing anything to a Western intelligence officer. So, by prearrangement, he would wander off during the reception and stash the secret documents in a concealed location in the bathroom water tank. Hugh Montgomery, an old friend of mine and veteran of the OSS who had parachuted with the Eighty-Second Airborne into France on D-Day, provided assistance. On what would be Penkovskiy's last visit to Spaso

House, the U.S. ambassador's residence in Moscow, as Montgomery would recall years later, he had considerable trouble extracting the documents from the tank, and his sleeve jacket was soaking wet when he finally located the package. He nonchalantly returned to the reception, where he proceeded to conceal his wet arm behind his wife and beat a hasty retreat from the residence, with the sensitive documents under his coat.

LESSON NINE

We must target and recruit spies from beyond military and intelligence circles and especially from the policy sphere.

The magnitude of their contribution can be measured, in part, by the fact that the peace was sustained during a most critical time.

—President JOHN F. KENNEDY, in a letter of commendation to DCI John McCone on CIA assets' contributions of critical intelligence

9

Policy Spies

Legacy of Spies

Many of our most valuable spies provided not only tactical and strategic intelligence but also information of great policy pertinence. Dmitri Polyakov, codenamed Top Hat, provided essential information on GRU intelligence operations and information on Soviet weaponry, including tanks and missiles and their capabilities. While in Burma in the late 1960s, he passed on everything the Soviets knew about the Vietnamese and Chinese armed forces. As he rose in the ranks, eventually becoming a general, he passed on astute assessments of the dynamics among the GRU, the KGB, the Communist Party, the Foreign Ministry, and the Kremlin. He also provided a commanding understanding of Soviet strategic thinking on foreign and economic policy, military strategy and doctrine, and the appetite for confrontation with the West. Polyakov furnished the CIA with copies of the classified version of "Military Thought," a monthly Soviet military strategy document. Through this and Polyakov's own insight, CIA analysts could demonstrate to the White House and the Pentagon that Soviet military leaders were not hardcore ideologues or great risk takers but were just as worried about a nuclear holocaust as the West. Perhaps most important, he gave detailed information on the deepening and enduring rift between the Soviet Union and China in the late 1960s and early 1970s. Henry Kissinger was particularly receptive to this intelligence, which greatly informed and helped shape President Richard Nixon's overtures toward China in 1972.[1]

In a similar way, Adolf Tolkachev's valuable work helped enable our military to understand, compete with, and prevail over the Sovi-

ets during the Cold War military technology race. The intelligence he
provided gave the Reagan administration a strategic edge, including
knowledge that the Soviets' actual level of technological prowess was
progressing at a snail's pace compared to U.S. capabilities. Armed with
his Pentax and trusty Tropel cameras, the latter hidden in an agency-
manufactured key fob that he smuggled into his office, Tolkachev
worked stealthily from within Russia from 1979 until 1985. His job as
an aeronautical engineer gave him seemingly limitless access to sensitive
classified military technology blueprints and related reports. Tolkachev's
work was so valuable to the United States at the time that a painting
of him stealing Soviet military intelligence, with his Pentax camera
clamped to the back of a chair in his home, hangs in CIA headquarters.

Arkady Shevchenko shared key Soviet leaders' insights—information
that in many ways is the most valuable type that spies provide. He is
exactly the type of asset we could benefit from today in our dealings
with Putin and his government when so few can claim a solid understanding of what makes Putin tick.[2] Shevchenko's observations revealed
the Politburo's philosophy and strategy in the late 1970s, which could
very well mirror some of Putin's thinking today. Shevchenko coun-
seled constructive engagement with the Soviet Union from a position
of force. He brought unprecedented insight into the Soviet foreign
policy process. He described how all interactions with the West were
viewed through a perceived existential battle between "two opposing
social and political systems" and with a deep belief that Soviet socialism would triumph in the end. Importantly, Shevchenko observed little
appetite in the Russian leadership for nuclear war or direct confrontation with the United States. He also said that it was America's "lack
of resolve" in Vietnam that spurred Soviet expansionist policies in the
1970s. This point should be kept in mind by U.S. policy makers today
when they consider how Putin views our resolve in crises abroad, especially in developing countries. Shevchenko's assessments also helped the
Reagan administration determine how best to engage Russia, establish normal relations, and mitigate the likelihood of confrontation.

With the advantage of hindsight, both the Soviet and U.S. sides
were primarily looking for sources of intelligence in each other's intel-

ligence and military services, and not enough attention was given to policy sources. This may be changing on both sides, as we have growing evidence of how heavily invested the Russians are in going after human sources in our government, in addition to continuing their technical and cyber operations and covert action. While Putin's calculus may be similar to that of the old Soviet leadership, our understanding of Putin's strategic thinking would be greatly augmented by having sources close to him in the Kremlin.

Nuclear Advantage

The stories of Polyakov, Shevchenko, and Tolkachev highlight the value of intelligence in foreign affairs. It is this hard-to-collect information that, once vetted and analyzed, gives decision-makers the best possible insight into a given policy priority or issue. These assets provided the United States with extraordinary information that gave us a marked advantage in policy generally and at key moments in history. Most significantly, their information was pivotal in helping avert nuclear disaster on at least two occasions.

When misinterpreting events poses existential risks, well-placed spies can provide a great service to our decision-makers by clarifying the intentions and policies of our adversaries. This point may be best exemplified by the Cuban Missile Crisis. After our Bay of Pigs fiasco, First Secretary Nikita Khrushchev decided to provide conventional weapons to Cuba in a defensive posture. Sometime in 1962, however, during a large buildup of Soviet arms in Cuba, he decided to initiate Operation Anadyr, a secret plan to deploy offensive nuclear weapons, including thirty-six MRBMs and twenty-four IRBMs, and forty-two thousand troops to Cuba. There had been agent and defector reports within the community of Cuban emigrants that the Soviets were planning offensive missile sites in Cuba, but the CIA was not able to confirm these reports. The intelligence community's assessment at that time was that the Soviets had no imminent plans to send nuclear weapons to Cuba, as they had no appetite to provoke the United States and potentially risk confrontation at a higher level. Most analysts within the intelligence community saw the conventional arms support as a defensive strategy by the Soviets, but DCI John McCone feared a worst-case scenario when in October 1962 Soviet offensive missile sites were detected in Cuba. It became clear that Khrushchev had taken very bold and aggressive action that threatened a direct military confrontation with the United States.[3]

Operation Anadyr at first went undetected because of restrictions placed on reconnaissance flights in September, but photos of the missiles and the construction for launch sites were detected during the very first U-2 flight after restrictions (imposed after the Gary Powers U-2 incident) were lifted on October 14. The CIA was quickly able to confirm that there were SS-4 MRBMs present because Penkovskiy had provided the schematics and manuals for these specific nuclear missiles. It was Ray Cline, the deputy director for intelligence, who gave the news to the national security advisor, McGeorge Bundy, on October 15. The Kennedy administration went into high gear, simultaneously ordering preparations be made by the Joint Chiefs of Staff for a military invasion of Cuba, as well as for another attempt by the CIA to start a revolution. Thanks also to the information provided by Penkovskiy, the CIA was able to determine that the SS-4s were not yet operational, giving Kennedy extra time to craft his strong yet famously diplomatic response. On October 23 Kennedy imposed a naval "quarantine," moved U.S. military readiness to DEFCON 3, and wrote a letter to Khrushchev demanding the removal of the missiles from Cuba.[4]

It is difficult to determine definitively what combination of information, timing, personalities, motivations, assessments of facts, and perceptions of the Russian threat and Soviet mind-set led Kennedy to respond the way he did and in doing so create an environment that prompted the Russians to back down. There is compelling evidence, however, that several critical elements in the decision process came from Penkovskiy: (1) none of the Soviet ICBMs were yet operational, (2) the Soviets lacked key warheads and guidance systems, and (3) the Soviets had no appetite for a possible armed conflict and were unprepared to stand their ground in Cuba. These elements—coupled with the CIA's analysis and interpretation of additional aerial reconnaissance imagery taken in the days that followed—gave Kennedy an important intelligence understanding of the growing readiness of the missile launch sites and the possible threat to the United States. Functional, up-to-date, and relevant intelligence gave Kennedy the information and data he needed to better calibrate his response to the Soviets and to respond forcefully and strategically, allowing him to negotiate for the removal of the missiles during the critical thirteen-day period.[5]

The Cuban Missile Crisis is now considered a watershed moment for the CIA. It demonstrated the reach and importance of the CIA's technical and HUMINT capabilities and served in part as redemption for the botched Bay of Pigs operation in Cuba earlier in Kennedy's presidency. It also showed the key role that technical collection would play in the new world of intelligence. The imagery gathered via aerial reconnaissance and related intelligence analysis allowed the agency to provide the president and his national security team with the information and insight—much of it derived from Penkovskiy's work—necessary to make the Soviets back down.

This crisis should be kept in mind by future administrations in dealing with Putin and his successors. It is critical to remember that Russians respect a forceful response, but only where there is credible resolve. Like Khrushchev before him, Putin may misjudge American resolve and take steps, including in the cyber sphere, that could bring us to the brink of conflict. The CIA will need to continue to stay ahead of the rapidly changing world of human and technical intelligence, especially in the critical theaters where we confront the Russians, places as varied as Belarus, Ukraine, Syria, Iran, North Korea, Cuba, Venezuela, and in the cyber sphere. The challenges facing spymasters have never been greater.

As an interesting footnote to the Cuban Missile Crisis, the fallout on the Soviet side came in October 1964. Supreme Soviet head Leonid Brezhnev, First Deputy Prime Minister and former KGB head Alexander Shelepin, and KGB chairman Vladimir Semichastny led a swift and bloodless coup d'état against First Secretary Nikita Khrushchev. Khrushchev's policies of relatively liberal reform—especially his de-Stalinization campaign—combined with his recklessness and perceived failure to prevail in the Cuban Missile Crisis prompted many Communist Party hard-liners to conclude that the Soviet Union was on the wrong path. Brezhnev succeeded him as First Secretary because even though Shelepin and Semichastny were the recognized kingmakers, there was no appetite for an intelligence chief as head of the empire. Brezhnev, hoping to secure political control of the security and intelligence services, in 1967 appointed party member Yuri Andropov as the next chairman of the KGB. Andropov was shrewd and effective, and his leadership signaled a new era for the KGB, one that would last fifteen years.

The second instance in which we came close to nuclear confrontation with Russia is less well known. When Ronald Reagan became president, his hard-line position against the communist world was underscored by his staunch refusal to reach out to Russian leadership. This was in stark contrast to the détente era, and Reagan's actions and rhetoric alarmed the Kremlin. The Soviet leaders of the Politburo, most notably Andropov, grew seriously concerned that the United States might launch a surprise, first-strike nuclear attack on the Soviet Union.[6]

In May 1981 the Politburo instructed the KGB and the GRU to carry out a substantial intelligence-gathering program known as Operation RYaN (the Russian acronym for Raketno-Yadernoye Napadenie, or nuclear missile attack) in order to detect if and when the United States and NATO might launch an attack. Soviet agents were dispatched to monitor individuals in the West who would be involved in a nuclear launch, and these targets of monitoring included decision-makers and technical and support staff at nuclear missile launch sites, military bases security sites, communication lines, and bomb shelters.[7]

Resources for Operation RYaN were deployed across the West and along the periphery of the Eastern Bloc, raising tensions higher. Meanwhile, the United States was engaging in psychological operations, or PSYOPS, which were random military acts of posturing intended to rattle the Soviets and keep them guessing as to Reagan's intentions. These PSYOPS involved sending American bombers to areas near the Soviet border and Western fleets to international waters near Soviet naval bases. The Soviets were indeed rattled by these maneuvers and on more than one occasion deployed countermeasures, signifying that the Soviet Union was so on edge that it was willing to respond with force to what it perceived as a real provocation. More generally, the Soviets—led in large part by Andropov—were ramping up preparations for a possible conflict, such as calling up reserve troops, deploying Spetsnaz (special forces), and deploying nuclear strike forces to its western front in East Germany, Poland, and Hungary.[8]

In an episode that should call to mind the events surrounding the 2016 elections, it was during this time, according to the Mitrokhin Archives, that the KGB sought to infiltrate the headquarters of the Republican and Democratic National Committees ahead of the 1984 election. In an effort to discredit President Reagan, they sought to disseminate the slogan "Reagan Means War!" By all accounts, in this pre-cyber era the effort was not only ineffective, it was also unlikely that the Soviets actually believed they could influence the 1984 election. At least on this occasion, the Soviets were leaving metaphorical "Chilean cats" on our doorstep. It was a nuisance conveying a message of disdain. Not much has changed in this mentality over the years.

Things nearly took a very dramatic turn in the fall of 1983, when NATO forces carried out a series of annual military exercises. These training exercises simulated an outbreak of conflict with the Soviet Union and Eastern Europe that would escalate into a conventional war. The culminating portion of the exercise was codenamed Able Archer 83, which simulated preparations for a nuclear conflict. The problem was that much of what must take place to conduct such a training exercise is exactly what must take place when preparing for an actual first-strike nuclear attack. It entailed the mobilization of nineteen thousand U.S. troops, consultation with heads of state, shifting of commands to alternative "war headquarters," and chatter that could imply significant escalation.

The Soviet Union, with its RYaN operatives in place, took note of the mobilization indicators but misread the West's intent, believing the training exercises to be an indication of preparation for a first-strike nuclear attack. Perhaps worse, the United States was not sufficiently sensitive to the fact that the Soviets might misconstrue NATO intentions. The Soviets then readied their nuclear weapons in Poland and

East Germany, transporting them from storage sites to delivery units via helicopter. All flights were suspended, save for intelligence flights, of which there were unprecedented numbers, over the Norwegian, North, Baltic, and Barents Seas to track the movement of U.S. naval forces.

Even though very few Americans were aware of this crisis, many experts will argue that Able Archer 83 was the closest we came to nuclear confrontation with the Soviets other than the Cuban Missile Crisis. It was avoided by the tempered actions of a senior NATO intelligence and U.S. Air Force officer, Lieutenant General Leonard Perroots, who was serving as assistant chief of staff for intelligence, U.S. Air Forces Europe. Perroots chose not to escalate the NATO threat level in response to Soviet mobilizations along the Polish and Eastern European borders, which greatly helped to calm Soviet angst. The Soviet threat posture progressively decreased as the Able Archer exercises finished, and a nuclear showdown was avoided.[9]

It is striking to note the apparent absence of both high-placed Russian policy sources and relevant dialogue among diplomats, intelligence services, and informal back channels during a period when tensions were exceptionally high. Able Archer or any similar event could plausibly have triggered a similar, potentially devastating response. Owing to the Soviets' genuine belief that the West might launch a surprise attack, there is significant information suggesting that they could have launched their own preemptive nuclear attack by mistakenly seeing indications of an American first strike where there was none. The argument for engaging in dialogue with one's enemies is as relevant today as it was back then. Putin's actions relating to the states along Russia's borders and his efforts to exacerbate NATO fault lines could also produce the miscalculation that we had in the 1980s. The same concern applies to the North Korean nuclear program.

The West came to appreciate the Soviets' genuine fear of a Western preemptive nuclear strike only because of reporting from a Soviet spy for Britain's SIS. In 1983 Oleg Gordievsky, mentioned earlier, was serving as the deputy chief of the London KGB *rezidentura* (residency). He told the SIS about increasingly alarming directives regarding Operation RYaN throughout the year. In early November he advised that

KGB central headquarters in Moscow had sent a flash cable inaccurately alerting the residency that U.S. forces in Europe had been placed on alert and mobilized either in response to the recent bombing of Western peacekeepers' military barracks in Beirut or possibly as part of the countdown for a surprise nuclear attack. Fortunately, the sober-thinking Perroots and his staff, along with his Washington counterpart, helped to deescalate the situation. But in the days that followed the Able Archer 83 exercises, Reagan took heed of the KGB's fear of a Western attack and became increasingly concerned about an accidental nuclear confrontation with the Soviets.

Reagan started to look for ways to warm up the relationship, including writing to Gorbachev to suggest a summit, which took place in Geneva in November 1985. This led to a string of summits that resulted in a thaw in overall Cold War tensions and a major breakthrough in arms control negotiations. Most notable was the INF agreement in 1987, which brought about the elimination of the intermediate-range nuclear weapons (this is the same nuclear treaty that President Trump withdrew from in October 2018, citing Putin's continuous and flagrant violation of its terms). It is hoped that the Russians will return to the negotiating table to work out a serious and verifiable agreement.

Putin should take heed of his own country's history in this misreading of competitors' intentions. It is his aggressive and provocative maneuvers that could lead to an unfortunate and potentially dangerous response if misunderstood. Russian Zapad war games, conducted in Russia and Belarus in September 2017 and mobilizing up to one hundred thousand troops along the borders of the Baltic states and Poland, provoked high anxiety in the United States, NATO, Finland, and Sweden. That anxiety was not unfounded, given that Russian had annexed Crimea following previous war games in 2014.

We also should not lose sight of the lessons of Able Archer. Given Putin's aggressive posture in Ukraine, in the Caucasus region, Syria, and elsewhere, there are ample opportunities for all parties to misread the intentions of the other, to provoke unanticipated responses, and start down a path where, once engaged, it is difficult to change course.

Patriot Spies

American intelligence during the Cold War was aided by a largely self-directed corps of individuals who came from within the heart of the Soviet system. What is unique is that many of the spies saw their spying as an act of Russian patriotism. They felt that the Soviet system had squandered the riches and greatness of Russia through corruption, hypocrisy, violence, and cynicism, and they wished to strike out against it.

According to his handlers, Polyakov perceived his role as that of a Russian patriot trying to assist the United States in undermining the Soviet regime that he had come to loathe. He believed that the United States was too weak during these turbulent years and feared that the Soviets could win the Cold War. He saw his intervention as essential in giving the United States the upper hand.

In a similar vein, according to Tolkachev's handlers and the treasure trove of notes he shared with the U.S. intelligence community, he was driven by ideological opposition to what the Soviet Union represented. Disillusionment with the "hypocritical demagoguery" and a deeply entrenched resentment over his in-laws' suffering under Stalin helped propel Tolkachev to do as much damage as possible in the shortest time possible. What is extraordinary about the Tolkachev story is his unwavering determination to execute his self-chosen task. In this respect he resembles Vasiliy Mitrokhin, who over the course of twelve years diligently copied a significant portion of the KGB First Chief Directorate's archive before smuggling it out after the fall of the Soviet Union, thereby providing the West with the most comprehensive view of Soviet intelligence during the Cold War.[10]

Neither Tolkachev nor Mitrokhin ever expected to see the fruits of their labors. They were working for a future that they were certain they would not see but hoped that perhaps the next generation might. More generally, though exfiltration plans were in place for most of these agents-in-place and arrangements for future financial remuneration had been set up, most of them knew that they would likely die in Russia because of their spying efforts.

Shevchenko defected in New York, and Gordievsky had a most extraordinary exfiltration from Moscow. On July 16, 1985, SIS agents in Moscow observed Gordievsky standing on a street corner. This was the signal that indicated that he had been discovered and needed to be evacuated immediately. Gordievsky had recently returned to Moscow, having been recalled from his post in London. He knew something was amiss when he felt certain that his apartment had been searched. A few days later his superior drove him to a dacha, where he was drugged, interrogated, and accused of being a spy but not arrested. He suspected that the KGB was hoping to catch him contacting his British handlers. Aware that he had little time to escape, he sent his family off on vacation and went to consult his hardbound copy of Shakespeare's sonnets. Even though Gordievsky was currently posted in London, the SIS had very astutely taken steps to put in place an exfiltration plan for him ahead of time, hiding the details in the binding of the book of sonnets. Gordievsky's confidence in the British served him very well. As a humorous aside, Gordievsky thought the SIS to be the best Western intelligence agency, citing its agents' British charm and elite educations as the foundational traits for excellence in espionage. He didn't think much of the CIA, stating that only one in ten CIA case officers had any sort of charm. He also charged that the CIA was too big and that it lost the best candidates for recruitment to Wall Street. But he reserved his most scathing assessment for the French, deeming them largely incompetent (except for their counterintelligence shop, *bien sûr*). Hidden under the flyleaf of the book of sonnets were instructions for him to stand on the designated corner at 7:00 p.m. and wait for a sign from a Brit who would be eating something. This would indicate that the SIS had received his signal.

Exfiltration from Russia was rare and extremely difficult because of the restrictive operating environment and the inherent security risks. On Gordievsky's first attempt to signal SIS, no one appeared, but on his second attempt, on July 16, a British intelligence officer carrying a Harrods shopping bag and eating a candy bar walked right by him. In the days that followed, Gordievsky managed to evade KGB surveillance and take a train to a meeting point near the Finnish border. Two British case officers and their spouses, aware that the KGB could be eavesdropping on their conversations by using technology, concocted a story of travel to Finland for shopping and a medical appointment. They managed to lose their KGB tail on their drive up from Moscow. They met up with Gordievsky outside the town of Vyborg and secreted him in one of their cars. They eluded heat-seeking cameras by covering Gordievsky with a "space blanket" at checkpoints and deflected the acute senses of Alsatian border guard dogs with the strategic use of potato chips and a timely diaper change for one officer's infant, also along for the mission. As they drove across the border, they changed the music on the car's sound system to Sibelius's "Finlandia," signaling to Gordievsky that he had successfully escaped.[11]

However, the majority of these men, like Tolkachev and Polyakov, paid a fatal price for their work with the West. In November 1958 Popov was recalled from East Germany, and everyone was concerned, particularly Kisevalter. Popov had recently provided information about the arrival in the United States of Russian illegal operative Margarita Tairova and her husband. An FBI surveillance operation to track Tairova and her husband in New York had been detected, and they managed to flee before they could be apprehended. Popov was Tairova's control officer, and Moscow began an aggressive investigation to determine how Tairova was compromised. Popov was an excellent source of information, but he took too many risks, never followed directions, and drank too much. Kisevalter was deeply concerned. In preceding months Kisevalter had expressed concerns about Popov's security and had on numerous occasions offered to help him and his family defect. Popov, however, never showed any interest in defecting.

A month after being recalled, in December 1958, Popov made contact with Russell Langelle, his default CIA contact in Moscow. He did so by calling a "wrong number," which signaled Popov would meet Langelle at one of several prearranged meeting spots at specific times. They met in the men's room of a restaurant, where Popov passed Langelle a note indicating that he had been dismissed by the GRU after having fallen under suspicion. Popov and Langelle agreed to meet again in a month's time at a bus stop. As a backup, a letter was mailed to Popov to provide him with other means to make contact should the "brush contact" not be made. This was highly questionable tradecraft, especially since Popov was under suspicion.

Nevertheless, Popov and Langelle continued to meet regularly, but uncharacteristically Popov did not provide any compelling intelligence and the notes in his notebook were written differently than his normal manner.[12] These were all signals that something was wrong—that he was possibly under hostile control.

On September 18, 1959, Langelle again met Popov in the men's room of a restaurant. When Popov shook Langelle's hand, he surreptitiously passed him what came to be known as the "cylinder message," written in pencil on eight small pieces of paper, rolled up, wrapped in cloth, tied with a string, and perfumed. In this letter he reported that he had been arrested in February and that all of their meetings since had been under KGB direction and surveillance. He also reported how much the KGB knew about Popov's cooperation with the CIA and that the entire U.S. embassy in Moscow was under surveillance. He also reported that he had been in prison for months and that it had taken him all that time to draft this message, which he had hidden under a bandage covering a self-inflicted wound he gave himself for that sole purpose. His last sentence was, "Could you not ask your kind President Eisenhower to see if he might cause restitution to be made for my family and my life?"[13]

On October 16, 1959, Langelle and Popov's regular brush contact was interrupted. Popov was arrested and Langelle was PNGed. Not long after, Popov was tried and convicted and then killed by firing squad in June. Some believed that it was the MI6 spy for the Soviets, George Blake, who had betrayed Popov.[14] Others suggested that the KGB's constant surveillance of the U.S. embassy was his undoing and that the game was over when someone at the U.S. embassy mailed the letter with the backup meeting instructions. I tend to believe it was the Tairova flap—once the KGB knew that someone had blown her cover, there could be only a limited number of suspects.

Penkovskiy would suffer a similar fate. On November 2, 1962, just as the Cuban Missile Crisis came to a close, the U.S. embassy in Moscow received a call on a special line. The caller blew three times into the telephone. Was this a signal from Penkovskiy that the Soviets were preparing for imminent nuclear war? The signal deviated slightly from the planned protocol, as the answer the embassy gave should have elicited a hang-up rather than three deep breaths. Still, there had been no news from Penkovskiy for nearly two months, and the CIA wanted and needed news of its agent. Case officers were quickly dispatched to see if the lamppost had been marked, and it had. As one officer proceeded to the dead drop location, a swarm of Soviet police descended upon him, whisking him off for interrogation. Because the officer was a U.S. diplomat with immunity, he was released and, along with a dozen other people, PNGed and expelled from the Soviet Union. Penkovskiy had been arrested on October 22, then convicted and sentenced to death. While there is some dispute about how he was executed, the prevailing belief is that he was shot by a firing squad and cremated.

Popov and Penkovskiy were among the most noteworthy of our agents-in-place to lose their lives, but there were many others. Although the stakes are incredibly high, their profile and dedication are what we continue to need to thwart Russia's aggressive actions. And given Russia's growing autocracy, set against its relatively weak economy and growing diplomatic isolation, it is a statistical certainty that there are disillusioned Russians who will become this generation's highly valuable "patriot spies." We must continue to be in a position to receive and handle them clandestinely and effectively wherever they appear.

LESSON TEN

The Russian strategic horizon is long, and covert action is the United States' most effective tool to counter it.

For the purpose of coordinating the intelligence activities of the several Government departments and agencies in the interest of national security, it shall be the duty of the Agency, under the direction of the National Security Council . . . **to perform such other functions and duties related to intelligence affecting the national security** as the National Security Council may from time to time direct.

—National Security Act of 1947

10

An American Covert Action Playbook

Current Posture

If we are to conclude anything about Russia today, it is that its intelligence assault, primarily in the form of active measures against the United States, has continued unabated. Covert action is the American cognate to Russian active measures. While Russia may be underpinning much of its foreign policy with the use of active measures, since the end of the Cold War the United States has largely been reluctant to deploy this vital mechanism to counter Russian aggression against our national interests, especially inside Russia.

Since the creation of the CIA's mandate in 1947 to combat Soviet aggression, American covert action has included such things as supporting oppositional political activities, designing and disseminating propaganda, aiding paramilitary activity, and fomenting regime change. It was and is a critical, if relatively underused, tool in U.S. foreign policy and one that needs to be exercised in blocking hostile behavior by adversarial national states, including Russia.

Covert action led the way at the agency in its early years, but after the failed Bay of Pigs operation in 1961 its primacy over intelligence collection and espionage started to wane. However, the unique and effective benefits covert action could offer would make it an essential tactic that would be used periodically and forcefully over the decades to come, as in the case of the Central American and Afghan programs in the 1980s, both of which I came to know firsthand.

That said, then as now the vast majority of CIA officers would prefer to stick to foreign intelligence collection and not get involved in action operations, which have high political risks when exposed, which almost always happens. As a result, there usually is a dearth of covert political and cyber action expertise in the agency at any given time. There has been much debate over the years as to which should be the primary mission of the agency. From my perspective, a hybrid approach works best, with both strong intelligence collection and covert action as essential levers of U.S. foreign policy. Frank Wisner, the CIA's second director of operations and an accomplished spymaster, saw this approach as "intelligence in action."[1]

Since September 11, 2001, the U.S. intelligence community's focus has been significantly reoriented to support counterterrorism and our military efforts abroad through paramilitary-type covert action and intelligence collection. What this means is that the bulk of our intelligence resources since 2001 have been focused on tactical targeting of our adversaries in Afghanistan, Iraq, Africa, and Syria, as well as providing tactical military support to forces on the ground.

The high point of American covert action during this time period was the 2011 raid in Abbottabad, Pakistan, that killed Osama bin Laden, America's most wanted terrorist for more than a decade. The successful raid was predicated on years of intelligence work—targeting potential sources, tracking down leads, and operating in hostile territories. According to reports, a spy for the Kurdish-led Syrian Democratic Forces (SDF) who had infiltrated ISIS provided the location for former ISIS head Abu Bakr al-Baghdadi, who was killed by U.S. forces in October 2019.[2]

Because of the central focus on counterterrorism, our attention was not as heavily weighted toward Russia or other, more traditional targets. For many years the general posture of American foreign policy identified terrorism as its most immediate threat. Therefore, we placed our intelligence assets primarily in the service of supporting that issue and our other military pursuits abroad.

We are slowly returning to the agency's original mandate of espionage and covert action abroad targeting some of our "big power" adversaries and their spheres of influence. Our focus is shifting to the assault on our democracy. One of our most effective tools on this strategic horizon is traditional covert action supported by modern technology, especially cyber operations, and we need to contemplate how best to reinvigorate and leverage it to serve our current and future foreign policy goals.

To better prepare for the future, it is worth recalling some major covert action operations we took against the Soviets during the Cold War. The first case that comes to mind exemplifies the type of thinking our covert action experts hopefully are contemplating today. It involves the targeting of the KGB's Line X.

By the 1960s the Soviet economy was faltering and the Soviet Union was falling woefully behind the West on scientific research, technical innovation, and industrial production. To counter these threats, in 1970 the KGB redoubled its efforts to obtain Western scientific and technical secrets. Agents in its operational arm in foreign embassies, in what was known as Line X, sought to acquire Western know-how so as to place the Soviet Union back on equal footing with the West. A massive intelligence effort was launched to recruit Western scientists and infiltrate Soviet delegations visiting U.S. firms and laboratories as part of détente. The Soviets and their proxies turned their focus to developing novel and circuitous ways of obtaining key U.S., European, and Japanese military, industrial, and computing secrets and conducting special activities operations against us. Dmitri Polyakov and Aleksei Kulak, as Russian spies working for the United States, confirmed this when they provided the CIA with a massive "shopping list" of all the military technologies that Soviet spies were seeking to obtain in the West. There were also a few notable cases that alerted us to a wider trend.[3]

In July 1981 French president François Mitterrand told President Reagan that the French had a spy operating within the heart of the KGB section in charge of infiltrating all major scientific and technical programs of Western private enterprise and government R&D programs. KGB colonel Vladimir Vetrov, codenamed Farewell, had identified more than two hundred KGB personnel stationed in the West and one hundred scientists associated with the KGB.[4] The level of access and successful penetration by the KGB and GRU was staggering. The Soviet

Union had essentially outsourced much of its R&D in radar, computers, machine tools, and semiconductors to the West via espionage. Our vital technological innovation that allowed us to maintain an industrial and military competitive advantage over the Soviet Union was being transferred to the Soviets right under our noses.[5] This same type of assault against our defense industry is ongoing today, albeit largely in the cyber arena.

In response to attacks in the 1980s, the CIA, Defense Department, and FBI, partnering with a few American companies, launched a major deception operation that was initiated by Gus Weiss, who served on the National Security Council. Because Vetrov had supplied detailed information on tech collection requirements, U.S. companies, led by the CIA, modified designs so that military technology would later fail. The project was hugely successful and resulted in the incorporation of defective technology into Soviet military equipment, pipelines, chemical plants, and even their space program. By cooperating with our NATO allies, we were able to compromise two hundred Soviet intelligence officers working across Europe and North America and send them packing. The work of the KGB was badly subverted. Some sovietologists consider this operation an important factor in impeding the Soviet Union's technical progress.

The formidable, persistent drive of our Soviet counterparts spurred our innovations in spycraft and counterintelligence, especially in the technology sector. This kind of inventive and ambitious covert action is applicable to countering Russian interference today; it is action that exploits Russia's strategic weaknesses and amplifies American strength. Examining key cases of American covert action from the Cold War can help us discern how U.S. political, technical, economic, and paramilitary action might be best leveraged to respond to the current Russian cyber and geopolitical challenge.

An Auspicious Start and an Enduring Playing Field

There are inherent tensions in the intelligence community between those who believe espionage is our most important craft and those who lobby for covert action. At the CIA's inception the nascent agency's leaders, as former OSS officers, were at first most at ease running covert actions. Empowered by success in influencing elections in postwar Italy, the CIA undertook two of the most high-profile and controversial covert action operations of the era: the 1953 coup in Iran, codenamed Operation Ajax, which reinstated the Shah, and Operations Fortune and Success, which oversaw the overthrow of Guatemalan president Jacobo Árbenz in 1954. At the time both operations were viewed as huge victories by the Eisenhower administration, as they successfully rolled back leftist governments that were increasingly hostile to U.S. interests and were perceived to be falling under the influence of the Soviets.

When I became CIA branch chief in Iran in 1985, I had an opportunity to review the agency's classified history of the Ajax operation and meet some of the Iranians who participated in the opposition movement. That history, along with a candid discussion I had had years earlier with the legendary cold warrior Rocky Stone, a key junior operator on the ground during the coup, left on me a deep impression of just how involved and important the CIA was in returning the Shah to power. Be that as it may, Stone went into considerable detail about how hard he and the head of Operation Ajax, Kermit "Kim" Roosevelt, had to work to persuade the Shah to risk returning to Iran (after his prime minister, Mohammad Mosaddeq, had refused to step down) and push himself back into power in coordination with key members of the military. Stone described rather vividly how on the day of the coup he had to help button General Fazlollah Zahedi's uniform because he was too nervous and his hands were shaking. If Stone and Roosevelt were that close to the Shah and Zahedi, our influence had to be proportionate to it. For many years thereafter the Shah and Zahedi were deeply grateful to the CIA and the officers who helped restore him to the throne, and he allowed the agency easy access to him throughout his reign. Because of Roosevelt's success in Iran, the CIA offered him a part in their plans for Guatemala, but he turned them down and remained focused on the Middle East for the rest of his life.[6]

When President Jacobo Árbenz of Guatemala instituted a massive land reform program that would undermine the United Fruit Company

(UFC), which owned a huge amount of land in Guatemala and was the country's largest employer, President Truman knew from intelligence reports that the Soviets had already made inroads among Guatemalan student and labor groups, and he feared that Árbenz was sympathetic to the Soviets. The UFC had tremendous sway in the country and extraordinary political links to Washington power centers. Both Secretary of State John Foster Dulles and DCI Allen Dulles worked on UFC business deals while practicing law at Sullivan and Cromwell in the 1930s. After his retirement, General Walter Bedell Smith, the CIA's formative DCI, was on the UFC's board of directors. Truman instructed the CIA to undertake a covert action operation (PBFortune), which was scrapped when Nicaraguan dictator Anastasio Somoza leaked that he was helping the United States to oust Árbenz from office. By summer 1953 Eisenhower and his advisors had resuscitated the plan to depose Árbenz, and the CIA was again told to execute a coup operation (PBSuccess). Frank Wisner, then the CIA's deputy director of plans (DDP), was put in charge of the overall operation, with help from insurgent operations expert and OSS veteran Jake Esterline and other legendary CIA officers, including Dave Phillips and Gerry Droller (aka Frank Bender).[7]

An external field office was set up in Florida to organize an insurgent group called the Army of Liberation, under Guatemalan colonel Carlos Castillo Armas. Training camps were set up in Nicaragua and Honduras, but the Army of Liberation was a figment of the imagination. To build up belief in this phantom force, the CIA set up a national radio network and a false insurgent radio, which was allegedly being broadcast from the jungles of Guatemala but was actually coming from Florida. These media outlets made it appear as though Colonel Castillo Armas had a large force heading toward the capital. This effort was buttressed by an elaborate international and local propaganda campaign designed to create the impression that Árbenz was facing a formidable opposition and that the United States would intervene militarily if Árbenz was not removed. This Guatemalan military, which was strongly anticommunist, had no stomach for a direct confrontation with U.S. military forces and ultimately preferred to stay in their barracks during the crisis. If they had chosen to fight the rebels, there is

AN AMERICAN COVERT ACTION PLAYBOOK

little doubt they would not have had any trouble destroying the ragtag "liberating" forces of Colonel Castillo Armas. Furthermore, the Guatemalan military was much less inclined to support Árbenz because throughout the crisis he had flirted off and on with the idea of providing arms to civilian militias, which was anathema to any national military institution. The psychological and propaganda campaign was combined with overflights and periodic airdrops of leaflets and crude bombs, which did little damage on the ground but had a devastating impact on civilian and military morale. Soon even Árbenz's most loyal generals changed sides. In a matter of a few days in late June, Árbenz stepped down as president and immediately sought asylum in the Mexican embassy. Castillo Armas was installed as the new president. Inside the CIA and throughout the administration, the CIA-orchestrated coup was—immediately and enduringly—considered a major success in the Cold War.[8]

Regardless of where one comes out on the long-term efficacy and righteousness of using these covert actions during the Cold War, CIA covert action programs blocked significant Sino-Soviet expansion, with two notable setbacks—Cuba and Vietnam. Although other ideological foes did emerge in places like Cambodia, Chile, Nicaragua, and a host of African countries, they did not become effective proxies of Soviet power. The strength of U.S. containment brought about an extraordinary time of relative peace, security, and prosperity in the world. We would be living in a different world if this effort had failed.

These successes helped define the agency. They drew a line in the sand for Soviet expansion and created theaters of competition between Russia and the West that endure to this day, including Iran, Syria, and even Latin America. These actions to counter Soviet influence operations also had the foundational effect of giving covert action an elevated standing in the enduring CIA culture. It is in the spirit of these strategic successes that the Iranian and Guatemalan covert action operations are evoked today. They were critically important for the Eisenhower administration and the agency in part because they provided concrete evidence of how an intelligence capability can provide a strategic advantage to American foreign policy priorities. We should be

161

alert for theaters where we might accomplish that again today, including Iran.

The covert action pursued in Iran was fundamentally driven by President Eisenhower's fear that allowing the Shah to fall would be the first step to ceding Iran to the Soviets—and with it a strategic footing in the oil-rich Middle East and a pathway to the Indian Ocean for the Soviet Union. We can see parallels with Russia's positioning today as an intermediary for the Iranians in their management of its enriched uranium for the Iran antinuclear deal, its alliance with Iraq, and its aggressive and empowering actions in Syria. The Russians have been making major progress in increasing their influence in Iran and Syria. Their actions, which have largely been met with limited resistance from the United States, are all consistent with the century-old Russian pursuit of a strategic footing in the region and access to the key waters of the Mediterranean and the Indian Ocean.

A tense conflagration between the United States and Iran in early 2020, which ended with Iran opting for a limited attack on a U.S. base in response to a U.S. drone strike that killed Iranian general Qassem Soleimani, may present an opening for the United States to reopen talks over Iran's nuclear program. The United States in this case employed an effective show of force, and Iran's response was calculated to de-escalate the situation. If the United States and Iran do not use this opportunity to return to the negotiating table, Russia will continue to press its advantage there to our detriment. Should talks with Iran fail, as they have in the past despite our best efforts, the United States should look to establish a robust and realistic covert action program to lay the groundwork for possible regime change should circumstances on the ground provide an opportunity for action.

The story of Guatemala in 1954 is not so different from what we see today in Nicaragua, Bolivia, Cuba, and most especially Venezuela. During the Cold War the Soviet intent to defeat the West in an ideological struggle, pitting communism against capitalism, resulted in strong bipartisan support in Congress for using our military and intelligence capabilities to block the spread of communism worldwide. Almost three-quarters of a century has passed, but the concern about leftist, socialist regimes under Russian influence in Latin America continues. In this regard the Cold War did not end. We still fear the shift of that region from the U.S. orbit and to that of our adversaries.

One of the most pressing strategic questions will be whether Russia will continue to prop up Nicolás Maduro's regime in Venezuela, acting as its de facto benefactor, just like it was for Fidel Castro's Cuba in the 1960s. Since 1999, when Venezuelan leader Hugo Chávez partnered with Cuba, Moscow-trained Cuban intelligence officers have been working in Venezuela. In October 2017 and again in December 2018 Maduro met with President Vladimir Putin in Moscow in a very public show of influence and partnership. To help Venezuela avert default on a series of loans, the Russian government sent the country a huge infusion of cash. Throughout 2018 the Russians and the Chinese continued to block any type of UN Security Council action sanctioning Venezuela and condemning Maduro's rule.

Most tellingly, Putin took explicit steps to express his support for Maduro in January 2019, hinting at Russia's willingness to provide military aid to Venezuela to reinforce the status quo and cement Venezuela's alignment with Russia after several nations, including the United States, recognized Juan Guaidó, head of the opposition-controlled National Assembly, as Venezuela's legitimate leader. Russia refused to recognize Guaidó, criticized the United States for imposing sanctions on the Venezuelan state-owned oil company PDVSA and freezing Venezuelan assets, and reportedly sent military contractors to Venezuela to support Maduro. These provocative steps to prop up an autocrat like Maduro mirror Putin's support for Syrian leader Bashar al-Assad.

Venezuela is shaping up as another potential source of U.S.-Russia confrontation. In supporting the Venezuelan opposition in the spring of 2019, indicating that all options were on the table, the United States sent a bold message to Putin not to interfere in the Western Hemisphere. Russia's support for Maduro and its counter "don't invade Venezuela" stance directly threaten the United States and seek to interfere in Western Hemisphere affairs. On this point Putin follows Russian dictators Khrushchev and Brezhnev, who saw it in their interest to try to weaken the United States at every turn. There is no doubt Putin is looking for another bastion in the hemisphere where he can plant Russia's flag, and he is betting that he will succeed in Venezuela.

How the United States decides to deal with Venezuela in the coming years will also be an indication of how we view Russia and Russian influence in the Western Hemisphere—a concern that is growing in some corridors within Washington. Thus far, the use of targeted sanctions appears to be somewhat effective in weakening Russia's level of support to Maduro. In February 2020 the United States imposed sanctions on two subsidiaries of the Russian national oil giant Rosneft for selling Venezuelan oil to Chinese refineries, thus hampering the company's ability to operate internationally. Rosneft, which had been one of Russia's primary channels of financial support to Maduro by being a purchaser and refiner of Venezuelan crude, announced in March 2020 that it was ending all operations and selling all assets in the country, citing sanctions as a driving factor behind the decision. Although the sale was made to a 100 percent Russian government–owned entity, oil market experts noted at the time that the purchasing entity has nowhere near the market reach, expertise, or financial heft of Rosneft and is unlikely to be able to provide the same level of support to Venezuela.[9] But it is not a complete victory, and to successfully counter Russia in Venezuela, as well as other countries in our backyard, policy makers will need to pursue additional means of ensuring that the realities on the ground support and promote regime change.

Never Underestimate Your Opponent's Resolve

I almost changed the title of my first book, *Good Hunting*, to *All It Takes Is a Spark*—alluding to the gross underestimation by many American and foreign officials of the work required to execute an effective covert action. Over the years I witnessed how many of these officials believed that a revolution or coup could be spawned by a single spark that miraculously works out to everyone's benefit. Nothing could be further from the truth.

Most of the early CIA deputy directors of operations, as well as its area division chiefs and chiefs of station, came from fairly wealthy backgrounds and had had excellent schooling and the self-confidence that often comes with financial privilege. This "gung-ho" confidence, however, sometimes leads to unrealistic optimism that underestimates the hard work needed to lay in the operational plumbing for covert action success. Some overconfident CIA officials learned hard lessons in Hungary, Indonesia, and then Castro's Cuba, the CIA's highest-profile covert action failure.

After Stalin's death in March 1953 and Khrushchev's rise to power, there was false hope within the Eisenhower administration and other Western governments for a "thaw" in the Cold War. Khrushchev's "secret speech" before the Communist Party Central Committee in February 1956 about Stalin and the cult of personality he engendered seemed to signal an easing in the Stalin-style iron-handed policy toward dissent. The highly restricted secret speech was obtained by Israeli intelligence, who dutifully passed it on to James Angleton, counterintelligence chief at the CIA. Angleton made sure that it received ample coverage in the *New York Times* and elsewhere, adding to the misperception that Soviet control over Eastern Europe could be reversed.

Secretary of State John Foster Dulles actively sought opportunities to abandon the "status quo" containment policy of U.S. diplomat George Kennan. It had been only about a decade since the end of World War II, and Dulles and his supporters perhaps naïvely hadn't recognized how entrenched the Soviets were in Eastern Europe and how much the Soviets were prepared to risk to hold on to the strategic gains made at Yalta. In many quarters this persistent underappreciation for Russia's attachment to its sphere of influence continues to this day. It has been very difficult to allay Russian concerns about NATO and European Union expansion, and it is through this optic that we should examine Putin's current actions in the Baltics, Ukraine, and Belarus.

In 1956 Secretary of State Dulles, along with his brother, CIA director Allen Dulles, made sure that Radio Free Europe (RFE) would push strong messages urging the people of Eastern Europe to cast off their communist occupiers, assuring them (mistakenly) that the United States and Western Europe would support them. While the CIA ran many propaganda operations into Hungary and had access to dissident groups, it lacked a well-developed infrastructure and internal capability to support an uprising. Moreover, quality intelligence sources who could provide insights on what was happening on the ground and help direct spontaneous unrest were few and far between. Both the CIA and the Kremlin were caught by surprise when a student demonstration in October 1956 erupted into a nationwide protest against the Soviets, resulting in dramatic armed confrontations between government forces and Hungarian citizens.

The Soviets hesitated briefly in responding but in the end acted with full force because they realized that a Hungarian revolution would likely spread to neighboring Soviet satellite countries. They believed that failure to suppress it would be seen in the West as weakness, which would promote uprisings elsewhere in Eastern Europe. After Egypt nationalized the Suez Canal, prompting Israeli forces, with British and French backing, to seize the canal on October 29, 1956, Moscow feared that a larger action against Soviet interests could be afoot. Six days later, on November 4, the Soviets invaded Hungary in a bloody suppression that killed more than twenty-five hundred Hungarians and caused two hundred thousand more to flee to the West. This put an end not only to the revolution but also to the dreams of those who thought Soviet power in Eastern Europe could be rolled back in the near future. Future KGB head Yuri Andropov, who was the Soviet ambassador in Budapest at the time, took note for future reference of how effective resolve was in squelching an attempted revolution.[10]

Be Mindful of Your Hubris

Those who might wish to dabble in intelligence activities and covert action to stem Russian influence by promoting regime change in Iran or elsewhere need to bone up on what can happen if the covert action is misaligned. The Bay of Pigs operation is a good place to start. Not long after taking office, President Kennedy approved what would become the CIA's worst covert action failure. Codenamed Operation JMATE, the Bay of Pigs was the botched effort to overthrow the communist government of Fidel Castro, who had come to power in a revolution that ousted corrupt dictator Fulgencio Batista on New Year's Day in 1959. Relations between the United States and Cuba deteriorated rapidly and worsened still when Castro proclaimed himself a communist in December 1961 and began to institute a communist-based economic system. He nationalized and collectivized the island's economy, confiscating and appropriating assets of Cuban citizens and American companies and prompting a huge exodus of Cubans. Castro and his communist government represented a new and dangerous force throughout Latin America, and as a consequence Cuba became the international center of attention for the White House and the CIA.

In 1959 Eisenhower authorized the CIA to draw up plans to oust Castro from power with force, but the plan's execution was handed off to the Kennedy administration. CIA director Allen Dulles and Richard Bissell, his deputy director of plans (the Plans directorate later became Operations), "father of the U-2," and my predecessor, enthusiastically began to organize, train, and arm a Cuban exile invasion force. President Kennedy received a briefing on the plan, which he approved shortly after he entered the White House. Kennedy agreed that the CIA should orchestrate an insurgent invasion force to overthrow Castro, but he substantially modified the scope of the Eisenhower plan by scrapping the use of any American air power. Kennedy was a fan and friend of Ian Fleming, the author of the James Bond spy novels, and had a wrong and naïve view about the supersized abilities of the CIA and covert action. He did not understand its limitations and grossly underestimated the potential downside of a failed operation.

Each time Dulles and Bissell briefed Kennedy in detail about the plan, new limitations were placed on the strategy. Kennedy eventually gave the go-ahead to implement a gutted plan, and it was Bissell's job to execute the operation. Bissell had an engineer's approach to operations, which he combined with high energy and intense focus, but he had no direct experience in covert action and agent activities. It didn't help that he was backed up by his deputy Tracy Barnes, whose perennial optimism about covert action capabilities had helped propel the planning forward.

Bissell and Barnes staffed the project with some of the key CIA players from the Guatemala operation, including Gerry Droller, Jake Esterline, Howard Hunt, and Dave Phillips.[11] I worked with all of them except Hunt. Not surprisingly, these experienced officers fell back on the Guatemala covert action blueprints and tried to apply them to the Cuba project—basically drawing on the concept of creating a small, essentially phantom insurgent force and using propaganda to scare Castro into packing his bags. In the wildly different political and military environment in Cuba, this scheme was unrealistic and a guaranteed failure. Esterline was appointed key line officer at headquarters and thus responsible for overseeing the Cuban operation. He shared this responsibility with Marine colonel Jack Hawkins. As the weeks went by, the watered-down action plan deteriorated further. Finally, Esterline and Hawkins confronted Bissell, stating that they believed the project was doomed to fail. Bissell heard them out but made it clear that the die was cast and there would be no retreat from the mission.

It seems clear now that the CIA leadership believed the operation would likely fail without U.S. air support. CIA planners should have walked away from the proposal, but Dulles and Bissell miscalculated Kennedy's resolve on U.S. air support and went ahead on the assumption that he would rescind the decision once combat began. It was a tragic miscalculation. The lesson for covert action operators and policy makers alike is never to go forward with any covert action plan on the hope that "higher authority" will change the policy in the future. It doesn't happen. The ill-fated invasion that began on April 17, 1961, collapsed quickly and proved to be a long-lasting embarrassment to the CIA and the Kennedy administration.

Richard Helms, who at the time was chief of operations (COPS), stayed on the sidelines and remained taciturn throughout the operational planning and execution. Helms, an experienced and respected operator from the OSS, was pessimistic about the project's likelihood of success from the outset and steered some of his closest allies, such as Desmond Fitzgerald, James Angleton, and Thomas Polgar, away from it. On the personal side, Helms was unhappy about being passed over when Dulles selected Bissell to be deputy director of plans (DDP, or what was then the Clandestine Service) and backed him up with Barnes for the Cuba dossier. Helms thought both of them were dilettantes in the espionage business and should not have been running the operational directorate. Below the surface, this friction had deeper roots in the continuing tug and pull between the espionage and covert action officers.[12]

In 1996 Helms invited me to lunch, and we discussed the state of world affairs and reminisced about his CIA experiences, including in Chile and Cuba. At the time it wasn't clear to me what was behind his invitation. I thought I detected a touch of empathy for my situation. The newly installed director, John Deutch, had just advised me that he was bringing in a non-Operations officer to replace me in my post as acting DDO and suggested I might want to go to a city in Europe as chief of station (COS). Helms talked about the Bay of Pigs fiasco and noted that something similar had happened to him back then, when Dulles brought in Richard Bissell instead of him. Dulles had asked him to "soldier on." Helms said he thought about resigning but decided against it. Instead, he "toughed it out," and he stayed to pick up the pieces after the Cuba failure and the subsequent firing of Dulles and Bissell. In addition to sharing his personal perspective from the top, Helms was, I suspect, looking for an in-close read from me on Deutch and his team. However, I wasn't prepared to kibitz about this, since I had developed a strong inside/outside mentality and felt it inappropriate to discuss confidential information about Deutch's plans. In the end Helms was right about Cuba, and in the aftermath of the fiasco he was finally appointed head of worldwide operations.

For those directly involved in the Bay of Pigs, there was a deep depression over the loss of life and the failure to complete the mission. I suspect that in its aftermath the senior officers in the Latin America Division felt less positive about Kennedy than they had at the outset of his administration. For those not involved, there was tremendous criticism about the poorly conceived and executed operation, and it remains the preeminent stain on the agency's history, cited still by critics wishing to take issue with the covert action mandate of the CIA.

The legacy of the Bay of Pigs serves as a cautionary tale, underscoring that more time and careful attention must be devoted to coordination, planning, and tradecraft. Its failure forced a more realistic assessment of the feasibility and possible success of covert action.

Speak Truth to Power

The Kennedy and Johnson administrations were fervent about halting the spread of communism and did not want to be held responsible for the "loss" of any country to communism and the Soviet sphere of influence. The domino theory—that if one country fell to communism, surrounding countries likely would as well—moved Kennedy and then Johnson to increase foreign aid to Latin America, Africa, and Southeast Asia, particularly Vietnam, to ramp up intelligence collection efforts, and to launch covert operations in an effort to roll back or contain the threat.

Every covert operation and U.S. intervention undertaken during the Cold War has to be seen through the lens of pushing back communism. Laos, Cambodia, and Vietnam are no exception. In Laos, a major covert effort was launched to train and arm the Hmong to counter communist forces in the region. In Cambodia, a bombing campaign was conducted against North Vietnamese forces. In Vietnam, Kennedy sought to help the South Vietnamese push back the encroaching communists of North Vietnam. The conflict in Vietnam started modestly during Kennedy's time in office, but by the time the Lyndon B. Johnson administration had taken the reins of power, Vietnam had turned into a full-scale U.S. military intervention.

For the CIA, obtaining good intelligence and sound analysis in Vietnam was difficult, and assessments were controversial. From the outset CIA analysts had a more pessimistic view of the situation in Vietnam than their military counterparts did. Early on DCI Allen Dulles recognized the strong support the Vietnamese rebels had in country, and several top field officers and analysts within the agency also believed that the North Vietnamese were drawing on a swell of nationalism that overwhelmed the support for the South Vietnamese. CIA officers had been working in former Indochina for a long time with a large network of on-the-ground sources, and they understood the strength of Ho Chi Minh's movement and the appeal of the Vietnamese communists in the north. By and large the CIA came to be known for having serious doubts about the possibilities for success in Vietnam, even as the agency was mandated to carry out covert operations and tactical intelligence collection efforts for the U.S. military.

The North Vietnamese had help from the KGB. The chief of station in Laos and then Vietnam during the Vietnam War, Ted "The Blond Ghost" Shackley, always believed that the North Vietnamese had advance warning of U.S. airstrikes and naval actions, and now we know he was right. The KGB had access to most American battle plans, war games, and strategic naval actions thanks to John Anthony Walker Jr., the chief warrant officer for the U.S. Atlantic Fleet HQ submarine base in Norfolk, Virginia. Walker provided the KGB, for which he would work for more than eighteen years, with ciphers, codes, and decrypted messages containing information at first just from the U.S. Atlantic Fleet but eventually from the U.S. Armed Forces, the CIA, the State Department, and the FBI. The information he provided allowed the KGB to break many U.S. military codes and essentially gave them the capacity to read U.S. military messages. The Soviets passed this information on to the North Vietnamese.[13]

The legendary spymaster Tom Polgar, who had wisely stepped away from the failed Bay of Pigs operation, later served as the CIA's last station chief in Saigon. His assessments of the prospect of success in country were controversial at the time. However, as he told me later when I worked with him during the 1970s, Vietnam heightened his long-standing drive to speak up on matters of principle. Imprinted in our collective memory is the last U.S. helicopter lifting off, carrying CIA station chief Polgar and other embassy staff. Polgar had just sent his historic cable back to Washington:

> This will be final message from Saigon station. It has been a long and hard fight and we have lost. This experience, unique in the history of the United States, does not signal necessarily the demise of the United States as a world power. The severity of the defeat and the circumstances of it, however, would seem to call for a reassessment of the policies of niggardly half-measures which have characterized much of our participation here despite the commitment of manpower and resources, which were certainly generous. Those

who fail to learn from history are forced to repeat it. Let us hope that we will not have another Vietnam experience and that we have learned our lesson.[14]

Polgar was a Hungarian immigrant who in the aftermath of World War II was heavily involved in debriefing Nazi military officers. He was easily and unwisely underestimated. He was short and somewhat pudgy, with a heavy accent. But he was smart, worldly, and wrote beautifully in English, German, and Hungarian. He had a hard-nosed way of looking at the world. In many ways he was Kissingeresque, and he had a long-standing friendship with Henry Kissinger. His clear assessments in country were controversial at the time. In a conversation with me at CIA headquarters in 1978, Polgar commented with conviction, "There comes a time when a senior official not only has a responsibility but an obligation to stand up and be counted." How right he was, especially as we look at just how bogged down the United States has become in recent years trying to force-feed costly nation-building in Afghanistan and Iraq. This sentiment should be etched in all senior intelligence executives' minds. While we likely will not have to leave these countries as Polgar left Vietnam, it is hard to envision a lasting peace in either place.

Case Study: An Important Domino in Chile

From the U.S. perspective at the time, and certainly within the CIA, driving out the threat of Soviet and Cuban influence in "our own backyard" was the overarching and critical objective in Latin America. The Johnson administration sent U.S. Marines into the Dominican Republic when civil war broke out following the ouster of leftist president Juan Bosch in 1965. While the U.S. intervention stabilized the country, its hard-charging tactics left a scar on the Latin American psyche and created much skepticism and even fear of U.S. intentions in the region.

Richard Nixon wanted to elevate concerns about the spread of Soviet communism in Latin America and the prospect of another Cuba in the Western Hemisphere. In the 1970s communist insurgencies like the FARC in Colombia and the Sandinistas in Nicaragua were flourishing. These insurgencies had their roots in the guerrilla warfare that took place in Cuba. Then the Marxist revolutionary Che Guevara, who sought to export the ideals and tactics of the 1959 Cuban Revolution across Latin America and Africa, began to champion communist rebels. As part of the Cold War competition, these insurgent activities were supported by Castro's Cuba and indirectly but very significantly by the Soviet Union.

Nixon, Kissinger, and many others in Washington looked with great trepidation at the prospect of the Chilean socialist Salvador Allende coming to power. Chile was home to the second-largest Communist Party in the West, and it was fertile ground for another Castro-like regime. There was great concern about Allende's ties to Cuba and his alliance with the Chilean Communist Party, which was a key part of his campaign coalition. The KGB and especially its surrogate, the Cuban intelligence agency (DGI), were openly and actively supporting Allende, who stood to provide them with a singular opportunity to establish a communist revolution in the West by the ballot box.

The Russians kept a close eye on the Chilean experiment, as the rise of the socialist model without direct Soviet intervention was seen as a victory by the Russians. The Soviet Union did not have the time to become as economically involved in Chile as it had with Cuba. But using Cuba as a model and the Cuban intelligence and military as surrogates, the Soviet Union engaged and encouraged the rise of Allende and South American socialism, eventually providing direct economic assistance to the Chilean government.

In a state visit to Moscow in December 1972, Allende negotiated with Leonid Brezhnev to secure additional economic assistance to Chile, and he received direct aid for food, as well as short-term credit.[15] Meanwhile, it was known that Moscow had been providing funding for the Chilean Communist Party for a very long time. Almost immediately after Allende's election victory, Fidel Castro had taken a twenty-five-day tour of Chile in 1971, and during this visit he gave multiple speeches and met with labor unions and stopped off at recently nationalized copper mines. The Soviet-trained Cuban intelligence service penetrated Chile in a meaningful way, and in the words of former KGB general Nikolai Leonov, Russian KGB officers were using Chile and all of Latin America primarily as a "hunting ground" for opportunities to work against the United States. The U.S. fear of the Soviet Union having another satellite in Latin America was real.[16]

In 1970 I was assigned to the Chile Task Force, a highly compartmented office inside of the Latin America Division, and it included Dave Phillips of PBFortune/Guatemala fame. Under Nixon's directive, the task force was responsible for trying to block Allende from assuming the presidency. At the time the CIA was pursuing two tracks. Track I consisted of a political and propaganda action against Allende. For Track II the Nixon White House had directed the CIA to organize a coup to block Allende from taking office, despite the local CIA chief's admonition that the conditions on the ground were not propitious.

With no real field operational experience up until then, it was like I had parachuted into unknown territory amid a firefight. It was my job in support of the task force chief to work the night shift and draft bullet points from reading the overnight cable traffic from around the world relating to this project. These bullet points detailed, among other things, how the Track II covert action effort turned out to be a fiasco.

In 1970 Allende was elected and took office, contrary to the White House's desire and the Track II effort. As the local CIA chief had forecast months earlier, the coup attempt fell apart when a rogue group of retired soldiers (with no connections to the CIA) led by a retired general, Roberto Viaux, foolishly attempted to kidnap General René Schneider, commander in chief of the Chilean army. In the heat of the attack the plotters shot and killed Schneider, which produced widespread outrage throughout the country, and virtually all the opposition to Allende collapsed, especially within military circles. This event was included in my daily bullet points. Shortly thereafter, Henry Kissinger, who was national security advisor at that time, sent a directive to the CIA instructing it to cease coup plotting altogether. Despite public perception to the contrary, the CIA immediately stopped the effort to overthrow Allende by force. The Chile Task Force was disbanded. Instead, the CIA concentrated its efforts strictly on the political action efforts of Track I. It was in this post–failed coup environment that my wife and I arrived in Santiago for my new position.

Not long after Pat and I settled into the new house, we learned that Cuban officials were renting the house adjacent to ours. Needless to say, we had to remain alert for any surreptitious attempts to enter our property and install listening devices. Even though we never had clandestine meetings in the house, through the ensuing years we had a constant stream of guests and social contacts who would have provided interesting content for any technical bug. A most dramatic incident occurred in 1973, when a right-wing paramilitary group tried to toss a bomb into the Cubans' garden but missed their target and hit our backyard, blowing plaster and siding off the wall that faced our patio. We didn't really register the precariousness of our situation; one feature of youth is to underrate physical risks.

The environment remained quite unstable. There were regular marches, mass demonstrations, violent clashes, mini coups, expropriation of property, and intimidation from all factions. Still, throughout 1973 it looked like Allende would limp through his term, and his party would be ousted in the next national election. Contrary to public understanding, the CIA had little early reporting indicating that the military would take action against Allende. A couple of days before the coup, a source of mine who was a prominent businessman and former military officer tried unsuccessfully to reach me. And so, in exasperation, he contacted Pat and advised her that the military would start the coup on the morning of September 11, and the navy would kick it off. He added that he was leaving the country that day because of his own precarious position. Pat ran me down and relayed the agent's information. The station immediately sent a CRITIC message—an extremely urgent message that supersedes all other cable traffic and goes straight to the White House and top policy makers—warning of the coming coup:

A COUP ATTEMPT WILL BE INITIATED ON 11 SEPTEMBER. ALL THREE BRANCHES OF THE ARMED FORCES AND THE CARA-BINEROS ARE INVOLVED IN THIS ACTION. A DECLARATION

WILL BE READ ON RADIO AGRICULTURA AT 7 A.M. ON SEPT.
II ... THE CARABINEROS HAVE THE RESPONSIBILITY FOR
SEIZING PRESIDENT SALVADOR ALLENDE.[17]

Later that night I received confirmation of the report, and in the following forty-eight hours the station received even more detailed reporting on what was about to happen.

Short of Track I efforts, the Chilean military received no support from the CIA for the coup. To our surprise, the coup ushered in the far-right military dictatorship of army general Augusto Pinochet, which stabilized the economy but used an unanticipated, violent, and heavy hand in suppressing civil liberties and consolidating power.

At first the U.S. government and the CIA welcomed the coup. American foreign policy interests had been realized, and Russian archival documents suggest that Chile was a significant milestone in arresting Soviet ambitions in Latin America at that time. Unfortunately, it also left lasting recrimination about the U.S. interference in Chile and the CIA's role in it.

Russian investment and influence in Venezuela and Cuba today are reminiscent of Soviet efforts in the early 1970s in Chile. While the communist-rooted Cold War is over, Venezuela under President Maduro can be compared to Chile under Allende, and the exertion of Russian influence via economic aid, military assistance, and political and ideological alignment continues. The same General Nikolai Leonov who worked Latin America for the KGB during the Cold War has since acknowledged Russian ambitions in the region at that time. He also served as a superior to the young Vladimir Putin and allegedly continues to serve in an advisory capacity to the Kremlin.

LESSON ELEVEN

The principles of a just war always apply.

Bellicose action can only be performed with wisdom
and ability, when done with prudence, which directs
man's action in life with rectitude.

—SAINT THOMAS AQUINAS

11

Best Practice

A Defining Moment in American Covert Action

The Chilean dust-up with the Russians and communists has stayed with me through my career, even as I look at Russia's moves against us today. That said, in the middle of my tenure I had the opportunity to observe the Russians at their worst—conducting a military invasion. This gave me a firsthand look at how best to push back, which is relevant today.

More than a decade after Chile, I undertook my assignment as head of the Afghan Task Force at headquarters in 1986. Overlooking the tragic mistakes of history—notably the failed British occupation in the three Anglo-Afghanistan Wars (1838, 1878, and 1917)—the Russians put their troops on the ground in Afghanistan in December 1979. This was a disastrous misjudgment. Controlling Afghanistan was a long-standing strategic goal of Soviet policy going back all the way to the Russian Revolution of 1917. Toward that end, the Russians tried to exert influence in Afghanistan by providing military and economic assistance to a series of Afghan governments and their armed forces, including during World War II.

Finally, in 1978 they orchestrated a coup, which installed as president Nur Mohammed Taraki, a pro-Soviet puppet who proceeded to crack down on Muslim traditionalists, imprisoning and killing thousands. This crackdown was hugely unpopular and led to outbreaks of violence throughout the country. By the spring of 1979 the Afghan government had lost control of the countryside and a civil war ensued. Brezhnev covertly sent in undercover KGB operatives and special forces to bolster the government, but it was too little, too late. Taraki was too weak to prop up, and his former deputy, Hafizullah Amin, carried out a countercoup. The revolt continued unabated, and on December 27, 1979, the Russian Fortieth Army invaded Afghanistan with more than sixty thousand troops. Amin was killed by a KGB Spetsnaz force, and Babrak Karmal was installed as the new president.

At the beginning of the Soviet invasion of Afghanistan the Soviets thought they could limit their engagement to just communication and transport support for the army of the Afghan Marxist regime. It quickly became clear to the Soviets that they would have to take to the battlefield themselves and engage the mujahideen directly in firefights. However, the Soviets' growing footprint only angered the Afghans, whose resistance began to grow in proportion to the Soviet troops on the ground. By 1985 the Soviet forces had increased to about 110,000 troops, including the elite Spetsnaz forces flying the lethal Hind MI-24 helicopters, which are similar to Blackhawks. On the other side of the battlefield the mujahideen fighters were estimated to be about 125,000 strong.

The Soviets' biggest miscalculation, however, was their belief that they could build a communist nation in their image. Nation-building is a policy mistake, one with which the U.S. has struggled since 9/11. As stated earlier, after many years of working abroad I came to the unwavering conclusion that, best intentions aside, you cannot force-feed how a foreign country should be run. This axiom became reality for the Soviets early on. The Marxist Afghan Army faced a high desertion rate, and its soldiers were generally reluctant to engage the mujahideen in combat. As the United States learned in Vietnam, Afghanistan, and Iraq, the success rate for building a fighting opposition force is dismal when the troops don't really have their hearts in the objective. The Afghan troops simply did not identify with the creation of a communist government, and they only signed up on a temporary basis for a paycheck, which meant they would duck when the firing started. As the war developed, a pattern unfolded in which the Soviets occupied the cities and communication centers, while the mujahideen formed bands to conduct an insurgency throughout the countryside. By the end of the war, most of the countryside was no longer under Kabul's communist control.

The international reaction to the Soviet invasion was swift and highly negative. In the United States, Zbigniew Brzezinski, who was national security advisor, almost immediately traveled to Pakistan to coordinate an overt and covert joint response. The British, Saudis, Egyptians, and Chinese joined us. First, severe sanctions were imposed on the Soviet Union. Second, the United States started providing a limited number of basic-level weapons to the mujahideen, from various sources, but especially from the Egyptians and the Chinese. We even managed covert procurement of Soviet arms from the Czechoslovak communist government, since it was susceptible to material incentives. Ultimately, our effort to arm militants through the Pakistani secret services, known as ISI, to fight off the Russians became the agency's longest and most successful covert operation to date.

At CIA headquarters the offices were located in a low-profile, sealed-off working area outside of public view. There was virtually no hall discussion about this major covert action operation. There had been a few public blips on the screen about it, but it didn't hold the headlines like the activities in Central America. So I was taken by surprise by its size and scope when Tom Twetten, the division chief and accomplished spymaster, asked if I would be interested in taking over from Gust Avrakotos, who was being replaced as chief of the Afghan program and moved to Africa Division. Twetten didn't go into the backstory about Avrakotos's clashes with DDO Clair George, several high-profile staff members in Congress, and the National Security Council staff, but he made clear that a change had to be made at headquarters and in Islamabad, especially in view of the huge buildup anticipated in the coming year. I knew Gust well and didn't have a hard time believing there were issues in the program. His interpersonal interactions could be quite confrontational at times. Avrakotos once told me that he got so annoyed while debating with a fellow officer that he took a pair of scissors from the desk, cut the officer's tie in half and walked out. I could believe it.

Avrakotos, a proud son of Greek immigrants, fashioned himself a blue-collar Pittsburgh guy, having worked for a while in a local steel mill. But once you got beyond his rather gruff manner, it was possible to appreciate his knowledge of the classics and general intellectual rigor, proven by having graduated from the University of Pittsburgh with honors. His personality had worked wonders with Charlie Wilson, a member of Congress from Texas and staunch supporter of the agency. The Texan was an effective congressional advocate for our successful Afghan operation, and his critically important effort steered funds to the CIA to carry it out. Wilson disdained what he often referred to as the "effete Ivy league" crowd at Langley and had a rocky relationship with the Near East Division for the first few years, until Avrakotos arrived on the scene.

The Afghan program strategy was straightforward: it armed the mujahideen with weaponry to wage an effective asymmetrical war against the formidable Soviet military. It was vastly complex to execute, however, given the terrain, multitude of parties involved, covert nature of the operation, and high stakes. As a reminder of this struggle and my involvement in it, I have on the wall in my office in New York City two plaques given to me by Representative Wilson. One is a quote from the last stanza of Kipling's "The Young British Soldier": "When you are wounded and left on the Afghanistan plains / And the women come out to cut up what remains, / Jest roll to your rifle and blow out your brains / An' go to your Gawd like a soldier."[1] This poem graphically captures the outcome that invading forces have faced for centuries when they have tried to conquer Afghanistan. The other plaque has a quote from Abdur Rahman Khan (ca. 1830–1901), the founder of modern Afghanistan: "My last words to you my son and successor. Never trust the Russians."[2] That is sage advice then as now and the epigraph for this book.

When I took over the task force, Twetten underscored that there were plans afoot to substantially ramp up the program. In fact, the budget almost tripled that year and the relatively small Afghan office was turned into a large task force. In a matter of weeks I was negotiating staff increases, traveling to Egypt, Pakistan, and China—and dealing with Charlie Wilson. In Islamabad we engaged in intense meetings with the ISI and mujahideen commanders. Concurrent with my appointment, a new senior CIA official, Milton Bearden, was sent out to Islamabad to take command of the field station. He was a strong and decisive leader who had a well-deserved reputation for working effectively with liaison partners. He was the right person for this key field operation. Bearden's innate swagger helped build a bond with fellow Texan Wilson, with whom he shared a zeal and optimism for prevailing over the Soviets. For his part, Bearden came quickly to realize that Wilson was far more knowledgeable on Afghanistan than had been portrayed in the press. He was also pleased to learn that contrary to the public perception of Wilson's role in the covert action activities, Wilson refrained from trying to direct its activities and wisely left it up to the CIA.

Nonetheless, in late 1985 the conventional wisdom in Washington was that the Soviets couldn't be beaten and that the momentum of the war was with them. Even the agency's top Soviet analysts shared this view. They were all wrong. The experts and policy makers consistently underestimated the determination of the mujahideen as well as the impact of the CIA's massive military weapons buildup, especially the Stinger missile. The introduction of the Stinger forced the Russians to curtail their air battle, leaving the playing field open to the mujahideen. It was a game changer.[3]

The buildup was a full-court press. With a budget going roughly from nearly $300 million up to $1 billion, the Afghan Task Force was able to undertake a sizable increase in its arms purchases from the Chinese and maintain our purchase level with the Egyptians. Early on in the program it was decided that the CIA would use only Soviet-type weapons, so as to reduce the U.S. footprint on the battlefield and provide the mujahideen with weapons that were interchangeable with those seized from Soviet and Afghan stores. This is a common practice in supporting insurgencies. The reversal of the 40–60 percent switch in weapons purchases between the Chinese and the Egyptians resulted in my receiving the only direct call of complaint from Charlie Wilson. Up until then, most of our interaction took place in his office or when we traveled abroad together.

Because he was such good friends with Egyptian president Hosni Mubarak, Wilson initially was annoyed with the switch, but he backed off once I explained that the Chinese produced a higher-quality product at a lower price and were more reliable in their packaging and delivery. We continued to make substantial purchases (40 percent) from the Egyptians because we could not afford to have only one major provider. We didn't want to be overly dependent on one country and run the risk of being shut down if the local political situation changed suddenly and restricted our procurements.

At the same time, we upped the purchase of four-wheel Toyota trucks that were needed for the rough terrain in Afghanistan. But even these trucks couldn't finish the last leg of the haul over the mountains. Consequently, we had to negotiate with the Chinese for the purchase of thousands of mules that had to be herded across China and delivered to camps in Pakistan. As the momentum for the mujahideen built up on the battlefield in 1986, it became clear that the Soviets would have to pull up stakes if we could keep the pressure on. Recently declassified Russian documents support this analysis.[4]

During the Afghan war, unbeknown to the CIA, a group of mujahideen drove a truckload of Qur'ans over the Soviet border and disseminated them throughout the region. I learned about this from initial Soviet grumbling but was unprepared for the furor it would create. It caused more immediate protestations and diplomatic headaches than even the introduction of the Stinger missile, which had changed the course of the war. In retrospect, this small action, which I had underweighted at the time, caused so much turmoil because it went to the heart of internal stability and legitimacy in the Soviet Union itself. Their deep sensitivity about introducing Qur'ans into the border states was rooted in the legitimate concern that the insurgency could spread to the largely Muslim repressed minority in those Soviet states. This gap in adequately understanding each other's sensitivities continues to this day.

The Soviet Union itself was undergoing a historic transformation. The Kremlin leadership was like a revolving door, with Leonid Brezhnev being followed quickly by two seriously ill leaders—Yuri Andropov and Konstantin Chernenko—both of whom died after each had served just a year in the top job. The timing of our buildup in Afghanistan roughly coincided with the selection of Mikhail Gorbachev as the new First Secretary of the Communist Party of the Soviet Union (CPSU). Gorbachev assumed power in 1985 with a reform mind-set. He set out to reform the Soviet system through his *glasnost* initiative to provide openness in public discourse, transparency in government activities, and a relaxation of censorship. Likewise, with *perestroika*, he sought to instigate political reform in the Communist Party and to open up the sluggish economy by easing central planning rules.

The desire to break the long-lasting fiscal stagnation and rebuild the Soviet Union's economy softened the Soviet resolve to prevail in Afghanistan, as the war came with a significant price tag. Major set-backs Soviet troops suffered in 1986 only intensified Gorbachev's desire to pull out. On July 20, 1987, the departure of Soviet troops was formally announced, and the process proceeded in a fairly orderly fashion. Negotiations were concluded in the 1988 Geneva Accords and the establishment of a UN program to monitor the withdrawal. The last Soviet troops left Afghanistan on February 15, 1989.

By this time I had moved on to Rome. Just as the final Soviet troops crossed the Friendship Bridge on their way out of Afghanistan, I received—along with the many others who had worked the Afghanistan War—a message from Islamabad station chief Milt Bearden: "We won." As I have repeated often, "we" meant a very large number of unsung heroes in the United States and abroad who were engaged for nearly a decade in executing the CIA covert action war. No one person alone or small group of people can take credit for the outcome.

There were several conditions on the ground that make this a model case for good covert action. First, there was a genuine national security imperative. The Soviets were vulnerable in Afghanistan, and it was important to take the opportunity to strike them in an area where we could really make an impact and still avoid direct confrontation. Second, we facilitated something that the population on the ground fundamentally desired. The mujahideen were already fighting at their own behest, and they were willing to fight to the death and for generations to rid themselves of the Soviet occupation. Third, the asymmetrical strategies and tactics afforded most notably by the Stinger missile were incredibly effective, and the cost for each missile relative to the damage it could render was very small. Fourth, the CIA personnel who were involved were endowed with the appropriate skills, experience, and expertise to effectively execute the action. Fifth, we had strong allies—in this case Egypt, Pakistan, and Saudi Arabia—who facilitated the operation. And in the end the action, though covert, remained within the legal parameters that were laid out for it, and it was in line with American public sentiment. Although the White House and Congress made a serious commitment of people and financial resources to the action, it was relatively autonomous.

As I look back over this time, it seems incongruous that the CIA director during this period, William Casey, had seemingly only passing interest in the Afghan program as we moved into the huge buildup in 1985. At the time, I didn't stop to think that it was unusual that the director as well as the White House, and Charlie Wilson for that matter, paid so little attention to the strategy on the ground, specific operations, decisive weapon acquisitions (Stinger missile and Milan antitank weapons), and major logistical challenges. Although in the early days (1981–85) Casey provided critical engagement on strategy with Congress and the president and took special and very important trips to see the king in Saudi Arabia to enlist his vital financial support, it is hard to identify after that where Casey exerted influence on the operational program, despite its complexity and many daily issues.

That Casey paid so little attention to the day-to-day running of the Afghan program was in sharp contrast with his almost daily involvement with Central America. I can count on two hands the number of times I spoke individually to the DDO, Casey, or the White House about the program. Like every program manager, I was grateful for the noninterference, but in hindsight I wonder about the fixation with Central America, despite its relatively modest budget. Perhaps Casey thought that because Central America was on our doorstep, events there represented more of a "clear and present danger," or perhaps he thought that since the Afghan program was running smoothly, with strong public and bipartisan congressional support, that no heavy lifting from him was required. Or perhaps because the program was already up and running when he became DCI, Casey felt it wasn't his creation or likely to become part of his legacy. This latter reasoning is hard to square with the fact that the Afghan program increased dramatically in size over his time as director, and on his watch the game-changing Stinger missile was deployed to counter Soviet aircraft, arguably leading the Kremlin to withdraw its forces. Whatever the reason, the Afghan Task Force, unlike Central America, was not subjected to the political machinations of Casey, the NSC, or Congress. It is perhaps this operational noninvolvement by the CIA's seventh-floor administrators and the NSC that contributed to it being the CIA's most successful covert action war in history. And amazingly, no Americans were killed or injured in this effort.

Today there exist lingering concerns in some quarters that the unintended consequence of our involvement in Afghanistan was the development of al-Qaeda. However, Osama bin Laden, Abdullah Azzam, and their associates never received military or financial support from the United States. Moreover, the contribution from the "Afghan Arabs"—foreign fighters traveling to Afghanistan to fight with the mujahideen—was insignificant, representing much less than 1 percent of the total fighting force. They were not part of the CIA Afghan program and left Afghanistan in late 1989.

In fact, they did not return until 1996, when they were expelled from Sudan and sought sanctuary in Afghanistan. That said, the use of non-state actor proxies did not begin or stop in Afghanistan. And there will always be unintended consequences to getting into bed with groups who share a temporary strategic goal with us but have their own long-term agendas. Although it is important to think strategically about which allies one might want to have, sometimes the operational situation requires problematic, short-lived alliances.

There is much from the covert action in Afghanistan that is relevant to our current military and paramilitary activities abroad. Policy makers will come to the agency, often as a last resort, asking that it undertake a covert action that would debilitate our enemies. Many of these programs entail huge costs, personnel commitment, and risks. They often are controversial actions sure to be debated vigorously for years when they eventually come to light. While these "special activities" regularly put the agency between a rock and a hard place, covert action remains a vital tool of statecraft that can be handled only by a disciplined clandestine force.

While covert action more than anything else helped frame the public image of the CIA as a swashbuckling, rogue organization, all covert action operations require the approval of the White House. Since the mid-1970s all operations have been directed and approved in writing by the president of the United States. This is probably the most misunderstood aspect of how the CIA really works. The CIA's role is to execute policy, not to make it. Policy making is the responsibility of the White House.

Principles of a Just War

On a personal note, the agency's use of covert action rarely caused me angst, and in many cases I raced to get in on it. But it is my strong belief that these types of operations, especially when force is included, must be carried out based on a clear set of strategic and ethical principles. From my vantage point, the most relevant framework to reference when considering covert action is the "just war" principles set out by Saints Augustine and Thomas Aquinas in their centuries-old writings. They are often-cited expositions on this theme.

In modern terms these principles require (1) a genuine national security threat, (2) a conviction that all other nonkinetic measures have been exhausted, (3) a belief that the potential gains outweigh the losses, (4) agreement that a measure of proportionality is exercised, (5) a commitment to ensure that noncombatant losses and bloodshed are kept to a minimum, and (6) a reasonable chance for success.

To these requirements, I have added a few that I believe need to be factored in before undertaking any CIA-directed covert action: (7) the need for broad public and bipartisan support, (8) a serious commitment of people and financial resources by the White House and Congress (no "dabbling" in covert actions), (9) an indigenous force that shares our goals and is prepared to fight, (10) experienced CIA personnel and

Special Forces with appropriate skills and area knowledge; and finally, (11) appropriate foreign allies to help execute the mission as needed.

There is little doubt that the United States will have to at least consider action in response to Russian and other nation-states' aggression for the foreseeable future. Our most seasoned intelligence officials will know from experience how important it is to keep in mind these principles and the American "rules of the road," including congressional oversight. Any efforts to circumvent Congress ought to be promptly quashed.[5]

LESSON TWELVE

Don't draw outside the legal lines.

The only things you can't tell Congress about are operations
you shouldn't be doing in the first place.

—Former CIA director RICHARD HELMS

12

A Cautionary Tale

Avoiding a Potential Misadventure

The cases of covert action described in the previous chapters illustrate the critical need for policy makers to show self-restraint in using intelligence tools and to use the government coordination process in developing thoughtful, principled, and pragmatic policies and CIA-directed covert action operations. Using the CIA to cut through the bureaucracy is tempting for most any administration.

If we are able to carry out the current policy plan to reduce the U.S. military footprint abroad, then ipso facto a more robust use of the CIA's traditional political and paramilitary covert action capabilities will likely be required to fill the inevitable vacuum, including blocking Russia's expansionist tendencies and desire for a controlling sphere of influence. The United States is fortunate to be able to draw upon the counsel of a deep bench of career experts and seasoned warriors who know how to analyze and execute policy "within the lines."

Many of our early covert action failures were rooted at least partially in the gung-ho and inexperienced hubris of early agency leaders who often didn't fully grasp the key factors that must be in place for covert action to be successful. Many of our career senior government officials and political appointees have absorbed the lessons of past failures, though there are always those whose hubristic confidence persists in spite of warnings and failures. In assessing how to tackle a problem as thorny as Iran, for example, it is worth remembering that the Iran of 2020 is not the Iran of 1951, and our national security strategy has to reflect an appreciation of the profound challenges of achieving regime change there today.

It is a worthwhile exercise to study one occasion when members of the White House staff and a few agency officers stepped outside the lines to seek to contain Soviet expansion. It is useful in considering how a combination of noble intentions, impassioned policy, real-world drama, and hubris can come together to lead key players astray. Such was the case in our Central American program in the 1980s.

Our fervent commitment to containing Soviet expansion, especially in Central America, dovetailed with a very emotional period when the United States was confronting hostage-taking in the Middle East. This confluence of circumstances created a perfect storm for what became known as the Iran-Contra Affair. Our rightful concern about Iran's nuclear proliferation and state sponsorship of terrorism, as well as Russia's expanding influence in strategic theaters such as Syria and Central and South America, could brew a similar storm.

Jihad and the Roots of the Iran-Contra Affair

The Iran-Contra scandal weighs heavily on the legacy of the CIA, and, as fate would have it, I saw both sides of the misguided Iran and Central America initiatives unfold from my postings in the Latin American Division and then as head of the Iran Branch.

Iran-Contra unfolded as the United States grappled with new geopolitical threats on opposite sides of the globe: terrorist attacks on Americans, including agency officers, in the Middle East and Soviet expansion in Central America. A handful of government officials stepped "outside the lines," skirting the strictures of official, legal procedures to address both problems, resulting in a scandal that almost brought down the Reagan administration.

This is how it started. In the midst of the Lebanese civil war, a suicide bomber drove a van loaded with about two thousand pounds of TNT into the American embassy in Beirut on April 18, 1983. The blast killed sixty-three people, including CIA personnel. Among the most senior officials killed in that attack were Kenneth Haas, a thirty-eight-year-old senior agency officer in Lebanon who was an experienced field operator and had earned a PhD from Syracuse University, and Robert "Bob" Ames, a highly respected and admired CIA Middle East expert and a close advisor to the director, William Casey. Ames was temporarily working in Beirut. He had excellent credentials, having worked the Middle East on both sides of the agency—analysis and operations— and he spoke Arabic. He was well known and well liked inside and outside the agency. His death came as a serious blow to morale within the CIA and among policy makers.

Then on October 23, 1983, another suicide bomber drove a Mercedes-Benz truck loaded with about 20,000 pounds of TNT into the U.S. Marine Corps barracks in Beirut. The tremendous explosion brought down the four-story building, killing 241 Marines and other service personnel. Concurrently, a suicide bombing at the French barracks housing parachute regiments killed 58. The American and French soldiers were in Lebanon as part of a UN peacekeeping force. The French retaliated immediately with airstrikes in the Bekaa Valley. An unknown group calling itself "Islamic Jihad," which would become the covert action arm of Hizballah, took credit for the attack, acting in part as a proxy for Iran and Syria. Hizballah and the Iranians denied any involvement for years, despite clear evidence to the contrary.[1]

The embassy bombing prompted strong statements of American resolve to remain in Lebanon and retaliate for this act of terrorism, but the American response did not come until December, with naval action against presumed terrorist targets in Lebanon. The delayed and limited response was due to uncertainty about who had carried out the bombings. Secretary of Defense Caspar Weinberger and Secretary of State George Shultz disagreed sharply on this point. Shultz wanted strong and immediate action, while Weinberger remained unconvinced that there was sufficient evidence to prove who was behind the attack.

This same issue confronts today's leaders when deciding how best to respond to a terrorist attack. Policy makers continue to struggle to establish a clear line of evidence to culpable parties, and even when one is identified, there is often a lack meaningful targets that would allow for a proportional response. Unlike nation-states, nonstate actors tend not to provide large, identifiable targets such as military installations or command centers. This is frustrating for Western leaders and often undermines both the decision-making behind the response and its effectiveness. In this case the U.S. response was too timid, and the perception of U.S. weakness was compounded by a withdrawal of the Marine presence from Lebanon in 1984. This left many to argue, convincingly, that the lasting lesson for Hizballah and other nonstate actors may have been that mass casualty attacks are an effective means of influencing American policy actions.

The terrorist tactics of the 1980s were as barbaric as those of ISIS today. Already in the crosshairs of the Lebanese civil war, Westerners became kidnapping targets for Hizballah and Islamic Amal (which eventually merged with Hizballah).[2] The most horrific example of personal barbarity was the 1984 Hizballah kidnapping, torturing, and killing of Beirut chief of station William "Bill" Buckley, who had stepped in to take charge of the CIA station after the embassy bombing.

Beirut was the highest-risk station in the world, and any chief was at high personal and physical risk serving there. Buckley was handpicked for the assignment by Casey, who knew him well, and, like all good soldiers, he stepped up to the job. At the time he was fifty-six years old and unmarried. Buckley was a person of simple tastes and a creature of habit, which opened up additional security vulnerabilities.

On March 16, 1984, Buckley left his apartment complex and decided to drive himself to work instead of being transported in an armored vehicle protected by security officers, which would have been the norm for such a high-risk location. He had attached to his wrist a briefcase of sensitive information. As he exited the elevator at the lower garage level, he was attacked from behind by an assailant in a business suit who was carrying a briefcase packed with stones. Two other attackers joined the struggle and pushed Buckley into a white Renault van, which sped off. They were able to transport him without incident to West Beirut, imprison him in dingy cellars, and gravely torture him for the next fourteen months.

It would have been hard for Buckley to spot his surveillance. When you are operating on the street, there are established moves you can make to smoke out surveillance. But a stationary stakeout is a different matter. While it is clear that the attack team had canvassed his building and Buckley's movement patterns, it is unlikely that he would have spotted a single assailant within his own building dressed in Western business attire. I know from personal experience the challenges of spotting surveillance. With enough experience, which Buckley had, your internal antenna often alerts you to something wrong in your surroundings. But it isn't failsafe by any means, and it wasn't for Buckley that day.

Over the next fifteen months the CIA received three tapes of Buckley filmed during his incarceration. They showed his progressive mental and physical deterioration under what agency analysts surmised was a complete deprivation of sunlight, being hooded or tethered much of the time, solitary confinement, repeated drugging, and torture. Under such extreme duress, his captors were able to extract from Buckley detailed information about CIA activities and agent identities. His kidnapping and torture were a very grave blow to agency morale, and Casey and DDO Clair George took the episode very personally. They pushed every button at their disposal in the effort to find Buckley, but to no avail. Casey regularly briefed President Reagan, who was likewise determined to get Buckley back. Despite these efforts, Buckley died in early June 1985, having succumbed to injuries incurred throughout his gruesome detention.

It is important to keep this horrific ordeal in mind when thinking about how Casey and the White House were drawn into the Iran "arms for hostages" deal in 1985. Throughout 1984 and 1985, while Casey was watching Buckley's captivity unfold via the tapes, six more Americans and several Europeans were taken hostage in Lebanon.[3] The memory of the American embassy hostages taken in Tehran following the 1979 Iranian Revolution and the frustration of having no means by which to recover Buckley despite enormous effort was certainly their overriding consideration in approving this White House–directed "arms for hostages" covert operation.[4] It played out poorly for the Reagan administration.

In 1985 an Iranian middleman made a secret request to purchase weapons from the United States in exchange for U.S. hostages. Although there was an embargo against selling weapons to Tehran—then embroiled in the Iran-Iraq War—members of Reagan's National Security Council and Casey at the CIA were open to the proposition, while Caspar Weinberger and George Shultz vehemently opposed it. Some thought that it was an avenue to create goodwill between the United States and Iran, but Reagan primarily sought to secure enough leverage for the release of the hostages. A deal was struck, and from the autumn of 1985 through the next year more than fifteen hundred missiles would be shipped to Iran, many via Israel. During the same period three hostages would be released, but three more would be taken.[5]

None Too Cautious

Halfway around the world, the Reagan administration was also deeply involved in blocking Soviet and Cuban expansion in Central America and the Caribbean. For months President Reagan had been making statements about the threat posed by "Soviet-Cuban militarization" in the Caribbean. In October 1983 U.S. forces invaded Grenada (at the official request of the prime ministers of Barbados and Dominica, as well as of Paul Scoon, the governor-general of Grenada) to thwart an attempted military coup supporting the Marxist-Leninist New Jewel Movement and rescue 233 American medical students on the island. No doubt the Iran hostage debacle still loomed large in Reagan's mind when he moved decisively to prevent a similar hostage crisis. At the time, I was serving in a neighboring country and was taken by surprise by the invasion, which seemed to me like an unnecessary overreach of U.S. power. One of my colleagues who had just participated in the invasion visited the station. He was still on an adrenalin high and touted its success. I appreciated his heroism but still had doubts about it. However, as I look back at the heavy Soviet and Cuban presence there, as well as the very real threat to our medical students, it seems now to have been a prudent move. It could well have proved disastrous if we had stayed on the sidelines and let it unfold.

Castro was furious that his cadres in Grenada surrendered to the American forces. He had expected them to fight to the death. There were mixed reactions within the CIA about the Grenada invasion, and there is no scientific way to measure agency support, though I suspect it probably mirrored the sentiment of Americans as a whole. However, the folks in the Latin America Division seemed to strongly support it.

While the Cuban military presence in Grenada was significantly larger than thought, the United States was able to quickly suppress Cuban and local resistance. Within relatively short order Grenada returned to normal without Soviet and Cuban influences.

Casey had arrived at Langley with the strong conviction that the Soviet Union and the Cubans were working to foment revolution throughout the region, starting with Nicaragua, where the Sandinista revolution had overthrown long-time dictator Anastasio Somoza in July 1979. Right from the get-go, President Reagan and Casey perceived the leftist Sandinista government as a serious threat to our national security.

On January 4, 1982, Reagan signed National Security Decision Directive 17 (NSDD-17), which authorized the CIA to recruit and support the Nicaraguan Contras with $19 million in military aid. In December 1982 Reagan delivered a speech in Costa Rica, broadcast throughout the region, calling on the nations of Central America to join in a "peaceful revolution for democracy."[6] The pointed statements, delivered amid rumors about the presence of CIA agents in Honduras, came as a warning to the communists in the region. Reagan would not confirm it at the time, but Casey was setting in motion a major covert action operation in Central America, one that became a hallmark of his tenure as DCI.

Casey also decided to shake up leadership in the Latin America Division. Nestor Sanchez, a highly respected officer and friend with fluent Spanish and rich experience in Latin America, was too cautious for Casey's taste, so Casey replaced him with Dewey Clarridge, a Middle East hand who matched Casey's OSS style of operating and had a reputation for pushing the envelope. Clarridge was only too eager to accept Casey's vision of the Soviet-Cuban threat, and he energetically threw himself into the job. Although Clarridge had no regional knowledge or Spanish-language skill, he was a strong leader and was able to develop a loyal following among many Latin America Division officers.

Clarridge was a flamboyant character. Having just left Rome as COS, he had an affection for colorful silk handkerchiefs and routinely tucked one into the pocket of his suit jacket, which on his most extravagant days was tan or white. Every day he parked his Jeep, which had an obscene gesture directed at Libyan leader Muammar Gaddafi on the rear tire cover, in his dedicated space in front of CIA headquarters. It was a way, I suppose, of setting himself apart from the rank-and-file. I remember in a discussion about leadership Clarridge saying that a leader "needed to create a folklore about himself," and indeed he did.

Based on the intelligence that Casey was viewing, it was clear that the Sandinistas had close ties to Fidel Castro in Cuba and that many Cuban, East German, and Soviet advisors were assisting Nicaragua. The key judgment of a Special National Intelligence Estimate, entitled "Soviet Policies and Activities in Latin America and the Caribbean" and published by the CIA in June 1982, found that the Soviet objective in the region was to encourage unrest and revolution and that it was "motivated by the USSR's global competition with the United States and its ideological and pragmatic commitment to support revolutionary causes worldwide." The intelligence estimate outlined a demonstrable increase in Soviet interest and activity in Latin America since the Sandinistas took power in 1979, with evidence of successful penetration by the Soviet Union and its Cuban proxies into Nicaragua. The Soviets had sent hundreds of Russians and thousands of Cubans to Nicaragua to train the Nicaraguan military and intelligence service, and the agency estimated that Soviet military assistance to Nicaragua in the form of Soviet-made weaponry was worth at least $100 million at that time. Moscow had also received high-level visits from representatives of the new Nicaraguan government and had entered into an economic assistance agreement that included a commitment of $480 million in nonconvertible currency credits to finance agriculture, roads, communications, and machinery.[7]

Casey saw growing evidence of Soviet ambitions in Central America and "became obsessed with Central America," according to former defense secretary and CIA director Robert Gates.[8] Gates said Casey seized on the idea that Soviet leaders believed the prospects for the success of revolutionary forces and Soviet-Cuban influence in Central America were much higher than they had previously believed.

From the moment Casey took over as DCI, he wanted to know about the flow of Soviet arms in and out of Nicaragua, how many guerrillas were being trained by Soviets and Cubans, and the impacts on other countries in Central America.[9] In retrospect, the focus was outsized for the threat, but the prevailing sentiment at the time was clear. Casey is quoted as stating, "If we can't stop Soviet expansionism in a place like Nicaragua, where the hell can we?"[10] This made sense to Clarridge.

Clarridge and I got along very well during the early part of his time as chief of the Latin America Division, but because of our differences about how to best handle the covert action program, we drifted apart. I badgered him that it would be more productive to put our emphasis on applying political and economic pressure inside Nicaragua. Instead, the Latin America Division focused on building up an exile force made up of disparate groups, including former Somoza National Guard soldiers and disillusioned erstwhile Sandinista insurgents who would be trained by Argentine military forces—a bad mixture under any circumstances. My reservations about the Central American program weren't about the objective but rather the means we chose to achieve it. It reminded me of the wrong-footed Bay of Pigs covert activities, and I saw the Central American effort as destined to fail.

As time went on, the Central America covert action program became increasingly controversial. Casey's and Clarridge's briefings to the House and Senate Intelligence Committees didn't help their cause. The committee members felt that they were routinely holding back under questioning, or at least not telling the full story, and soon came to distrust Casey and Clarridge. The CIA mining of Nicaragua's harbors in 1983, designed to support the Contras by cutting off the flow of weapons and fuel to the Sandinista government, became a fiasco as mines damaged commercial shipping vessels and local fishing boats that continued to use the harbors. When I heard of this operation, I was incredulous and convinced that it would lead to lasting problems with Congress and the media. At one point Senator Barry Goldwater (R-AZ) wrote in a letter to Casey, "This is no way to run a railroad . . . I am pissed off."[11] The Republican and Democratic members grew ever more unhappy with what they viewed as the CIA officials' disdainful and untruthful behavior, which virtually guaranteed that they would take punitive action against the Central American Task Force.

Congressional opposition eventually led to the Boland Amendment legislation (1982–84), which proscribed CIA assistance to the Contras "for the purpose of overthrowing the Nicaraguan government" and ultimately outlawed providing any U.S. government funds to the group at all. CIA operational activity was forced to stop. Casey should have listened to Helms's advice that "the only thing you can't tell Congress about are operations you shouldn't be doing in the first place."[12]

"Say Yes"

After the Boland Amendment cut off U.S. funds to the Contras, the White House and Casey reached out to third-party countries and private donors and raised about $35 million for military supplies. This was technically legal, even though it ran against the spirit of the Boland Amendment.

Since the CIA was sidelined, the National Security Council, in the person of Lieutenant Colonel Oliver "Ollie" North, took charge. Having the NSC running operations was unheard of. North appropriately called the project "The Enterprise," which became a secret arm of the NSC staff, and for the first (and hopefully last) time in history the NSC had direct control over operational activity. The idea that the NSC on its own should or could run clandestine operations out of the White House was absurd. Why this wasn't tied off by experienced senior government officials remains a conundrum for me to this day.

Partly to get away from Central America operations, I decided in 1985 to depart Latin America, my "home division," to take over Iranian operations in the Middle East Division, which again brought me into contact with Casey. Little did I know that instead of removing myself from the troubling Central America program, I was jumping back into the thick of things. As chief of the Iran Branch, I would become an unenthusiastic part of the "arms for hostages" deal, which became known as the Iran-Contra Affair and almost brought down the Reagan administration.[13]

It all started with a call I received in December 1985 from Clarridge, who by then had moved on to become chief of the Europe Division. His call was brief and cryptic, basically, "The DCI will be calling you soon on a very important matter, and say 'yes.'" Almost immediately, I was called to Casey's office, where he informed me that I needed to meet an NSC contract employee at his Georgetown residence. Casey believed he had sensitive information about the hostages being held in Beirut, which I knew was a hot-button issue for him. It turned out to be one of the most extraordinary and disturbing meetings I have had in my agency experience.

The NSC contractor, Michael Ledeen, laid out in considerable detail how he, Ollie North, and Iranian arms dealer Manuchehr Ghorbanifar had engaged in covert action activity, coordinated out of the NSC, and had orchestrated a shipment of TOW missiles to Iran with Israel's help. He reported that the deal had led to the release of Presbyterian minister Benjamin Weir, who had been kidnapped in 1984. This was a stunning "outside of the lines" revelation by any standard, but in the context of long-standing U.S. public policy to not negotiate with terrorists, it was over the top. Later we were joined by North and Ghorbanifar, who rattled on about their spectacular operation. It didn't take long for me to develop a strong dislike for Ghorbanifar, an unprincipled wheeler-dealer who would betray anyone or anything without batting an eye. Moreover, I had been well briefed by folks in the Iran Branch about his track record of deception. His reputation was so bad that the CIA had put out a "burn notice" on him a few years earlier, saying that he was a serial fabricator who couldn't be trusted.[14] Everyone should have paid attention to this notice, but they didn't.

After my meeting with Ledeen, North, and Ghorbanifar, I went directly to the home of Middle East chief Bert Dunn. When I informed him about the meeting, he was as thunderstruck as I. We agreed that DDO Clair George and Casey needed to be briefed first thing the next day. As planned, I went to the director's office, where George was already seated across the desk from Casey. While George seemed to be hearing the news for the first time, Casey showed no reaction to it. In fact, he was unmoved by my briefing about Ghorbanifar's background and the surprising revelation that we were negotiating with terrorists for the release of hostages. Casey felt we should continue to deal with Ghorbanifar because, he said, "he might have information about the hostages." In one last attempt to cut off further dealings with Ghorbanifar, I suggested that we polygraph him. From a professional standpoint, it was a difficult proposition for Casey and his senior team to turn down, so in early January 1986 I arranged to have Ghorbanifar meet with me and an experienced CIA polygrapher.

The polygrapher and I spent a good deal of time going over the relevant questions so as to get them just right. We wanted to make sure there was no ambiguity that would allow Ghorbanifar to squeeze by in his answers. It was a grueling exercise for all, lasting about two hours. In the end it was no surprise that he flunked the polygraph test hands down, including on the key questions about the hostages and his Iranian contacts. George reportedly briefed Casey on the results and then told me that the Operations Directorate was "out of it." It is a matter of historical record that this was not quite the case. But at the time I was greatly relieved and believed, foolishly, that I had successfully killed this ill-conceived NSC initiative. Instead, Casey turned the Ghorbanifar relationship over to Charlie Allen, a seasoned analyst in the Intelligence Directorate, to pursue information about the hostages. Ghorbanifar had no information of value to share on this sensitive issue.

To my surprise, the deputy chief of the Near East Division, Tom Twetten, called me to his office in February to tell me that Admiral John Poindexter, who was serving as national security advisor, told him President Ronald Reagan had signed a "finding" authorizing the trade of missiles for hostages. Twetten said that he and Clair George, the DDO, had been summoned to the White House and told that President Reagan had authorized the finding for this trade, the foundation for which was the reported promise that Iran would arrange for American hostages in Beirut to be released. Since that promise came from Ghorbanifar, Twetten and George saw little to no likelihood of success. In addition, Admiral Poindexter said that Congress was not to be advised and that the only copy of the finding would be retained in the White House. The next week Twetten insisted that he be permitted to retain a copy of the finding on the grounds that he intended to read it again each time a step was taken, to ensure that all actions were within the boundaries of the written instruction. Fortunately, Poindexter agreed, and the finding enabled the Iran part of this covert action to remain legal. Unfortunately, North had already made one shipment using an aircraft approved quickly over a weekend without proper vetting. Ed Juniewicz, the ADDO (deputy chief of CIA worldwide operations) involved, resigned. Deputy Director John McMahon, who protested, also decided to leave government service soon after. However, Director Casey reportedly arranged for an agency lawyer to write a retroactive covert action finding, which appeared to have been signed before the first shipment. Thus, the making of the scandal was well under way.[15]

Twetten knew I would not deal with Ghorbanifar, but he asked if I would coordinate the logistics of getting the mission completed with Colonel North and air force general Richard Secord. Even though I thought it was a terrible policy, the president had made a decision, and it was now our job to help execute. I also held out hope that someone in authority would pull the plug on such a foolhardy operation before long. No one did, and despite my misgivings, I helped make the mission happen.[16]

What I was never apprised of until its public revelation to the world was that North had sold Poindexter on the idea of upcharging the price of the missiles. A portion of the profits from this transaction went to the Contra forces in Central America, a clear violation of the law and the Boland Amendment. Despite various investigations, it remains unclear exactly what Reagan, Vice President George H. W. Bush, and Casey knew about the illegal transfer of funds.

The operation, which the president signed off on in January 1986, sent a shipment of arms from the United States to Iran without informing Congress and thus raised a fair amount of cash. The Pentagon charged $3,500 per missile, and Ghorbanifar sold each one to the Iranians for $10,000. The first thousand of the planned four thousand TOWs were delivered to Iran in February 1986.[17] By summer the Iranians had begun complaining about the huge markup we were charging. Charlie Allen recalled that at the time he began to suspect that Secord and Iranian businessman Albert Hakim were involved in diverting the profits in the upcharge account to the Contras to get around the Boland Amendments laws. Allen wrote a memo to Casey outlining his concerns and suspicions, but the operation began to spiral out of control before he could deliver it.

By November 1986 a pro-Syrian magazine in Lebanon, *Ash-Shiraa*, had published a piece about the secret arms deal with Iran, and the American press began to go after the story. The Justice Department got involved, and investigators found a memo describing the diversion of $12 million from Iran arms sales to the Contras. On November 25 President Reagan stated publicly that he had not been fully informed about the sale of arms to Iran and that up to $30 million had been used to support the Contras.[18]

As mentioned previously, one of the many sad truths about the arms deal is that few hostages were released and still others were abducted to replace them, creating what George Shultz called a "hostage bazaar." Nearly everyone from the U.S. government who had been involved came to realize what a mistake the operation had been. Especially within the CIA, the operation had come at a significant cost in terms of congressional and public trust. As for Ghorbanifar, despite being universally discredited for having misrepresented every party in his "arms for hostages" negotiations, he reemerged in 2006 as a Pentagon subject matter expert on Iranian matters. The CIA again disputed his bona fides, and he was eventually let go. Michael Ledeen—the NSC consultant who first brought Ghorbanifar to the NSC—has also resurfaced, along with his wife Barbara, in the Mueller Report, demonstrating that some political operators have at least nine lives.[19]

The Nicaraguan side of the equation was much worse because it was illegal, run explicitly to get around congressional funding cutoffs. Unlike the Iran side, this action was not covered by a finding signed by the president. It was an NSC covert operation, although at that time the CIA was the only entity authorized to run covert actions. Furthermore, the impact of the effort does not stand up well to historical scrutiny. Despite years of covert funding, by the end of Reagan's presidency the Contras were politically divided, accused of corruption and human rights violations, and had made little impact in Nicaragua. The many setbacks for the Contras—and the fact that they were never able to secure ground in Nicaragua—also meant that the rebel forces were never able to act as an important political and economic force in Nicaragua. Eventually, the rebels and the Sandinistas agreed to negotiations.

The Contras eventually demobilized in 1989, ahead of elections in 1990. Violeta Chamorro, from the National Opposition Union (UNO), won a surprising victory over incumbent Sandinista National Liberation Front (FSLN) leader Daniel Ortega. How much of an influence the Contras ultimately had in creating the conditions for a resolution to the conflict and a democratic transition in Nicaragua is debatable. In contrast, a strong case can be made that the failed socialist economic policies of the Sandinistas, coupled with the collapse of the Soviet model, had much more to do with the defeat of the Sandinistas at the polls in 1990 than U.S. support to the Contras. Ironically, midway through the Central America program, the leaders of its task force argued with me that they wanted the Chamorro family to shut down the highly influential newspaper *La Prensa* and leave Nicaragua to fight from outside the country and serve as a symbol of the country's lack of a free press. It was vastly more important for the family to stay and keep *La Prensa* fighting from inside Nicaragua, as Chamorro's election clearly demonstrated. They wisely ignored the agency's advice and kept the struggle going.

Shultz and Weinberger, both staunch anticommunists, declined to have anything to do with this covert program from the beginning of the effort (even before the finding was signed). But they were kept apprised in some detail by the NSA director, who shared with them the intercepts of the foreigners with whom North was conspiring, so they just waited for the inevitable scandal to break. Although it was a White House operation involving only a few CIA personnel, all of whom were working with the NSC off the books and of their own accord, the agency suffered greatly from the scandal.

There are many lessons in the Iran-Contra Affair that future administrations should keep in mind in policy formation, but the most wrong-footed actions were using the NSC as an operational arm of policy and keeping Congress in the dark.

The decision to violate our long-standing foreign policy against negotiating with terrorists had repercussions that endure today. Terrorists took solid note that mass casualty attacks prompt military withdrawals and that kidnappings can extract extraordinary bounty for a single American life. If there is anything to be learned from the illegal support of the Contras, aside from the obvious fact that illegal actions come with consequences, it is that CIA covert action officers should always exercise caution when faced with politically inspired covert action that emphasizes expediency and ideology over pragmatic, on-the-ground realities and ignores the professional advice of career professionals and Congress.

LESSON THIRTEEN

Never trust the Russians.

I cannot forecast to you the action of Russia. It is a riddle wrapped
in a mystery inside an enigma; but perhaps there is a key.
That key is Russian national interest.

—WINSTON CHURCHILL, October 1939

It wasn't a single attempt. They're doing it as we sit here,
and they expect to do it the next campaign.

—Special Counsel ROBERT S. MUELLER III,
testimony before Congress, July 23, 2019

13

Onward
- - - - - - - -

Unrelenting Kremlin

In August 2016, in an effort to persuade the Russians to cease their interference in the 2016 elections, CIA director John Brennan reportedly spoke to his SVR counterpart, Aleksandr Bortnikov, about the emerging evidence that Russia was attempting to meddle in the U.S. election even though we were maintaining our long-standing, hands-off approach relative to theirs. "If you go down this road, it's going to have serious consequences not only for the bilateral relationship but for our ability to work with Russia on any issue, because it is an assault on our democracy," he said.[1]

Yet we know that the Russians proceeded. What is perhaps most disconcerting is that Russia did so with relative impunity, and there is a growing body of evidence that it continues its election interference and efforts at democratic subjugation to this day. In addition to the evidence of Russian interference in U.S. elections, there is convincing data that Russia has meddled in the internal affairs of other Western countries, including Britain, the Czech Republic, France, Germany, Greece, Italy, Montenegro, Norway, Spain, and others in the form of cyber attacks, disinformation campaigns, and funding for pro-Russian parties. Whether Russia will continue to actively interfere in our elections and other political processes depends on whether Putin accepts a new set of Moscow Rules and whether he believes it is worth the consequences of continuing to antagonize the United States.

The United States was initially slow to acknowledge the extent of the Russian escalation of its aggressive foreign policy aimed at undermining U.S. influence across the globe.[2] But the interference in the 2016 election made it patently clear that steps had to be taken to curtail Russian actions. In December 2016, in retaliation for Russian cyber attacks targeting our election, President Obama decided to expel 35 Russian diplomats and close two Russian diplomatic properties that were used in intelligence operations. In July 2017 Congress passed a law, the Countering America's Adversaries through Sanctions Act of 2017 (CAATSA), imposing sanctions "against entities doing 'significant' business with Moscow's defense and intelligence sectors."[3] Almost immediately, Russia responded by cutting 755 personnel at U.S. diplomatic missions in Russia, which in turn prompted the United States to force Russia to close three consular offices. A promising next step came in December 2017, when the Trump administration issued the National Security Strategy and acknowledged that Russia was seeking to "challenge American power, influence, and interests, attempting to erode American security and prosperity."[4]

One month later the triumvirate of the Russian intelligence services—SVR head Sergei Naryshkin, FSB head Aleksandr Bortnikov, and the GRU head, Colonel General Igor Korobov—traveled to Washington DC to meet with their American counterparts and discuss counterterrorism cooperation. It is unclear if they set aside time to talk about resetting the Moscow Rules, including frank conversations about Russian intelligence interference in Western elections and the American resolve to counter it. This type of behind-the-scenes meeting, however, is the best forum in which to adjudicate our differences and reestablish a baseline for a reasonable intelligence modus operandi. If it was discussed, Russia seemingly still did not heed the message.

In March 2018, very shortly after this promising meeting, an exceptionally powerful class of Russian nerve agent called Novichok was used in an attempt to assassinate a former GRU spy for the British, Sergei Skripal, and his daughter in Salisbury, England, at the likely hand of Russian intelligence agents. In solidarity with Britain, 27 countries and NATO headquarters expelled more than 150 Russian diplomats—many who are believed to work for Russian intelligence services. The United States alone expelled 60 Russians. Russia predictably responded in kind, booting out 150 Western diplomats and closing consulates in Russia. Importantly, Britain vowed to more tightly oversee Russian financial interests in Britain—especially those held by allies of Putin. The U.S. Treasury Department also imposed new sanctions targeting a number of Russians who had attempted to access sectors of the U.S. government, as well as the "energy, nuclear, commercial facilities, water, aviation, and critical manufacturing sectors."[5]

Following Trump's 2018 meeting with Putin in Helsinki, his administration engaged in more behind-the-scenes efforts to pressure Russia. These efforts included a punitive sanctions regime that followed in August 2018 and an executive order in September 2019 focused on combating interference, largely through sanctions. Other promising developments included the indictment of Elena Khusyaynova by the Counterintelligence and Export Control Section of the Justice Department's National Security Division for attempted interference in the 2018 election.[6] Another effort was the NATO Trident Juncture war games off Norway's coast in November 2018, the largest activity of its kind since the end of the Cold War. The U.S. imposed new sanctions on the trading arm of the Russian state-owned oil company Rosneft, along with one of its board members, in February 2020 for its support of Venezuelan president Nicolás Maduro.[7]

Although this succession of punishing initiatives, punches, and counterpunches was significant, they do not seem to be producing the desired effect of deterring Russia from its aggressive activities, and they are also creating a more volatile environment. A stronger response will be needed for the Russians to change course, unless an external factor like the COVID-19 pandemic brings a temporary reduction of their efforts. Furthermore, the implications of the Mueller Report and the first section of the Senate Intelligence Committee report on the 2016 Russian election interference suggest that Russia has not been deterred from interference and has set out a road map for other nations—including China, Iran, and North Korea—seeking to interfere in our elections. Evidence of these interference efforts has already emerged. Microsoft Corporation says it has delivered nearly 750 notifications of nation-state attacks on federal, state, and local political candidates, party committees, election-oriented technology vendors, and select nonprofit and nongovernmental organizations in the United States since August 2018.[8]

Above all, strong leadership from the United States and its allies is required to contain Russia's actions. In that regard, there is one instance of presidential leadership in the past that might well be applicable today, as it had a powerful impact on both morale and policy effectiveness. President Reagan intuitively understood that Moscow would be moved only by an American show of strength. Reagan held a strong belief that détente wasn't working and that the United States needed to apply a more aggressive policy toward the Soviet "Evil Empire." As soon as he was elected, he moved quickly to reassert American power abroad. In addition, Reagan rightly felt that the Soviet economy was much weaker than generally believed by Washington experts and that the Soviets couldn't keep up with us economically. He was convinced they would fold if we raised the defense budget across the board, particularly if we moved forward with the Strategic Defense Initiative (SDI), a missile defense system that would put a "Stars Wars" shield over the continental United States. Reagan, with NATO support, also moved Pershing and Cruise missiles into Europe within range of Soviet territory. This approach was coupled with a strong desire to combat Soviet puppet states (especially Afghanistan) and leftist regimes around the world. The policy became known as the Reagan Doctrine.

At the time, I was serving in Latin America as chief of station, and I regularly ran into Russian officials on the diplomatic circuit who expressed concern about the Reagan Doctrine, especially the SDI issue, and their conviction that it represented a real threat to them. Not wishing to lessen their angst, I noted my certainty about Reagan's determination to build such a capability and that American technical know-how would make it a reality.

A similar posture will be needed to ensure that Russia is in no doubt of American resolve to protect its democratic institutions and its allies, to respond forcefully to Russian interference, and to willingly deploy incrementally more aggressive measures to deter Russia from acting against U.S. interests in the future. To accomplish this, we need to take heed of the extent to which our political processes have been penetrated and whether they remain vulnerable to future penetration. We also need to better measure what aggressive activities Russia continues to engage in, especially in the cyber field, against the United States and our allies. And while we should always pursue a reset in our relationship with the Russians to draw Russia into a genuine relationship with the West where it rightfully belongs, we must understand that a reset will come only if we are able to negotiate with Putin from a position of strength and if Putin recognizes a reset as a strategic benefit for Russia. What this will require is a long-term change in U.S. foreign policy timbre and follow-through that will consistently hold Putin to account, including dedicating robust intelligence resources to counteracting Russia's actions.

In any case, Putin's strategic objectives will be challenged by Russia's inherent economic and political weakness and that of his "fair weather" allies. Putin's interference in the internal politics of the West and military adventurism have put him at the margins of "big power" relationships and dramatically narrowed the prospects for Western investment in and trade with Russia, with major negative impacts on Russia's economic growth potential. Putin's deprecation of the democratic rule of law and restrictions on a free press inside Russia set him conspicuously and unfavorably apart from the United States and Europe.

Regarding Putin's purported allies, we need to understand that no matter how much Putin woos China, Beijing will continue to view Russia with great suspicion as a proximate potential military adversary. As far as Iran, Venezuela, Syria, and Cuba are concerned, their weak economic and political systems certainly don't make them good long-term bets for strategic alliances. While one can make a short-term deal with Iran for trade purposes or to resolve a specific problem, such as curbing Iran's nuclear development program, its ample support for terrorism makes it inherently incompatible with any government that is not a Shia theocracy.

Putin's thinking is badly out of date and out of sync with today's reality. Although he appears confident and unabashed, Putin is in a race against time to undermine the Western democratic order before his own government fades into history.

We no longer live in an ideologically driven bipolar world involving a fierce struggle between two diametrically opposed ideological political and economic systems. Russian communism is dead, as a vision and as a system. A Russia aligned with Europe and the United States in a democratic capitalistic system would not be suffering under sanctions or seeing its alliances limited to other struggling economies, like Iran's and Venezuela's. On the U.S. side, it's hard to see how anything meaningful will change in our relationship with Russia unless Putin is able to take a hard strategic look over the horizon and develop a fresh game plan that enables him to sit at the table with the West as a partner and not an adversary.

Intelligence Lessons from the Cold War

My agency career was immersed in the struggle between the CIA and the KGB and GRU. Moreover, my focus over the last three years has been spent revisiting the history of American and Russian intelligence efforts since World War II. As discussed, there is much to be learned from our past intelligence successes and failures that enables us to know how best to respond to Russia today.

Much like in the post–World War II period, we underestimated the Russian threat until significant and systemic penetrations were perpetrated across our government and throughout our defense structure.[9] Fully appreciating Russia's determination today to undermine Western democracy and its essential institutions will give us the strategic footing we need to respond. If there is one thing to take away, it is that Russia's intelligence actions against the United States remain elaborate, unyielding, and damaging. Russia endeavors to penetrate all echelons of the U.S. government and the private sector. Fortunately, most of our national security policy makers, members of Congress, and the intelligence community have awakened to the need to address the threat of Putin's aggressive actions abroad and to counter Russian intelligence activities in the United States more forcefully.

The most effective manner by which we thwarted the Russian expansionist strategy during the Cold War was by ensuring that we had a strong economy and military. Another important element to our

Cold War success was that we had countervailing assets and capabilities against the Russians in every possible theater. Espionage, covert action, and counterintelligence—the foundational elements of the intelligence business—are essential levers of American foreign policy. They greatly contributed to our ability to prevail in the Cold War and will greatly serve us in confronting the Russian challenges that lie before us.

Unlike at the onset of the Cold War, today we have the intelligence infrastructure, tradecraft expertise, and counterintelligence capability to thwart Russia, but even greater efforts toward Russia and other "hard target" nation-states will be required in the future. Because of 9/11, the United States of necessity has been bogged down for too long in costly wars in Iraq and Afghanistan, which has caused a shortfall on what is needed to counter Russian (and Chinese) goals to expand their spheres of influence and weaken ours. Russia never reduced its personnel or resources in our country, whereas until recently we devoted only about 10 percent of our intelligence resources to Russia.[10] Press reports suggest that U.S. intelligence agencies are expanding their budget allocation against the Russian threat to repair the acknowledged deficit. Unfortunately, as we saw in the 1950s and 1960s, it can take years for recalibration to take meaningful effect.

We will likely need to increase our expenditures and activities, not only in the cyber world but also in traditional intelligence collection, political and paramilitary covert action, and counterintelligence. In the years ahead we need well-placed sources in adversarial foreign powers' leadership circles and in their military and intelligence institutions. Without such sources, we will not be prepared for the increasing competition among major powers and the concomitant crisis that naturally will unfold from this competition.

Looking ahead, we will hopefully be able to scale back major military endeavors combating terrorism. Moreover, a worldwide wave of renewed nationalism and the resurgence of "big power" struggles seem ever more apparent as Russia continues to reassert its regional and global objectives and as China uses its growing economic and military might to exert power in Asia and across the world. As this unfolds, U.S. policy makers and the intelligence community will no doubt intensify their focus on these "big power" issues. A look back at the lessons learned from the Cold War—principal among them being the cutting-edge importance of intelligence in developing an effective response to these new challenges—will be most instructive. A continuing reprioritization will be essential. In this effort we must not lose sight of the fact that although China is the bigger of the "big powers" and a more potent adversary over the long term, Russia, at least for now, is the greater aggressor.

Regarding our counterintelligence posture at home, it is likely that the Russians continue to seek to suborn Western officials. Russian intelligence officers will take full advantage of the obliging operating environment afforded by the porous nature of our democracy, which allows freedom of movement and association. No doubt as in the past there are currently high-value traitors within our government, including within the intelligence agencies, who are providing high-value intelligence about national security matters as well as secrets about our military, science and technology, and economic capabilities. It is critical for us to maintain a formidable counterintelligence posture and to be ever vigilant against foreign spies inside our national security structure. It is a discipline often underweighted in the intelligence business.

New Moscow Rules

Both diplomatic isolation and economic sanctions can be effective tools to bring Russia back from this neo–Cold War and into a less aggressive political posture. We have seen in the past that a forceful U.S. containment policy response that challenges Russian interests is highly effective and that reinforcing our alliances with NATO partners and the democracies in eastern Europe and recommitting to U.S. missile defense are also among the most significant steps the United States could take to signal its commitment to defending itself against Russian aggression. An increased presence with partners along Russia's borders and bolstered support for Ukraine and the Baltic states would send a clear message to Moscow.

At the same time, the free flow of information in our society can blind us to Putin's concern, which mirrors that of his Soviet predecessors, about the impact on his own citizens of the alternative worldview and quality of life Western democracy offers in comparison to his corrupt autocracy, which threatens his hold on power. The United States has been consistent in promoting democratic institution-building generally, but there is a growing need to redouble these efforts, especially in eastern Europe and its neighboring countries. We need to promote the rule of law, freedom of the press, and the right to free and fair elections. Russia's badly flawed electoral system, its assault on domestic free expression, and its arbitrary system of justice are all fair targets for well-publicized scrutiny.

If Russia continues its cyber attacks on the United States, we will need to invest more in defensive cybersecurity infrastructure and offensive cyber initiatives through the U.S. Cyber Command, aided by robust intelligence coordination with allies in partnership with our European and NATO allies. Without such counterpunching, the Russians will persist in cyber political actions and military collection efforts inside the United States.[11]

Sub-rosa, high-level intelligence meetings are almost certainly being attempted, and could already be under way, to set out new Moscow Rules. They would need to establish revamped rules of the road, particularly with regard to interference in each other's internal political affairs. If so, and if Russia were to remain inured to our efforts, it may well be necessary for us to consider mirroring Russia's cyber operations on the same scale as it is interfering in the United States.

In closing, after revisiting the greatest cases of espionage and covert action of the Cold War, it is clear in most cases, with the important exceptions of the Cuban Missile Crisis and the action in Afghanistan, that there was no singular intelligence action that tipped the balance in the Cold War. Cumulative intelligence actions, however, had a critical impact on the outcome, just as a persistent and strong intelligence action can help us prevail in today's environment.

The calculus of victory falls in the favor of the United States, not only because of how the Cold War ended but also because of how the Cold War was lived. In Russia life went from bad to worse with episodes of deprivation and a general state of oppression. Conversely and by contrast, the quality of life in the United States was exceptionally good in comparison to any country in any period in human history. This was attained in large measure by virtue of our economic and military power as well as our democratic institutions, including the rule of law, a free press, and fair elections. This combination of freedom, quality of life, and aspirational wish for a more fair and just world lies at the heart of the concept of American exceptionalism.

This reality remains fundamentally the same today. How we respond to the Russia challenge has profound and long-lasting implications. Our reality is quickly becoming a world of renewed "big power" competition and the management of dangerous nation-states, like Iran and North Korea, that have potentially significant nuclear weaponry. For this contest, it is worth highlighting that the explosion of high-tech capabilities in the defense and intelligence industry will be an overarching tactical test of the current generation of leaders and spymasters alike.

The intelligence business is but one reflection of the United States, but if history is our guide, we can expect that the cloak-and-dagger intelligence world of spymasters, spies, espionage, counterintelligence, and covert action will be just as indispensable in the shaping of history going forward as it was in the twentieth-century Cold War. What is more, the powerful concept of American exceptionalism, which was deeply engrained in and underpinned the sense of mission in combating communism during the Cold War, was the glue that held together the Cold War covert action operations. Today, as in the past, Russia is trying to take advantage of the divisions at home and within our alliances and is working to undermine the integrity of the institutions that underpin American democracy and its uniqueness. Through this spymaster's prism, it is clear that Putin gravely underestimates the inherent strength and resiliency of American democracy, and if he doesn't change course, he will fail in his ambitions just as did his communist predecessors. For America is indeed exceptional.

APPENDIX

Russia's Known Elicitation Attempts in Trump's Inner Circle

- Putin spokesperson Dmitri Peskov had several discussions with members of the Trump Organization—including Donald Trump, Ivanka Trump, Donald Trump Jr., Trump's personal attorney Michael Cohen, and longtime Trump associate Felix Sater—during the organization's efforts to build a Trump Tower in Moscow.

- Cutouts for Russian intelligence operatives sought out low-level foreign policy advisor George Papadopoulos as soon as he was publicly affiliated with the Trump presidential campaign in March 2016.

- Russian proxy Natalia Veselnitskaya arranged and held a meeting with Trump's son-in-law Jared Kushner, Donald Trump Jr., and Trump campaign head Paul Manafort in June 2016.

- Russian SVR agents who were part of a spy ring exposed in 2015, including Victor Podobnyy, had several interactions with Trump campaign foreign policy advisor Carter Page. Page traveled to Moscow to deliver a commencement address at the New Economic School in July 2016.

- Konstantin V. Kilimnik, a former GRU officer, met twice, in May and August 2016, and had several other interactions with his longtime associate Paul Manafort while Manafort was leading the Trump campaign. Manafort caused for internal polling data to be shared with Kilimnik. And Kilimnik on several occasions broached a proposed peace plan for Ukraine. Kilimnik also corresponded with Manafort partner and RNC official Rick Gates in October 2016. (Manafort is known to have longtime contacts with individuals having links to the Kremlin and to Ukraine.)

- The GRU-created Guccifer 2.0 persona corresponded about his leaks with "a person who was in regular contact with senior members of the presidential campaign of Donald J. Trump"—later identified as Trump advisor Roger Stone—in the summer of 2016. WikiLeaks—identified in a Justice Department indictment as "Organization 1," which released information that was hacked by the GRU—corresponded with Stone as well as Donald Trump Jr.

- Convicted Russian access agent Mariia Butina and Russian SVR officer Alexander Torshin met with Donald Trump Jr. at an NRA dinner in May 2016. Butina also had several interactions with J. D. Gordon. Butina unsuccessfully tried to arrange a meeting between Trump and Putin on two separate occasions. Butina's American boyfriend and Republican operative Paul Erickson and a Butina associate, conservative Christian activist Rick Clay, both individually reached out to Trump campaign advisor Rick Dearborn in hopes of creating a back channel to Moscow during the transition.

- Sergei Kislyak, the Russian ambassador to the United States and a suspected SVR agent, met or spoke with future NSC head Michael Flynn on several occasions during the transition from the Obama administration to the Trump administration.

- Kislyak also met with Kushner, his aide Avi Berkowitz, and Flynn during the transition. (Kislyak had met with candidate Trump and with Kushner just before Trump's first foreign policy speech, in April 2016. Kislyak also met with future attorney general Jeff Sessions, future national security advisor J. D. Gordon, and Carter Page at the Republican National Convention in 2016, but the Mueller Report concluded that these meetings were nonsubstantive.)

- Similarly, Sergei N. Gorkov, head of VneshEconomBank (VEB), the bank involved in the 2015 case of SVR agents seeking intelligence in New York, met with Kushner during the transition.

- Kirill Dmitriev, the chief executive officer of Russia's sovereign wealth fund, attempted several times to make contacts with the Trump transition team. Notably, Dmitriev met with Erik Prince, a supporter of the Trump campaign and associate of senior Trump advisor Steve

Bannon, in the Seychelles in January 2017 and discussed U.S.-Russia relations. Dmitriev also sought out a friend of Jared Kushner and worked on a "reconciliation plan for the United States and Russia, which Dmitriev implied had been cleared through Putin. The friend gave that proposal to Kushner," who shared it with Bannon and the incoming secretary of state, Rex Tillerson, as detailed in the Mueller Report.

- Konstantin Sidorkov, an executive at Vkontakte, or VK, a Russian social media company, emailed Donald Trump Jr. and social media director Dan Scavino in January 2016 and again in November 2016 with offers to help promote Trump's campaign.

- Victor Vekselberg, a Russian oligarch and reported Putin crony, met with Michael Cohen in Trump Tower, wired funds to Cohen, and attended the inauguration.

NOTES

Introduction

1. Martin Matishak and Andrew Desiderio, "Senate Intel Report Confirms Russia Aimed to Help Trump in 2016," Politico, April 21, 2020, https://www.politico.com/news/2020/04/21/senate-intel-report-confirms-russia-aimed-to-help-trump-in-2016-198171.

2. Aliaksandr Kudrytski, "Belarus Leader Decries Russia's 'Hints' at Merger for Cheap Oil," *Bloomberg News*, February 14, 2020, https://www.bloomberg.com/news/articles/2020-02-14/belarus-leader-decries-russia-s-hints-at-merger-for-cheap-oil?srnd=premium&sref=lER6Tslz.

3. Shane Harris and Delvin Barrett, "Justice Department Investigates Sci-Hub Founder on Suspicion of Working for Russian Intelligence," *Washington Post*, December 19, 2019, https://www.washingtonpost.com/national-security/justice-department-investigates-sci-hub-founder-on-suspicion-of-working-for-russian-intelligence/2019/12/19/9dbcb6e6-2277-11ea-a153-dce4b94e4249_story.html.

4. In recent years the term "Moscow Rules" has also been used to refer to how the CIA runs its operations in Moscow.

5. Adam Goldman, Julian E. Barnes, Maggie Haberman, and Nicholas Fandos, "Lawmakers Are Warned That Russia Is Meddling to Re-elect Trump," *New York Times*, February 20, 2020, https://www.nytimes.com/2020/02/20/us/politics/russian-interference-trump-democrats.html?action=click&module=Top%20Stories&pgtype=Homepage.

6. Julian E. Barnes and Adam Goldman, "Russia Trying to Stoke U.S. Racial Tensions before Election, Officials Say," *New York Times*, March 10, 2020, https://www.nytimes.com/2020/03/10/us/politics/russian-interference-race.html.

1. Our Strategic Intelligence Shortfall

1. Mueller et al., *Mueller Report*, executive summary to volume 1, 4.

2. According to Tretyakov, the SVR recruited and ran sources from Germany, Greece, Iran, Poland, Sweden, Tajikistan, Turkey, and Uzbekistan, among others, out of UN headquarters. Earley, *Comrade J*, 92.

3. Earley, *Comrade J*, 192–93.

4. Like many of our most important intelligence sources from Russia, Tretyakov came to the United States a Russian patriot who had soured on the ruling class in Moscow. Born and bred for Russian intelligence, Tretyakov had a grandmother who was a member of the

NKVD (the KGB predecessor intelligence agency), and his mother worked for the KGB. Recruited at the height of the Cold War in the 1980s, he deftly maneuvered through the post-Soviet transition. By the time he became the deputy-resident in New York, he was deeply lamenting the endemic corruption and cronyism that made the new system no more noble than the last. He came to resent his privileged position among the corrupt elite and regretted the apparent fate of the Russian people. Tretyakov felt compelled to do something. After his mother died in early 1997, he made contact with the U.S. intelligence community. After he defected with his wife and daughter in 2000, he remained in hiding in the United States until his death in 2010.

5. Earley, *Comrade J*, 319.

6. Ken Dilanian, Carol E. Lee, Courtney Kube and Kristen Welker, "Russia Intel Mystery: How Strong Is the Case Russia Bribed the Taliban to Kill Americans?," *NBC News*, June 29, 2020, https://www.nbcnews.com/politics/national-security/russia-intel-mystery -how-strong-case-russia-bribed-taliban-kill-n1232452.

7. Throughout the 1940s and early 1950s Russian intelligence was focused on empowering the Soviet Union with the political and technological intelligence necessary to keep growing U.S. power at bay and to allow the communist union to carry out its plans of expansion. The plans to do this had been laid in the 1930s, when intelligence agents sought to identify and recruit promising students from elite U.S. educational institutions and talented young professionals just starting out in their careers, all with the hope that an intricate espionage network could then penetrate throughout the U.S. government. One key element was the large pool of susceptible candidates for recruitment—upwards of seventy-five thousand official members of the American Communist Party as of 1938. Only later would we learn that these American communists acted under direct instruction from Moscow. Certainly not all but more than a few of Moscow's spies would not have seen themselves as traitors but rather sympathizers with the "noble" idea of communism that they hoped to support, without any sort of view of undermining their own government.

The FBI, which had been slow to fully appreciate the emergent threat, was compelled in 1945 to respond when a Soviet cipher clerk in Ottawa named Igor Gouzenko and a disillusioned and self-confessed American spy for Russia named Elizabeth Bentley separately defected and named scores of individuals in the U.S. government they claimed were Soviet assets. As a consequence, the FBI re-interviewed Whittaker Chambers, who had confessed to being a spy for the Soviet Union seven years earlier, and opened up a proper investigation into alleged Soviet infiltration of the U.S. government, seven years after his initial confession.

8. Lauchlin Currie, codename Page, was a White House economic advisor. He is believed to have convinced the White House to provide the Soviets with plates for engraving German occupation currency. Treasury executive and Bretton Woods system architect Harry Dexter White regularly passed sensitive treasury information to the Soviets. And Duncan Chaplin Lee, codename Koch, was special assistant to OSS head Bill Donovan and provided information on anti-Soviet work carried out by the OSS during the war.

Among the many people identified during the investigation was State Department official Alger Hiss, who became the emblematic figure of this period. From an intelligence perspective, Hiss's most sensitive and possibly history-changing access to policy secrets was his advisory role for Roosevelt at the 1945 Yalta Conference. Roosevelt, Stalin, and Churchill met to develop the strategy to defeat Hitler, end the war, and carve up postwar Europe. This position placed Hiss at the center of U.S. policy and decision-making relative to the Soviets. This role would have enabled Hiss to provide invaluable intelligence to Stalin during these difficult negotiations and undoubtedly would have given Stalin and his team key insights into just how far the Allies were prepared to go in accommodating the Soviets. Most critics on the right, even to this date, see the Yalta agreement as a sellout to the Russians and attribute much of this failure to Hiss's alleged cooperation with Soviet intelligence. It is often difficult to draw a clear line to the fallout from espionage, but in this instance it is indisputable that the Soviets had a direct line into the heart of U.S. interests and considerations in these negotiations.

For more information on early Soviet spying in the United States, Whittaker Chambers, Alger Hiss, and others, see Weinstein and Vassiliev, *Haunted Wood*; and Klehr, Haynes, and Firsov, *Secret World of American Communism*.

9. In February 1943 the U.S. Army's Signal Intelligence Service started a top-secret project codenamed Venona to decode previously transmitted encrypted wartime Soviet diplomatic, NKVD, GRU, naval GRU, and Trade Ministry cables. Impressive work by the American cryptographers in Arlington Hall, later joined in 1948 by their British counterparts at Bletchley Park, decrypted a trove of information outlining Soviet espionage activities all over the world, including key information on recruitment, tradecraft, and their assets or sources of information in the United States. In addition to learning of efforts against the Manhattan Project, they found that Soviet agents were targeting the U.S. jet aircraft program and technological advances in radar and rockets. Particularly alarming were reports that hundreds of GRU and NKVD agents were working in the United States.

A notable example of the Venona Project's impact can be seen in the Hiss case. Ambiguity and uncertainty about Hiss's guilt persisted for decades. The protracted and fraught debate over his likely guilt or innocence was only settled in the public sphere in 1996, when the CIA and National Security Agency (NSA) released a Venona cable (no. 1822) that clearly implicated Hiss. Espionage, for issues of national security, must play a very long game of vindication at times. Dated March 30, 1945, the cable describes an American agent codenamed Ales who had been working for the GRU since 1935, attended the Yalta Conference, and then traveled to Moscow. According to an open-source CIA analysis of the Americans at Yalta who then went to Moscow with Secretary of State Edward Stettinius, only Hiss fit this profile. Other Soviet intelligence files make several mentions of Ales, corroborating Soviet defector Hede Massing's 1935 encounter with Ales. They describe Ales as a "strong, determined man with a firm and resolute character, who is aware that he is a communist with all the consequences of illegal status." Quoted in Haynes and Klehr, *Venona*, 171.

The Venona decryption program was known to the Soviets not long after it began, thanks to the treachery of Russian agent William Weisband, an American army officer who was fluent in Russian and who had been assigned to assist cryptanalysts at Arlington Hall. Soviet awareness of our Venona successes prompted them to alter their trade-

NOTES TO PAGES 7–8

craft and close down many of their U.S. networks proactively. New, "clean" officers and illegals were being sent instead.

10. For more on Venona, see Benson, *Venona Story*; and Haynes and Klehr, *Venona*.

11. Burton Gerber, interview by and correspondence with the author about the foundations of the CIA, the Cambridge Five, Soviet tradecraft, and key spy cases in Moscow, and key moments in American covert action, 2016.

12. The Cambridge Five were uncovered after decrypted Venona reports suggested that an individual codenamed Homer had provided high-level intelligence to the Soviets on the U.S. and British atomic programs. Homer was a senior British diplomat who was posted to Washington during the 1940s. He is mentioned in several Venona cables from New York and Washington. After nearly two years of investigation, U.S. intelligence officials and the British security service had strong evidence to believe that Homer was Donald Maclean, a senior British foreign ministry official who served as First Secretary at the British embassy in Washington in 1944 and worked specifically on the issue of nuclear security. Philby, the British MI6 liaison to the CIA in Washington, tipped off Maclean before MI5 could move to have him apprehended, and Maclean fled with another official, Guy Burgess. The so-called "Case of the Missing Diplomats" garnered headlines until Maclean and Burgess reappeared in Moscow, heralded as heroic Soviet spies, four years later, in 1956. Despite the strong beliefs of many intelligence officials in both the United States and Britain, doubt about Philby's culpability endured. MI6 relieved Philby of his intelligence duties in 1951 but did not dismiss him until 1955.

After Soviet KGB officer Anatoliy Golitsyn defected to the West in 1961, he confirmed Philby's treachery, and Philby defected to the Soviet Union in 1963. Philby has the detestable and remarkable distinction of being the only person to have received both the Order of the British Empire and the Order of the Red Banner.

In the early 1930s the Soviet Union had the idea of recruiting people from "Oxbridge," with the hope that one day their recruits would be in positions of influence. While studying at Cambridge University in the early 1930s on the heels of the Great War, the Great Depression, and the rise of fascism in Europe, Blunt, Burgess, Cairncross, Maclean, and Philby were drawn to the Soviet socialist experiment. This attraction was largely due to their belief that Stalin was the best hope to defeat fascism. Blunt, Burgess, and Cairncross were all members of a debating society called the Cambridge Apostles, which reportedly leaned toward Marxism. All five recruits advanced quickly in the small and closed world of Britain's privileged class. By the early 1940s Blunt was an officer for MI5, Burgess worked in the news department at the Foreign Office, Cairncross had worked at Bletchley Park before joining MI6, Maclean was well established in the Foreign Office, and Philby was an officer in MI6.

It is deeply ironic that, according to the Mitrokhin Archive, the Soviets could not believe their good luck. They worried the Cambridge Five's recruitment had been too easy. They feared their easy advancement in the British government's top echelons was too facile for individuals who had such openly left-wing backgrounds. What is more, they found their behavior completely unruly—excessive drinking, sexual promiscuity, and mental instability were open and obvious red flags to the Soviets—but not, appar-

228

ently, to the British. The Soviets thought that perhaps the Cambridge Five were double agents of a British conspiracy. The Soviets considered the group's intelligence potentially duplicitous and at best unreliable. Declassified files show that the Soviets spent an enormous amount of time trying to vet and verify information coming from the Cambridge Five, thereby making it occasionally less timely and less useful.

The Venona files implicating Maclean are Venona decrypt nos. 915, 1105–1110, 1146, 1263, 1271–74, all sent during 1944. Declassified Documents, Venona (1943–80), National Security Agency Central Security Service, https://www.nsa.gov/news-features/declassified -documents/venona/. The most authoritative and meticulous research on the Cambridge Five can be found in Andrew and Mitrokhin, *Mitrokhin Archive*; and Andrew, *Defence of the Realm.*

13. There were many iterations of the NKVD during its lifetime, including the OGPU, the MGB, and the KI (Committee of Information), in which the NKVD and GRU were briefly reorganized into one entity before being separated again. These shifts reflect the many different iterations of organization based on the different intelligence heads and periods when army intelligence and state security functions were integrated with the intelligence function.

14. Solzhenitsyn's famous works featuring life in the gulags include *One Day in the Life of Ivan Denisovich* (originally published in the literary magazine *Novy mir*, 1962) and *The Gulag Archipelago* (three volumes written between 1958 and 1968 and published in Paris from 1973 to 1975).

15. Serge Shmemann, "Gorbachev Says Bush Called Him to Give Early Warning of a Coup," *New York Times*, November 13, 1991, https://www.nytimes.com/1991/11/13/world /gorbachev-says-bush-called-him-to-give-early-warning-of-a-coup.html.

16. For example, upon the collapse of the Soviet government, Marshal of the Soviet Union and armed forces chief of staff Sergei Akhromeyev committed suicide.

17. Quoted in Wise, *Spy*, 139.

2. Shaping and Reshaping the CIA

1. "An Act to promote the national security by providing for a Secretary of Defense; for a National Military Establishment; for a Department of the Army, a Department of the Navy, a Department of the Air Force; and for the coordination of the activities of the National Military Establishment with other departments and agencies of the Government concerned with the national security." National Security Act of July 26, 1947, Public Law 80-253, 61 Stat. 495, available at https://research.archives.gov/id/299856.

2. Tim Weiner, "F. Mark Wyatt, 86, CIA Officer, Is Dead," *New York Times*, July 6, 2006, https://www.nytimes.com/2006/07/06/us/06wyatt.html.

3. For an interesting assessment of the history of intelligence reform in the United States since 1947, see Werner and McDonald, *US Intelligence Community Reform Studies since 1947.*

4. Helms and Hood, *Look over My Shoulder*, 59–60.

5. For more information on this period of American governance, see Herken, *Georgetown Set.*

6. Authorization for Use of Military Force against Iraq Resolution of 2002, Public Law 107–243, 116 Stat. 1498, https://www.congress.gov/107/plaws/publ243/PLAW -107publ243.pdf.

3. A Study in Russian Spycraft

1. Mueller et al., *Mueller Report*, 1:4.

2. Huib Modderkolk, "Dutch Agencies Provide Crucial Intel about Russia's Interference in US Elections," *Volkskrant*, January 25, 2018, https://www.volkskrant.nl/tech/dutch -agencies-provide-crucial-intel-about-russia-s-intereference-in-us-elections~a4561913.

3. DCLeaks information was disseminated via the Guccifer 2.0 persona, which was created and controlled by the GRU.

4. Mueller et al., *Mueller Report*, 1:26.

5. Snyder, *Road to Unfreedom*, 228–31.

6. Philip Bump, "What's Russia Still Doing to Interfere with U.S. Politics—and What's the U.S. Doing about It?" *Washington Post*, May 3, 2019, https://www.washingtonpost .com/politics/2019/05/03/whats-russia-still-doing-interfere-with-us-politics-whats-us -doing-about-it/?utm_term=.65b9402c04e2.

7. Davey Alba and Sheera Frankel, "Russia Tests New Disinformation Tactics in Africa to Expand Influence," *New York Times*, October 30, 2019, https://www.nytimes.com/2019 /10/30/technology/russia-facebook-disinformation-africa.html.

8. Philip Ewing, "Report: Russian Election Trolling Becoming Subtler, Tougher to Detect," NPR, March 5, 2020, https://www.npr.org/2020/03/05/812497423/report-russian -election-trolling-becoming-subtler-tougher-to-detect.

9. Julian E. Barnes and David E. Sanger, "Russian Intelligence Agencies Push Disinformation on Pandemic," *New York Times*, July 28, 2020, https://www.nytimes.com/2020 /07/28/us/politics/russia-disinformation-coronavirus.html.

10. Evan Osnos, David Remnick, and Joshua Yaffa, "Trump, Putin, and the New Cold War," *New Yorker*, February 17, 2020, https://www.newyorker.com/magazine/2017/03 /06/trump-putin-and-the-new-cold-war.

11. Julian E. Barnes and Matthew Rosenberg, "Charges of Ukrainian Election Meddling? A Russian Operation, U.S. Intelligence Says," *New York Times*, November 22, 2019, https://www.nytimes.com/2019/11/22/us/politics/ukraine-russia-interference.html?auth =login-email&login=email&smid=nytcore-ios-share.

12. Barnes and Rosenberg, "Charges of Ukrainian Election Meddling."

13. Snyder, *Road to Unfreedom*, 139–205.

14. Bittman's career began with his work as a Czechoslovak agent in Berlin in 1961, and he rose in the ranks to become a major and the deputy director of the Czechoslovakian Disinformation Department. According to Bittman, his first kernel of doubt about the Soviet system was planted when President John F. Kennedy spoke in Berlin in June 1963. Like many of his colleagues in the intelligence service, Bittman was cautiously optimistic when the events in Prague in the spring of 1968 started. When the Warsaw Pact forces rolled into Prague in August with such brutality, Bittman was crestfallen. He immediately drove to the German border and crossed over to the West. Bittman was not the

only casualty; agents Frantisek August and Josef Frolik followed him out a year later and echoed many of Bittman's tales.

15. He attributed his alienation with the CIA to his Catholic education, including at the University of Notre Dame, which supposedly instilled in him a moral conflict with CIA activities. It is a stretch to accept that this belief would lead him to collaborate with the communists, who are diehard antagonists of Catholicism.

16. Agee was expelled from Britain, the Netherlands, France, and Italy and eventually settled in Germany and Cuba, where he supposedly ran a travel agency.

17. A Law to Amend the National Security Act of 1947 to Prohibit the Unauthorized Disclosure of Information Identifying Certain United States Intelligence, Officers, Agents, Informants, and Sources, Public Law 97–200, 96 Stat. 122 (1982).

18. Mueller et al., *Mueller Report*, 1:42.

19. Snyder, *Road to Unfreedom*, 205.

20. Steven Eke, "Russia Law on Killing 'Extremists' Abroad," *BBC News*, November 27, 2006, http://news.bbc.co.uk/2/hi/europe/6188658.stm.

21. "Soviet Use of Assassination and Kidnapping: A 1964 Review of KGB Methods," approved for release September 22, 1993, CIA Historical Records Program, https://www.cia.gov/library/center-for-the-study-of-intelligence/kent-csi/vol19no3/html/v19i3a01p_0001.htm.

22. Andrew, *Sword and Shield*, 470.

23. Kalugin and Montaigne, *First Directorate*, 207.

24. Lyalin reportedly accepted, provided that he was furnished a safe house where his affair with Teplyakova could continue.

25. Andrew, *Sword and Shield*, 496–502.

26. U.S. Department of Homeland Security, CSISA (Cybersecurity and Infrastructure Security Agency), "Alert (TA18–074A): Russian Government Cyber Activity Targeting Energy and Other Critical Infrastructure Sectors," March 15, 2018, https://www.us-cert.gov/ncas/alerts/TA18–074A.

27. The Mitrokhin Archive was a compilation of handwritten notes accumulated over thirty years by KGB archivist Vasiliy Mitrokhin. He turned these notes over to British intelligence when he defected in 1992.

28. Wolf's prolific use of handsome East German Romeos to seduce and sometimes even marry female West German students and government secretaries began in the early 1960s and has been well documented. His use of secretary spies was successful in penetrating Konrad Adenauer's chancellery; the office of his secretary of state, Hans Globke; Chancellor Helmut Schmidt's private office, as well as the Ministry of Defense, the Foreign Office, the Ministry of Finance, and prominent German political parties. Vulnerable, single secretary spies became such a systemic security risk that Germany launched Operation Registration in 1979 to vet the partners of single secretaries holding key positions with access to sensitive material. But even as late as 1987 an analyst from within the West German Service, Gabrielle Gast, was revealed as having worked for the East Germans since 1968.

29. Wolf with McElvoy, *Man without a Face*, 124–38.

30. Andrew, *Sword and Shield*, 593.

31. Ashley, *CIA SpyMaster*, 98; Sulick, *American Spies*, 23.

32. Although he was not confronted over his relationship with Keeler specifically, Profumo ended the affair immediately by writing to Keeler what came to be known as the "Darling Letter."

33. For more on the Profumo Affair, see Knightley and Kennedy, *Affair of State*; and Summers and ʃDorril, *Honeytrap*.

34. Andrew E. Kramer and Andrew Higgins, "In Ukraine, a Malware Expert Who Could Blow the Whistle on Russian Hacking," *New York Times*, August 16, 2017, https://www.nytimes.com/2017/08/16/world/europe/russia-ukraine-malware-hacking-witness.html.

35. Andy Greenberg, "The Untold Story of NotPetya, the Most Devastating Cyberattack in History," *Wired*, August 22, 2018, https://www.wired.com/story/notpetya-cyberattack-ukraine-russia-code-crashed-the-world/.

36. David E. Sanger and Nicole Perlroth, "U.S. Escalates Online Attacks on Russia's Power Grid," *New York Times*, June 15, 2019, https://www.nytimes.com/2019/06/15/us/politics/trump-cyber-russia-grid.html.

37. Aaron Mehta, "What Is DARPA Doing in Ukraine?," *DefenseNews*, March 1, 2018, https://www.defensenews.com/global/europe/2018/03/01/what-is-darpa-doing-in-ukraine/.

4. A Spymaster President

1. For more on Putin, see Gessen, *Man without a Face*; Hill and Gaddy, *Mr. Putin*; and Putin et al., *First Person*.

2. Wolf with McEvoy, *Man without a Face*. Historical analysis suggests that during this reign of fear, there was one Stasi informant for every fifty people living in East Germany and as many as ten thousand informants operating at any given time.

3. Putin first expressed interest in joining the KGB before he graduated from high school and was told go to law school if he wanted a career in intelligence. The KGB recruited him shortly after his graduation from law school. He worked in counterintelligence and was sent to the Andropov Red Banner Institute in Moscow, where he was selected for field operations in Dresden, East Germany.

4. Snyder, *Road to Unfreedom*.

5. Martin Matishak and Andrew Desiderio, "Senate Intel Report Confirms Russia Aimed to Help Trump in 2016," Politico, April 21, 2020, https://www.politico.com/news/2020/04/21/senate-intel-report-confirms-russia-aimed-to-help-trump-in-2016-198171.

6. Evan Osnos, David Remnick, and Joshua Yaffa, "Trump, Putin, and the New Cold War," *New Yorker*, February 17, 2020, https://www.newyorker.com/magazine/2017/03/06/trump-putin-and-the-new-cold-war.

5. Spies among Us

1. "Russian National Charged in Conspiracy to Act as an Agent of the Russian Federation within the United States," press release, U.S. Department of Justice Office of Public Affairs, July 16, 2018, https://www.justice.gov/opa/pr/russian-national-charged-conspiracy

-act-agent-russian-federation-within-united-states; Jessie K. Liu, U.S. Attorney, to Robert Driscoll and Alfred Carry, McGlinchey Stafford PLLC, re. United States v. Mariia Butina, Criminal Case No. 18–218 (TSC), December 6, 2018, https://www.documentcloud .org/documents/5626092-US-v-Butina-Plea-Agreement-and-SOF-EXECUTED.html.

2. U.S. Department of Justice, Sealed Complaint: United States of America v. Evgeny Buryakov aka "Zhenya," Igor Sporyshev, and Victor Podobnyy, defendants, Violations of 18 U.S.C. §§ 371, 951, 2, January 23, 2015, https://www.justice.gov/sites/default/files/opa /press-releases/attachments/2015/01/26/buryakov-complaint.pdf.

3. When clandestine operators are sent abroad, they are given cover documentation to disguise their true affiliation with the KGB or CIA. They are often given authentic official positions and carry out legitimate diplomatic responsibilities. After hours and during innocuous breaks during the day, these operators carry out clandestine activities, such as meeting agents and surveilling targets. Their government passport provides diplomatic immunity against arrest or prosecution. They commonly work out of a station or *rezidentura* in the case of the Soviets. These offices are mainly housed inside an official installation. By contrast, the much smaller group of illegals—in CIA parlance we call this status nonofficial cover (NOC)—integrate into the local economy and play the role of a permanent resident, often under a false name and foreign citizenship. The illegal has no diplomatic immunity and is subject to the full weight of the law if discovered.

4. "Ten Alleged Secret Agents Arrested in the United States," press release, U.S. Department of Justice Office of Public Affairs, June 28, 2010, https://www.justice.gov/opa/pr /ten-alleged-secret-agents-arrested-united-states; "Russian National Pleads Guilty in Connection with Conspiracy to Work for Russian Intelligence," press release, U.S. Department of Justice Office of Public Affairs, March 11, 2016, https://www.justice.gov/opa/pr /russian-national-pleads-guilty-connection-conspiracy-work-russian-intelligence; Garrett M. Graff, "The Spy Who Added Me on LinkedIn," *Bloomberg*, November 15, 2016, https:// www.bloomberg.com/news/articles/2016-11-15/the-spy-who-added-me-on-linkedin.

5. In 1953 the New York Police Department and FBI were flummoxed by a hollowed-out nickel found by a young Brooklyn newspaper boy. It was a 1948 Jefferson nickel and had a tiny hole drilled in the R of the word *trust* on the obverse side; the reverse of the coin was made from another nickel, of a copper-silver alloy used between 1942 and 1945. When the halves were separated, they revealed a very small photograph of a series of numbers. The FBI forensic investigators feared this was an indication of the presence of a sophisticated espionage threat within the United States. Despite persistent efforts, no progress was made in identifying the origin of the nickel or the meaning of the coded message within it until Häyhänen confessed to U.S. intelligence investigators that he had lost the nickel.

6. Michael Sulick, former deputy director for operations for the CIA, indicated in correspondence to me that Pavlov convinced Treasury department official Harry Dexter White to emphasize to the FDR administration his concern about the rapidly growing Japanese aggression. The goal was to provoke more hostility between the United States and Japan and divert the glare of the "Rising Sun" from Russia's eastern front. Pavlov later wrote a book about this covert action plan, titled after its codename, Operation Snow.

7. All that was known for years about Abel was that he was reportedly a colonel in the NKVD who had traveled to the United States via Canada in November 1948 under the alias of Andrew Koyotis. (The real Koyotis was born in Lithuania in 1895, was naturalized as a U.S. citizen in 1930, and died while visiting family in Lithuania in 1947.) Abel also assumed the identities of Emil Robert Goldfus, an American who had died in infancy, and of Martin Collins, whose birth certificate was actually a forgery. Abel had worked as an aspiring artist and had been Häyhänen's superior for the preceding three years. What Abel was actually doing and with whom remained a mystery.

8. Francis "Gary" Powers had been shot down while on a CIA photographic reconnaissance flight over the Soviet Union in 1960. The shoot-down became a major foreign policy embarrassment for President Eisenhower because he publicly denied the flight was a U-2 spy mission and instead described it as a misdirected weather plane. Eisenhower and the CIA wrongly assumed Powers had been able to hit the self-destruct mechanism on the U-2 and had taken the poison pill, a special coin containing a shellfish toxin, which had been provided to him for this purpose. His capture and the reconstruction of the plane led to a show trial in Moscow at which Powers received a ten-year prison sentence. While Powers received a cool reception upon his return because he had not destroyed himself and his airplane, he was later recognized by the CIA and Congress as a brave hero of the Cold War. Allen Dulles later said that he never expected a U-2 pilot to take his own life. Everyone expected that if there was a crash or a shoot-down, the pilot would be killed. In 1977 Powers died in a helicopter crash in California while covering brushfires in Santa Barbara for KNBC.

9. It is unknown whether, after the arrest of the Rosenbergs, Fisher's efforts yielded any significant intelligence of value.

10. Details for the Häyhänen and Abel cases can be found in Richard S. Friedman, "A Stone for Willy Fisher," Central Intelligence Agency Library, posted May 8, 2007, last updated August 3, 2011, https://www.cia.gov/library/center-for-the-study-of-intelligence/kent-csi/vol44no4/html/v44i4a08p_0001.htm; Andrew and Mitrokhin, *Sword and the Shield*; and a 1958 video by the U.S. Department of Defense, *Rudolf Abel and His Life in Brooklyn*, available at https://www.awesomestories.com/asset/view/Rudolf-Abel-and-His-Life-in-Brooklyn.

11. Gordon Lubold and Shane Harris, "Russian Hackers Stole NSA Spy Secrets," *Wall Street Journal*, October 6, 2017, https://www.wsj.com/articles/russian-hackers-stole-nsa-data-on-u-s-cyber-defense-1507222108; United States v. Harold T. Martin III, twenty-count indictment for willful retention of national defense information, violations of 18 U.S.C. §§ 793 and 981, U.S. District Court for the District of Maryland, February 8, 2017, https://www.justice.gov/opa/press-release/file/937581/download.

12. The third major breach came in 1964, when a former NSA employee published a very detailed account of NSA activities in the Soviet newspaper *Izvestia*. Victor Norris Hamilton (born Victor Hindali) was a Palestinian immigrant who was recruited into the NSA because of his Arabic-language skills but suffered a mental breakdown in 1959 and had to resign. Hamilton defected to the Soviet Union in 1962, but it is unclear whether his defection was even known until his account's publication in *Izvestia*. Hamilton's exposé

included information on the U.S. effort to spy on countries other than the Soviet Union, including Egypt, Greece, Lebanon, Saudi Arabia, and Turkey. It was later learned that Hamilton was hospitalized for schizophrenia almost immediately after his defection and was first sent to a hospital for high-ranking officials but was later transferred to the more prosaic psychiatric prison known as Special Hospital No. 5, in Troitskoye, where he was only rediscovered in 1992 and found to be completely incoherent. Although he may have been of little real use to the Soviets, he certainly was useful as a compelling propaganda tool and had laid bare the striking security vetting vulnerabilities within the U.S. intelligence apparatus.

For more on the third breach by Victor Hamilton, see the Associated Press article, "American Defector Is Found in Russian Prison," *New York Times*, June 4, 1992, http://www.nytimes.com/1992/06/04/world/american-defector-is-found-in-russian-prison.html.

13. Martin and Mitchell had first met during their military service, when they both worked at the Naval Radio Intercept Station in Kamiseya, Japan, and they were thrown together again when they were recruited to work for the NSA in 1957. Although it was long suggested that the two were lovers whose sexual relationship drove them to defect, in fact they were probably just two mathematicians who objected to American nuclear policies, which most notably included spy plane flights over the Soviet Union and U.S. determination to seek a first-strike capability. They first sought to alert Rep. Wayne Hays of Ohio about what they felt were dangerous and aggressive military actions that could provoke a nuclear war. When nothing resulted from their whistleblowing, they came to believe they had few good options that would not leave them further ostracized, out of a job, and possibly in prison, so they sought to defect. Mitchell traveled to Mexico in December 1959 and made contact with the Soviets, who encouraged him to remain at the NSA and spy for them. Mitchell and Martin weren't actually interested in becoming spies, however. They instead embraced the misguided notion that they would level the playing field. They defected in June 1960, and after a thorough debriefing the Soviets held an impressive press conference that September parading the two as heroes. Both Martin and Mitchell sought without success to return to the United States, and both died thoroughly disabused of the wisdom of their treachery.

14. Rick Anderson, "The Worst Internal Scandal in NSA History Was Blamed on Cold War Defectors' Homosexuality," *Seattle Weekly*, July 17, 2007, http://www.seattleweekly.com/home/887442–129/story.html.

15. William Martin and Bernon Mitchell. "Text of Statement Read in Moscow by Two U.S. Security Agency Workers," *New York Times*, September 7, 1960, https://www.nytimes.com/1960/09/07/archives/text-of-statements-read-in-moscow-by-former-us-security-agency.html.

16. Dunlap's covert activities on behalf of the Soviet Union seemed primarily motivated by money. Spying provided him access to a luxurious lifestyle, which included a yacht, fast cars, and a mistress. To explain his newfound wealth, Dunlap concocted a ridiculous story about an estranged uncle who had bequeathed him a thriving plantation in his native Louisiana. Everyone apparently believed him and no one looked into it. Amazingly, using one crime to commit another, Dunlap managed to gain access to highly sensitive docu-

ments by assisting NSA officers who were interested in "misappropriating" furniture and other items from their offices. Through this "service," Dunlap was able to gain access to their offices and their files.

17. Edward Jay Epstein, "The Spy Wars," *New York Times Magazine*, September 28, 1980, available at http://www.edwardjayepstein.com/archived/spywars_print.htm.

18. The most sensitive information was kept in an impenetrable steel vault, heavily guarded and protected by a series of combination locks and keys. Still, the prospect of penetrating this vault represented a potential intelligence boon so great that the KGB provided enormous resources and undertook significant effort to empower the underwhelming Johnson to do their bidding. First Johnson had to apply for top-secret security clearance, which, despite his checkered past and volatile marriage, he obtained swiftly. Next, Johnson managed to be assigned to weekend guard duty, during which he would be alone guarding the vault and fewer people would be coming and going into it. Once on this posting, he shifted his efforts to obtaining the keys and combinations. Over time, he was able to make wax copies of the keys, and according to one account he came across one of the combinations, which had been left in a drawer. For the last combination lock, the KGB gave Johnson a portable x-ray device that he managed to use to take a picture of the last combination lock. With that, the Soviets were able to deduce the numbers to breach the vault, and Johnson then had everything he needed to come and go undetected from the vault with some of the West's greatest secrets in hand. His Soviet handlers would copy, reseal, and pass the materials back to Johnson so he could return them to the vault.

19. John Barron, "The Sergeant Who Opened the Door," *Reader's Digest*, January 1974, 187–94; Campbell, "Robert L. Johnson"; Stanley Johnson, "Book Tells of Soviet Spy Coup," *St. Petersburg (FL) Times*, January 18, 1974, available at https://news.google.com/newspapers?nid=888&dat=19740118&id=5-pRAAAAIBAJ&sjid=L3MDAAAAIBAJ&pg=7202,1696535&hl=en; Associated Press, "Man to Be Tried on Charge of Slaying Father in Prison," *New York Times*, May 27, 1972, http://query.nytimes.com/gst/abstract.html?res=940DE6DD153AE73ABC4F51DFB3668389669EDE; Gustaf Hildebrand, "The Spy Who Loved Nothing," Damn Interesting, February 18, 2013, http://www.damninteresting.com/the-spy-who-loved-nothing/.

20. Unlike my own background, Aldrich "Rick" Ames's interest in intelligence stemmed from his father, Carlton Ames, who worked at the CIA on counterintelligence matters for years, on James Angleton's counterintelligence staff. Ames even accompanied his father on Carlton's first undercover assignment, to Rangoon, where by all accounts his father underperformed and cultivated an alcohol problem. He apparently was able to socialize well enough but couldn't bring himself to convert any of the contacts into agents. A senior official in Burma at the time wrote a highly critical report about him and suggested that he didn't belong in the intelligence business and should not be assigned abroad again. Rick Ames supposedly became aware of this highly critical write-up years later, and it left a deep scar and bitter feelings.

A month after first offering his services to the Russians, on June 13, 1985, Ames gave the Russians the identities of nearly every Soviet source the United States had. As a result, eleven of our most valued agents were executed and dozens of lower-level operations were compromised, along with several highly valuable technical operations. Sadly, Ames was able to successfully operate unobstructed for the KGB between April 1985 and February of 1994, though his access to information about the agency's Soviet operations was limited after he entered Italian-language training in September 1985 and was sent to serve in Rome.

21. Hanssen's first major coup for the Soviets was to betray Dmitri Polyakov, an extremely important spy for the United States within the GRU. Hanssen broke off his contact with the GRU after three years but would write again, this time to the KGB, in 1985.

He would work on and off for the Soviets for twenty-two years. He betrayed scores of American intelligence assets and sensitive operations. One of his greatest revelations was that the FBI had constructed a high-value, multi-million-dollar technical collection operation in a tunnel, codenamed Monopoly, beneath the new Soviet embassy on Mount Alto in Washington DC. It took Hanssen nearly a decade to put together a mosaic of information that enabled him to uncover this highly sensitive and tightly controlled operation. Hanssen's treachery wouldn't be revealed until 2001, several years after the end of the Cold War and after I had left the agency.

22. For more on Ames, see Grimes and Vertefeuille, *Circle of Treason*, 140; Earley, *Confessions of a Spy*; and Maas, *Killer Spy*. For more on Hanssen, see Wise, *Spy*. For a comparison of the two, see Grimes and Vertefeuille, *Circle of Treason*, 183–87.

23. Despite his uninspired performance as an operations officer, Ames received high praise for his handling of Soviet foreign service officer Arkady Shevchenko when he defected.

24. Notable Soviet spies who defected included army major Dudinka, Lieutenant Colonel Andrey Dudin, Vladimir Sintov, naval captain Gregoryiev Pasko, Alexander Litvinenko, Igor Sutyagin, Valery Oyanyea, and Lieutenant Colonel Aramentko. Perhaps the most emblematic episode of long-held intelligence sources laid bare in the post-Soviet era is the case of Melitta Norwood, aka the "Red Granny." Norwood was recruited by the NKVD in 1934. She spied on and off for forty years, providing information that greatly advanced Soviet atomic research and allowed the Soviet Union to replicate the British nuclear bomb within two years. She was a prized resource and received the Order of the Red Banner. Norwood retired in 1972, never having disclosed to anyone but her husband that she was a Russian spy. Norwood's treachery was only discovered in 1992, when Vasiliy Mitrokhin brought his archive to the West. When the story broke in 1999, she was eighty-seven and still unrepentant. She told the BBC in an interview, "I did what I did not to make money but to help prevent the defeat of a new system which had at great cost given ordinary people food and fares which they could afford, good education and a health service." Quoted in Andrew, *Sword and the Shield*, 24.

25. A sampling of those convicted of spying against the United States includes David Sheldon Boone, a U.S. Army intelligence analyst; Daniel King, a U.S. Navy petty officer; George Trofimov, a U.S. Army Reserve colonel; Brian Patrick Reagan, a signals intelligence specialist in the army; and Ana Montes, a Defense Intelligence Agency analyst.

26. Martin Roeber, correspondence with and interview by author about Harold James Nicholson, 2016.

27. Yudhijit Bhattacharjee, "My Father and Me: A Spy Story," *GQ*, June 15, 2012, http://www.gq.com/story/my-father-and-me-spy-story-russia.

6. A Spymaster's Rules in Counterintelligence

1. Karen Yourish and Larry Buchanan, "Mueller Report Shows Depth of Connections between Trump Campaign and Russians," *New York Times*, April 19, 2019, https://www .nytimes.com/interactive/2019/01/26/us/politics/trump-contacts-russians-wikileaks.html.

2. Mueller et al., *Mueller Report*, 1:13, app. D.

3. For more on the Fuchs/Gold/Greenglass/Rosenberg cases, see Venona cable dated September 21, 1944, release 1, National Security Agency Declassified Documents, https:// www.nsa.gov/news-features/declassified-documents/venona/; "Atom Spy Case/Rosen-bergs," Famous Cases & Criminals, FBI History, https://www.fbi.gov/history/famous -cases/atom-spy-caserosenbergs; Doug Linder, "Trial of the Rosenbergs: An Account," University of Missouri Kansas City School of Law, 2011, http://law2.umkc.edu/faculty /projects/ftrials/rosenb/ROS_ACCT.HTM; and Eric Pace, "Klaus Fuchs, Physicist Who Gave Atom Secrets to Soviet, Dies at 76," *New York Times*, January 29, 1988, http://www .nytimes.com/1988/01/29/obituaries/klaus-fuchs-physicist-who-gave-atom-secrets-to -soviet-dies-at-76.html.

Of great interest to investigators was Gold's mention that in addition to regularly meeting with Fuchs in New Mexico, he was instructed on one occasion in June 1945 to meet with another scientist from Los Alamos. Yatskov provided Gold with an onion-skin paper with the source's name written on it, a street address, half a torn cardboard side of a Jell-O box, and a code phrase: "I come from Julius." When Gold found his contact, he had in his possession the matching side of the torn Jell-O box and provided Gold with papers and sketches from Los Alamos. This is another element to the intelligence game: capitalizing on human error. The Americans were focused on confirming Fuchs's espionage but came across an entirely separate and distinct spy network outside of Gold's orbit thanks to one illicit meeting outside his own spy network. This discovery resulted in one of the most significant trials for espionage in U.S. history: that of Julius and Ethel Rosenberg.

The Venona cables clearly implicate Julius (codename Liberal), Ruth Greenglass (code-name Wasp), and David Greenglass (codename Caliber). Much was made (and, since then, strongly debated) at the Rosenbergs' trial about whether their treachery provided key nuclear secrets to the Soviets. In truth, they were part of a different network. None-theless, it is unquestionable that the Rosenberg network provided essential information on radar technology that was instrumental to developing countermeasures against the American U-2 spy plane program. We also now know that this technology contributed significantly to accelerating the development of the Russian atomic bomb.

What distinguishes the Rosenbergs is that even when all the evidence had been mounted against them and they faced imminent death, they resolutely maintained their silence. By 1950 there was little doubt that Stalin was a tyrant, yet the Rosenbergs remained unyield-ing and deeply devoted to their cause. Although Soviet and American declassified docu-ments suggest that Ethel Rosenberg was only passively complicit in Julius's spying, neither she nor Julius wavered in their final moments before their execution. Such ideological devotion is fairly rare in the world of espionage. The Rosenbergs were the only spies in the United States put to death for espionage during the Cold War.

4. William J. Broad, "Fourth Spy at Los Alamos Knew A-Bomb's Inner Secrets," *New York Times*, January 27, 2020, https://www.nytimes.com/2020/01/27/science/manhattan -project-nuclear-spy.html?algo=identity&fellback=false&imp_id=142719995&imp_id= 243270345&action=click&module=Science%20%20Technology&pgtype=Homepage.

5. Donie O'Sullivan, "Facebook: Russian Trolls Are Back; And They're Here to Meddle with 2020," CNN Business, October 22, 2019, https://edition.cnn.com/2019/10/21 /tech/russia-instagram-accounts-2020-election/index.html.

6. Leonid Poleshchuk, a KGB counterintelligence agent, went on leave from his post in Lagos, Nigeria, and returned to Moscow. Codenamed Run and Weigh, he had first worked with the CIA in the early 1970s, when he was a KGB political officer in Kathmandu, Nepal. Poleshchuk had recently reinitiated contact and provided significant information on KGB penetrations of and operations against foreign intelligence services in Africa. He was arrested upon his return to the Soviet Union and was tried and executed in 1986. Gennadiy Smetanin, codenamed Million, a GRU officer in Lisbon, Portugal, had volunteered in 1983. He was arrested in Moscow just before he was slated to return from his home leave, and he too was tried and executed. Valeriy Martynov had been working with the FBI and CIA since 1983. The KGB was trying to find a way to lure him home without arousing his suspicions and to keep him from defecting. When Yurchenko decided to reverse his defection and return to Moscow in November 1985, Martynov was chosen as part of the "honor guard" to accompany Yurchenko home. He was arrested as soon as he returned. Martynov too was tried and executed. Gennadiy Varenik, who had just started working for the CIA in March 1985, was invited to a KGB conference in East Germany that same year. There he was arrested, returned to Moscow, tried, and executed.

7. Grimes and Vertefeuille, *Circle of Treason*, 86–87, 87–89, 91–92.

8. Sergei Motorin, codenamed Gauze, was a KGB political intelligence officer who had been recruited by the FBI after he was posted to Washington DC. The FBI had exploited Motorin's womanizing and his trading of his vodka allowance for stereo equipment to persuade him to work with them. He was tried and executed. Sergei Vorontsov (codenamed Cowl), a KGB officer in the Moscow Directorate, volunteered to the CIA in Moscow in early 1984 and provided his handler with the infamous "spy dust" used to track CIA Moscow station personnel. The CIA learned that Vorontsov was compromised when CIA Moscow station officer Mike Sellers was arrested on his way to meet with Vorontsov. Vorontsov was tried and executed. Vladimir Vasilyev, a GRU colonel codenamed Accord, volunteered to a U.S. military representative in Hungary in 1982 and worked with the CIA until December 1985. He provided information that would later expose the treachery of U.S. Army sergeant Clyde Conrad. Vasilyev was first betrayed by CIA defector Edward Lee Howard, but the KGB was unable to identify him because they had assumed that he was a KGB colonel and not from the GRU. Vasilyev was tried and executed. Dmitri Polyakov, one of our most valuable spies, having been forced into retirement six years prior, was arrested, tried, and executed.

9. Vladimir Potashov, codenamed Median, a researcher at the Institute of the United States in Canada, had volunteered five years earlier when he was living abroad. He was

arrested and imprisoned but eventually amnestied. Grimes and Vertefeuille, *Circle of Treason*, 93–94.

10. Boris Yuzhin, codenamed Twine, worked for the FBI from 1979 until 1982, when he returned to Moscow. Yuzhin is considered the luckiest unmasked spy in history: he almost gave himself up when he misplaced a spy camera hidden in a cigarette lighter in the Soviet consulate in San Francisco. In fact, he was betrayed not only by Aldrich Ames and Robert Hanssen but also by Edward Lee Howard and another spy, Earl Edwin Pitts. Yuzhin was arrested and sentenced to fifteen years in a labor camp. After the fall of the Soviet Union, he was repatriated to the United States. Lieutenant Colonel Vladimir Pigusov, codenamed Jogger, had been recruited in Indonesia in 1978, but the CIA had not had contact with him since 1979. He too was tried and executed. Grimes and Vertefeuille, *Circle of Treason*, 70–72.

11. Burton Gerber, correspondence with author, 2016.

12. Edward Lee Howard, in preparation for his posting, was read in on the top spy cases being run in Moscow. Howard was also given extensive, specialized training on how to operate in Moscow, including countersurveillance training. After he failed his polygraph, CIA management took the questionable step of immediately firing him, a drastic and unwise move in light of just how much he knew about the agency's most sensitive Russian sources and methods. While there is no totally safe place in the CIA to stash an "unfit for duty" officer, more thought should have been given to providing a softer landing for such a high-risk individual. It might have been more sensible to have put him in an administrative position and provide him in-house counseling with a goal of reintroducing him into the private sector, taking whatever time was needed to make it a smoother transition. Instead, Howard returned to New Mexico and became deeply embittered about the agency's treatment of him. Not only did the CIA apparently mishandle his dismissal, they failed to signal to the FBI that he could be a security risk even after he made drunken threats to his superior and admitted to an agency psychologist that he had considered going into the Soviet embassy in Washington.

Howard reached out to the KGB out of spite, as well as in pursuit of money and excitement, which apparently was an important driver in his psychosocial makeup.

When Yurchenko provided enough detail to identify Howard, the FBI was notified immediately. The FBI quickly put surveillance on Howard, tapped his home phone in Santa Fe, and asked Howard to come in for an interview. Shortly after the interview, Howard defected to the Soviet Union. In 2002, at age fifty-one, the Russian media reported that Howard had died at his apartment, apparently from a broken neck incurred in a fall. It's possible, I suppose.

13. Grimes and Vertefeuille, *Circle of Treason*, 140, 169–71.

14. Many of these details stem from Sandra Grimes and Jeanne Vertefeuille's personal account of the hunt for Aldrich Ames, memorialized in their excellent book *Circle of Treason*.

15. Grimes and Vertefeuille, *Circle of Treason*, 108–11.

16. Grimes and Vertefeuille, *Circle of Treason*, 117–19, 123–24.

17. Grimes and Vertefeuille, *Circle of Treason*, 129.

18. Grimes and Vertefeuille, *Circle of Treason*, 127–30.

19. Grimes and Vertefeuille, *Circle of Treason*, 140–43.

20. Maas, *Killer Spy*, 134.

21. Maas, *Killer Spy*, 182.

22. Grimes and Vertefeuille, *Circle of Treason*, 108; Wise, *Spy*, 220.

23. Wise, *Spy*, 63.

24. There has never been sufficient evidence to support the view that Colonel Bokhan (officially on duty in the Athens GRU post while spying for the CIA) and Gordievsky were betrayed by Ames, as the time line of their recalls to Moscow doesn't line up with Ames's purported "big dump." While Gordievsky returned to Moscow and was later exfiltrated, Bokhan did not return and defected to the West. Grimes and Vertefeuille, *Circle of Treason*, 72–75, 169–70; David Wise, "Thirty Years Later, We Still Don't Truly Know Who Betrayed These Spies," *Smithsonian Magazine*, November 2015, http://www.smithsonianmag .com/history/still-unexplained-cold-war-fbi-cia-180956969/?no-ist.

25. Cherkashin, *Spy Handler*, 253–54, 334.

7. Limits of Counterintelligence

1. Goleniewski provided information that exposed not only SIS spy George Blake but also Harry Frederick Houghton, whose discovery led to the detection of Gordon Lonsdale and his Portland Group in the United Kingdom, West German intelligence spies Heinz Felfe and Hans Clemens, Swedish spy Stig Wennerstrom, British Civil Service spy John Vassall, and U.S. State Department traitor Irvin Chambers Scarbeck.

2. "KGB Exploitation of Heinz Felfe: Successful KGB Penetration of a Western Intelligence Service," Central Intelligence Agency, April 13, 1977, http://www.foia.cia.gov /sites/default/files/document_conversions/1705143/FELFE,%20HEINZ%20%20KGB %20EXPLOITATION%20OF%20HEINZ%20FELFE_0002.pdf; Helms and Hood, *Look over My Shoulder*, 193.

3. The only person who was beyond suspicion in the whole affair was George Kisevalter. Yet, ironically, he probably was the only one to fit the profile Golitsyn provided, as he was of Slavic origin, his name began with K, he had a foreign-born wife, and he had been posted in West Germany!

4. Mangold, *Cold Warrior*, 332–34; [author's name redacted], "James J. Angleton, Anatoliy Golitsyn, and the 'Monster Plot': Their Impact on CIA Personnel and Operations," *Studies in Intelligence* 55, no. 4 (2011): 39–54, https://nsarchive2.gwu.edu/NSAEBB /NSAEBB431/docs/intell_ebb_019.PDF.

5. Key information provided in Nosenko's first meetings included information about John Vassall's work as a Soviet spy in the British admiralty; that recent CIA recruit and Radio Moscow correspondent Boris Belitsky was in fact a Soviet double agent; that Robert Lee Johnson and James Allen Mintkenbaugh were spies; and that there were fifty-two microphones secreted in the walls of the U.S. embassy in Moscow.

6. Robarge, "Moles, Defectors, and Deceptions."

7. Heuer, "Nosenko."

8. There was a "Sasha" discovered later—a former contract employee of Berlin Operating Base in the 1950s—but this person had nowhere near the level of access that Golitsyn purported and Angleton feared.

9. Weiner, *Legacy of Ashes*, 270.

10. Cherkashin, *Spy Handler*, 254.

11. Jolie Myers and Monika Evstatieva, "Meet the Activist Who Uncovered the Russian Troll Factory Named in the Mueller Probe," NPR, March 15, 2018, https://www.npr.org/sections/parallels/2018/03/15/594062887/some-russians-see-u-s-investigation-into-russian-election-meddling-as-a-soap-ope.

12. William M. Arkin, Ken Dilanian, and Cynthia McFadden, "U.S. Officials: Putin Personally Involved in U.S. Election Hack," NBC News, December 14, 2016, https://www.nbcnews.com/news/us-news/u-s-officials-putin-personally-involved-u-s-election-hack-n696146; Greg Miller, Ellen Nakashima, and Adam Entous, "Obama's Secret Struggle to Punish Russia for Putin's Election Assault," *Washington Post*, June 23, 2017, https://www.washingtonpost.com/graphics/2017/world/national-security/obama-putin-election-hacking/?utm_term=.a632b9f54caa; David. E. Sanger and Matthew Rosenberg, "From the Start, Trump Has Muddied a Clear Message: Putin Interfered," *New York Times*, July 18, 2018, https://www.nytimes.com/2018/07/18/world/europe/trump-intelligence-russian-election-meddling-.html?module=inline.

13. Julian E. Barnes, Adam Goldman, and David E. Sanger, "C.I.A. Informant Extracted from Russia Had Sent Secrets to U.S. for Decades," *New York Times*, September 9, 2019, https://www.nytimes.com/2019/09/09/us/politics/cia-informant-russia.html?auth=login-email&login=email.

8. Agents-in-Place

1. Browder, *Red Notice*.

2. Samantha Schmidt, "Outrage Erupts over Trump-Putin 'Conversation' about Letting Russia Interrogate Ex-U.S. Diplomat Michael McFaul," *Washington Post*, July 19, 2018, https://www.washingtonpost.com/news/morning-mix/wp/2018/07/19/trump-putin-conversation-about-russian-interrogation-of-u-s-diplomat-prompts-outrage-astonishment/.

3. At the age of twenty, Penkovskiy, fresh out of artillery school, fought in World War II. During his convalescence from a war injury, he met Colonel General Sergei Varentsov and became his aide de camp. After the war Varentsov sent Penkovskiy to Frunze Military Academy (the Russian West Point) and then to the Military Diplomatic Academy, setting him up for a career in the GRU. However, during his first assignment abroad in Istanbul, he became embroiled in an episode of political infighting that resulted in his recall to the Soviet Union, which prompted his rivals to look into his background, where his father's ignominious past in the Russian White Army was discovered. In large part due to Varentsov's sponsorship, Penkovskiy survived this revelation but was unable to obtain another international post and felt forever slighted and marginalized by the GRU and, now cognizant of his father's fate, ever more disdainful of the Soviet system.

4. Ashley, *CIA SpyMaster*, 77–82, 142–71.

5. Cherkashin, *Spy Handler*, 114.

6. Shevchenko, *Breaking with Moscow*, 19.

7. Gordievsky, *Next Stop Execution*.

8. Ashley, *CIA SpyMaster*, 70–71.

9. Garbler's career suffered after his return to Washington; he was a casualty of James Angleton's quixotic quest to unmask the elusive (and likely fictitious) Soviet mole Sasha.

10. Ashley, *CIA SpyMaster*, 242–50.

11. Quoted in Ashley, *CIA SpyMaster*, 132.

12. Ashley, *CIA SpyMaster*, 129, 130–42.

13. The first was Aleksei Kulak, codenamed Kayo, a chemist and KGB officer working at the UN for nearly fifteen years. He had been a long-term source for the FBI in the United States, under the codename Fedora, and when he returned to Moscow in 1977 he was able to maintain a productive contact with the CIA. The second asset was Aleksandr Ogorodnik, codenamed Trigon, a Soviet diplomat who had been recruited and trained in Bogotá in 1974 before returning to the Soviet Foreign Ministry in Moscow that same year. He provided a steady stream of secret cables after his return. The third asset was Anatoly Filatov, a GRU officer who had been caught in a honeytrap in Algiers and had agreed to spy upon his return to Moscow.

14. Hoffman, *Billion Dollar Spy*, 24–38.

15. Hoffman, *Billion Dollar Spy*, 51.

16. Ashley, *CIA SpyMaster*, 112–13; "A Look Back: CIA Asset Pyotr Popov Arrested," Central Intelligence Agency News and Information, January 21, 2011, https://www.cia.gov /news-information/featured-story-archive/2011-featured-story-archive/pyotr-popov.html.

17. Ashley, *CIA SpyMaster*, 184.

18. When the West wanted to communicate with Penkovskiy, his handlers would send a message using truncated Morse code numbers from a radio transmitter in Western Europe at a predetermined date and time. Penkovskiy, the CIA, and the SIS each had one of three unique copies of a cipher notebook with pages designated for different days. To decode the transmission, each would consult the page correlating with the day the transmission was sent, and the cipher would produce a new series of numbers. These sets of numbers would then produce a third set of numbers that stood for specific letters in the Cyrillic alphabet. When spelled out, these letters were the message for Penkovskiy. Ashley, *CIA SpyMaster*, 180, 190.

9. Policy Spies

1. Elaine Shannon, "Death of the Perfect Spy," *Time*, June 24, 2001, http://content .time.com/time/magazine/article/0,9171,164863,00.html; Ben Fenton, "FBI Betrayed Top Spy," *The Telegraph*, October 4, 2001, http://www.telegraph.co.uk/news/worldnews /northamerica/usa/1358475/FBI-agent-betrayed-top-spy.html; Sandy Grimes interview, "Episode 21: Spies, National Security Archive Interviews," George Washington University Library, January 30, 1998, http://nsarchive.gwu.edu/coldwar/interviews/episode-21 /grimes1.html; Cherkashin, *Spy Handler*, 112.

2. We had some other important defections as well: KGB major Stanislas Levchenko defected in 1979 while stationed in Tokyo and named more than two hundred KGB officers and agents. He also detailed how the Soviet disinformation machine operated to discredit the United States in Asia and the developing world throughout the 1970s. There was also KGB officer Ilya Dzhirkvelov, who defected to the British from his post in Swit-

zerland and revealed covert action operations from Iran and India to Tanzania and Turkey, as well as counterintelligence operations in Moscow. Gary Thatcher, "A Soviet Defector Provides Firsthand Look at the KGB," *Christian Science Monitor*, April 23, 1987, http://www.csmonitor.com/1987/0423/akgb.html; John Gross, "Books of the Times: Memoir of a Soviet Life Undercover," *New York Times*, June 3, 1988, https://www.nytimes.com/1988/06/03/books/books-of-the-times-memoir-of-a-soviet-life-undercover.html.

3. Guided Missile and Astronautics Intelligence Committee, Joint Atomic Energy Intelligence Committee, and National Photographic Interpretation Center, "Joint Evaluation of Soviet Missile Threat in Cuba," CIA Library, October 18, 1962, https://www.cia.gov/library/readingroom/docs/CIA-RDP78T05449A000200030001-8.pdf; Schechter and Deriabin, *Spy Who Saved the World*.

4. Defensive Readiness Condition (DEFCON) is a system ranking situations of military severity from 5 (least severe) to 1 (most severe). Joint Chiefs of Staff, Memorandum for the President: Evaluation of the Effect on U.S. Operational Plans of Soviet Army Equipment Introduced into Cuba, November 2, 1962, https://nsarchive2.gwu.edu/NSAEBB/NSAEBB397/docs/doc%2022%2011-2-62%20memo%20to%20JFK%20re%20invasion%20plans.pdf.

5. Garthoff, "Intelligence and the Cuban Missile Crisis."

6. There has been serious debate about whether this fear of a U.S. first strike was a reasonable concern grounded in analysis, the result of the aging Politburo's paranoia, a political tool for internal maneuvering between rival factions, or an orchestrated posturing against the West to keep NATO Pershing and Cruise missiles at bay. With the advantage of hindsight, it seems there is evidence to believe that there was indeed a real fear within the Politburo. "The Soviet 'War Scare,'" President's Foreign Intelligence Advisory Board, February 15, 1990, https://nsarchive2.gwu.edu/nukevault/ebb533-The-Able-Archer-War-Scare-Declassified-PFIAB-Report-Released/2012–0238-MR.pdf.

7. Committee of State Security of the Union of Soviet Socialist Republics, "Report on the Work of the Committee of State Security of the Union of Soviet Socialist Republics in 1981" [in Russian], April 10, 1982, https://nsarchive2.gwu.edu/NSAEBB/NSAEBB426/docs/8.%20Report%20of%20the%20Work%20of%20the%20KGB%20in%201981-May%2010,%201982.pdf; Jones, *Able Archer 83*.

8. "Soviet 'War Scare.'"

9. "Soviet 'War Scare.'"

10. Hoffman, *Billion Dollar Spy*, 5, 67, 72, 79, 91, 100, 119, 162, 175, 176, 207: Andrew and Mitrokhin, *Sword and the Shield*.

11. Guy Walters, "Spy Who Came in from the Cold Thanks to a Packet of Cheese and Onion Crisps: A True Story More Gripping Than Le Carre," *Daily Mail*, July 7, 2015, https://www.dailymail.co.uk/news/article-3151625/Spy-came-cold-thanks-packet-cheese-onion-crisps-true-story-gripping-Le-Carre.html; "Thirty Years Later, We Still Don't Truly Know Who Betrayed These Spies," *Smithsonian Magazine*, November 2015, http://www.smithsonianmag.com/history/still-unexplained-cold-war-fbi-cia-180956969/?no-ist.

12. Popov's new notes were written in a conventional front-to-back manner, whereas he had previously always written from the back to the front. In addition, his new messages were unnumbered, unlike his earlier ones.

13. Ashley, *CIA SpyMaster*, 136.

14. George Blake's treachery had exposed as many as forty people working for MI6, along with possibly as many as four hundred Soviet sources. He also undermined one of the greatest wiretapping endeavors attempted by the Western intelligence corps and quite possibly exposed Popov. Blake had accidentally come across intelligence that the CIA had a source in East Germany who was a senior Soviet intelligence officer. "A Look Back: CIA Asset Pyotr Popov Arrested," Central Intelligence Agency News and Information, posted January 21, 2011, last updated June 20, 2013, https://www.cia.gov/news-information /featured-story-archive/2011-featured-story-archive/pyotr-popov.html.

10. An American Covert Action Playbook

1. Ambassador Frank Wisner Jr., interview by and correspondence with author about Frank Wisner Sr., the Georgetown Set, and Kim Philby, 2016.

2. "Abu Bakr al-Baghdadi: IS Leader's Underwear 'Stolen' for DNA Test," *BBC News*, October 29, 2019, https://www.bbc.com/news/world-middle-east-50218637.

3. For more information, consider the cases of Amos Dawe, a Hong Kong businessman dispatched by the KGB to gain access to American technology companies' IT destined for the U.S. military, and William Holden Bell, an employee of Hughes Aircraft Radar Systems Group successfully recruited by a Polish intelligence officer to provide important details on top-secret American defense projects.

4. Not much is known about the motivation of Colonel Vetrov, but he certainly took enormous risk to share this information with the West, and his contribution to assuring our advantage in the Cold War is considerable. Sadly, he met with a dramatic and inglorious end. While details are fuzzy (and quite possibly a KGB cover story), the most reliable account suggests that Vetrov was fighting with his mistress in his car when he was interrupted by a KGB militiaman. Thinking his espionage activities had been discovered, he stabbed the man and his mistress (though she survived). He was convicted for murder, and while in prison, likely through his own statements, his espionage was discovered. He was executed shortly thereafter.

5. Gus Weiss, "Farewell Dossier: Duping the Soviets," Central Intelligence Agency Library, posted April 14, 2007, https://www.cia.gov/library/center-for-the-study-of -intelligence/csi-publications/csi-studies/studies/96unclass/farewell.htm#rft4.

6. Irvin Molotsky, "Kermit Roosevelt, Leader of C.I.A. Coup in Iran, Dies at 84," *New York Times*, June 11, 2000, http://www.nytimes.com/2000/06/11/us/kermit -roosevelt-leader-of-cia-coup-in-iran-dies-at-84.html; Gwen Kinkead, "Kermit Roosevelt, Brief Life of a Harvard Conspirator, 1916–2000," *Harvard Magazine*, January– February 2011, http://harvardmagazine.com/2011/01/kermit-roosevelt; Roosevelt, *Countercoup*, 154.

7. Helms and Hood, *Look over My Shoulder*, 114.

8. Helms and Hood, *Look over My Shoulder*, 118–19.

9. Anatoly Kurmanaev, Clifford Krauss, and Andrew E. Kramer, "Russian State Oil Company Rosneft, in Sudden Move, Sells Assets in Venezuela," *New York Times*, March 28, 2020, https://www.nytimes.com/2020/03/28/world/americas/venezuela-rosneft-oil.html.

10. R. W. Apple Jr., "Some Insights into Andropov Gleaned from Budapest Role," *New York Times*, December 28, 1982, https://www.nytimes.com/1982/12/28/world/some-insights-into-andropov-gleaned-from-budapest-role.html.

11. Proof of Hunt's poor judgment surfaced years later during the Watergate scandal, when he was identified as a principal organizer of the "plumbers" who broke into the Democratic headquarters during Nixon's presidential campaign in 1972.

12. Helms and Hood, *Look over My Shoulder*, 163–64.

13. Kalugin and Montaigne, *First Directorate*, 84–89; Andrew and Mitrokhin, *Sword and the Shield*, 283–84.

14. Quoted in William Yardley, "Thomas Polgar, C.I.A. Officer, Dies at 91; Helped Lead U.S. Evacuation of Saigon," *New York Times*, April 7, 2014, https://www.nytimes.com/2014/04/07/world/asia/thomas-polgar-cia-officer-dies-at-91-helped-lead-us-evacuation-of-saigon.html.

15. Chile received approximately $30 million in direct aid for food and cotton and a $20 million increase in short-term credit. According to CIA data, the Soviet Union had provided $98.5 million in short-term credit and $162 million in long-term supplier's credit to Chile between 1971 and 1973.

16. Paul E. Sigmund, "Strategic Issues Research Memorandum: Soviet Policy in Cuba and Chile," Strategic Studies Institute of the Army War College, October 30, 1980, http://www.dtic.mil/dtic/tr/fulltext/u2/a090958.pdf; "The Soviets Abandon Allende," Central Intelligence Agency Library, September 25, 1974, https://www.cia.gov/library/readingroom/docs/DOC_0000307740.pdf; "Soviet Policies and Activities in Latin America and the Caribbean," Special National Intelligence Estimate, Director of Central Intelligence, June 25, 1982, https://www.cia.gov/library/readingroom/docs/19820625.pdf; Nikolai Leonov, "Soviet Intelligence in Latin America during the Cold War," lecture to the Centro de Estudios Públicos, trans. Tim Ennis, Santiago, Chile, September 22, 1998, http://www.hacer.org/pdf/Leonov00.pdf.

17. Quoted in Kornbluh, *Pinochet File*, 112.

11. Best Practice

1. Rudyard Kipling, "The Young British Soldier," first published 1890, accessed at Kipling Society, http://www.kiplingsociety.co.uk/poems_youngbrit.htm.

2. Quoted in Payind, "Soviet-Afghan Relations from Cooperation to Occupation," 108.

3. The CIA and the State and Defense Departments initially opposed supplying the mujahideen with Stingers, but in 1985 a GRU officer informed the agency that an agent it ran in Greece had provided them the full transparencies for Stinger (a Greek company was to produce only a certain part, but the German contractor sent them the full set). There was no longer a need to protect the Stinger; the Soviets already had it. This discovery eventually helped in the final decision to deploy the missiles.

4. Devine, *Good Hunting*, 37–39.

5. During a budget extension negotiation at the end of January 2018, the White House, through its Office of Management and Budget, requested language (that was then submitted by the House Ways and Means Committee) that sought to refer to Section 504 of

the 1947 National Security Act as "notwithstanding." This simple word sent the intelligence committees in both the House and Senate reeling because Section 504 is in fact the section that grants Congress oversight over all intelligence actions ordered by the White House and by extension the NSC. This was a temporary budget extension, and there is no current language that permanently removes congressional oversight. But close attention needs to be paid to any attempt to water down congressional oversight. There is troubling precedent when the White House and the NSC have chosen to ignore Congress and go their own way, and we ought to heed the lessons from it. Karoun Demirjian and Shane Harris, "Short-Term Budget Would Give Trump Authority to Change Intel Spending, Lawmakers Say," *Washington Post*, January 18, 2018, https://www.washingtonpost.com /powerpost/short-term-budget-would-give-trump-sweeping-power-to-secretly-change -intel-spending/2018/01/18/5c5bbc8c-fc55-11e7-8f66-2df0b94bb98a_story.html?utm _term=.db213fa7e18e.

12. A Cautionary Tale

1. In 2004 the Iranians built a monument in Tehran commemorating the attacks and their "martyrs," leaving no doubt about their culpability.

2. The motivations for the kidnappings were many, but first among them was to discourage reprisal attacks for the bombings. Another was to create collateral for Iranian and Lebanese militants being held by the Phalange militia in northern Lebanon and in Kuwait.

3. These hostages included the Rev. Benjamin Weir, age sixty, a Presbyterian minister, kidnapped May 8, 1984; Peter Kilburn, also sixty, the librarian at the American University of Beirut, who disappeared on November 30, 1984; the Reverend Lawrence Martin Jenco, fifty, director of Catholic Relief Services in Lebanon, kidnapped on January 8, 1985; Terry A. Anderson, thirty-seven, chief Middle East correspondent for the Associated Press, kidnapped March 16, 1985; David Jacobsen, fifty-four, director of the American University Hospital, kidnapped May 28, 1985; and Thomas M. Sutherland, fifty-three, dean of agriculture at the American University, kidnapped June 9, 1985.

4. "Hostages in Lebanon: Israelis Are Guarded; Another Seven Americans Held Hostage in Lebanon," *New York Times*, June 27, 1985, http://www.nytimes.com/1985/06/27 /world/hostages-lebanon-israelis-are-guarded-another-seven-americans-held-hostage.html.

5. It is a noteworthy comparison that the Soviets' response to hostage-taking in Beirut may have been more effective. On September 30, 1985, four Soviets, including KGB operative Arkady Katkov, were abducted by a radical Sunni group that hoped the Soviet Union would use its influence to stop an ongoing offensive in Tripoli, in northern Lebanon. Katkov died of wounds he sustained during his abduction, and the other three hostages were released a month later. There are conflicting accounts of how the Soviets secured their release. Some say they threatened to attack Qom if Hizballah and the Iranians did not use their own intelligence networks and influence to arrange for their release. The more gruesome account is that KGB operatives hunted down relatives of the kidnappers and subjected them to harsh treatment until their hostages were released. "KGB Reportedly Gave Arab Terrorists a Taste of Brutality to Free Diplomats," *Los Angeles Times*, January 7, 1986, http://articles.latimes.com/1986-01-07/news/mn-13892_1_soviets; Freedman,

Moscow and the Middle East, 221–22; Serge Schmemann, "Freed Russians Tell of Beirut Captivity," *New York Times*, November 3, 1985, http://www.nytimes.com/1985/11/03 /world/freed-russians-tell-of-beirut-captivity.html.

6. Steven R. Weisman, "Reagan Denounces Threats to Peace in Latin America," *New York Times*, December 5, 1982, https://www.nytimes.com/1982/12/05/world/reagan -denounces-threats-to-peace-in-latin-america.html.

7. "Soviet Policies and Activities in Latin America and the Caribbean," Special National Intelligence Estimate, Central Intelligence Agency, June 25, 1982, https://www.cia.gov /library/readingroom/docs/19820625.pdf.

8. Gates, *From the Shadows*, 242.

9. For example, the fear that the Soviets would deliver fighter jets and other military aircraft to Nicaragua by way of the Punta Huete airfield—constructed in the early 1980s with Soviet and Cuban funds—was very real, and the intelligence community monitored the movements at the airfield closely. Vickers, "Intelligence and Punta Huete Airfield," 13.

10. Quoted in Persico, *Casey*, 264.

11. Quoted in Doyle McManus and Robert C. Toth, "Setback for Contras: CIA Mining of Harbors 'a Fiasco,'" *Los Angeles Times*, March 5, 1985, https://www.latimes.com /archives/la-xpm-1985-03-05-mn-12633-story.html.

12. Waller, *Disciples*, 499. The following acts of legislation are collectively known as the Boland Amendment: Public Law 97–377, 96 Stat. 1830; Public Law 98–212, 97 Stat. 1453; Public Law 98–215, 97 Stat. 1477; Public Law 98–473, 98 Stat. 1837; and Public Law 98–618, 98 Stat. 3298.

13. Interestingly, there was an operational precedent of Western intelligence agencies working with the Khomeini regime for common purpose. In 1982 KGB major Vladimir Kuzichkin defected to MI6 because he was reportedly being set up by his superior to take the fall for a security breach in the Soviet embassy in Tehran. Kuzichkin worked in the KGB's illegal operations in Tehran and was working to prop up Tudeh, which was the Iranian Communist Party. MI6 and the CIA passed information from Kuzichkin to the Khomeini government, which resulted in the dismissal of nearly all Soviet personnel from Tehran and the banning of Tudeh. But little interaction had taken place subsequently, until 1985.

14. A copy of the redacted burn notice for Manuchehr Ghorbanifar is available at George Washington University's National Security Archive, http://nsarchive.gwu.edu/NSAEBB /NSAEBB210/12-Ghorbanifar%20Fabricator%207-25-84%20(IC%2000505).pdf.

15. John M. Poindexter, "Covert Action Finding Regarding Iran," White House memorandum, January 17, 1986, accessed at Brown University Research, https://www.brown .edu/Research/Understanding_the_Iran_Contra_Affair/documents/d-all-1.pdf. This finding and the associated background memo from Admiral Poindexter (prepared by Colonel North) were not shared with Congress.

16. Kuzichkin, *Inside the KGB*; Vladimir Kuzichkin, letter to the editor, *New York Times*, July 21, 1991, http://www.nytimes.com/1991/07/21/books/l-inside-the-kgb-938391.html.

17. Persico, *Casey*, 495.

18. Nora Boustany, "Beirut Magazine Says McFarlane Secretly Visited Tehran," *Washington Post*, November 4, 1986, https://www.washingtonpost.com/archive/politics/1986

/11/04/beirut-magazine-says-mcfarlane-secretly-visited-tehran/f066d68b-a1d3-4afc-a84e
-182843107ab4/.

19. Barbara Ledeen is a staffer for Senator Chuck Grassley (R-IA). She engaged in a 2016 effort
to locate Hillary Clinton's missing emails and provided updates on her endeavors to Michael
Flynn during that time. Michael Ledeen was a member of the Trump transition team who advised
on foreign policy and national security matters and spoke with Michael Flynn before Flynn
decided to call Russian ambassador Sergei Kislyak. Mueller et al., *Mueller Report*, 1:162, 170.

13. Onward

1. John Brennan, interview by Chuck Todd, *Meet the Press*, July 9, 2017, http://nbcnews
.com/feature/meet-the-press-24-7/meet-press-july-9-2017-n781106.

2. David Jackson, "Trump Doubts Russian Meddling in 2020 Election, Disputing Robert
Mueller," *USA Today*, August 1, 2019, https://eu.usatoday.com/story/news/politics/2019
/08/01/donald-trump-questions-whether-russia-interfere-2020-election/1893638001/.

3. U.S. Department of Treasury, "Imposition of Sanctions with Respect to Persons
Engaging in Transactions with the Intelligence or Defense Sectors of the Government of
the Russian Federation," 22 U.S. Code § 9525, 31.

4. White House, "National Security Strategy of the United States of America," December 2017, 2, https://www.whitehouse.gov/wp-content/uploads/2017/12/NSS-Final-12
-18-2017-0905.pdf.

5. Administration of Proliferation Sanctions and Amendment of Executive Order
12851, Exec. Order No. 13883, August 1, 2019, 84 Federal Register 38113 (August 5, 2019),
https://www.federalregister.gov/documents/2019/08/05/2019-16879/administration
-of-proliferation-sanctions-and-amendment-of-executive-order-12851.

6. "Russian National Charged with Interfering in U.S. Political System," press release,
U.S. Department of Justice Office of Public Affairs, October 19, 2018, https://www.justice
.gov/opa/pr/russian-national-charged-interfering-us-political-system.

7. Lara Jakes, "U.S. Imposes Sanctions on Russian Oil Company Supporting Venezuela's Leader," *New York Times*, February 18, 2020, https://www.nytimes.com/2020/02/18
/world/americas/venezuela-russia-sanctions-trump.html.

8. Tom Burt, "New Cyberthreats Require New Ways to Protect Democracy," *Microsoft on the Issues: The Official Microsoft Blog*, July 17, 2019, https://blogs.microsoft.com
/on-the-issues/2019/07/17/new-cyberthreats-require-new-ways-to-protect-democracy/.

9. Shane Harris and Devlin Barrett, "Justice Department Investigates Sci-Hub Founder
on Suspicion of Working for Russian Intelligence," *Washington Post*, December 19, 2019,
https://www.washingtonpost.com/national-security/justice-department-investigates-sci
-hub-founder-on-suspicion-of-working-for-russian-intelligence/2019/12/19/9dbcb6e6
-2277-11ea-a153-dce4b94e4249_story.html.

10. Greg Miller, "As Russia Reasserts Itself, U.S. Intelligence Agencies Focus Anew on
the Kremlin," *Washington Post*, September 14, 2016, https://www.washingtonpost.com
/world/national-security/as-russia-reasserts-itself-us-intelligence-agencies-focus-anew-on
-the-kremlin/2016/09/14/cc212c62-78f0-11e6-ac8e-cf8e0dd91dc7_story.html.

11. Harris and Barrett, "Justice Department Investigates Sci-Hub."

BIBLIOGRAPHY

Andrew, Christopher. *The Defence of the Realm: The Authorized History of MI5*. London: Penguin Books, 2012.

———. *For the President's Eyes Only*. New York: HarperCollins, 1996.

Andrew, Christopher, and Oleg Gordievsky. *KGB: The Inside Story of Its Foreign Operations from Lenin to Gorbachev*. New York: HarperCollins, 1990.

Andrew, Christopher, and Vasiliy Mitrokhin. *The Mitrokhin Archive: The KGB in Europe and the West*. 2 vols. London: Allen Lane, Penguin Press, 1999.

———. *The Sword and the Shield: The Mitrokhin Archive and the Secret History of the KGB*. New York: Basic Books, 2000.

Ashley, Clarence. *CIA SpyMaster*. Gretna LA: Pelican, 2004.

Bearden, Milt, and James Risen. *The Main Enemy: The Inside Story of the CIA's Final Showdown with the KGB*. New York: Ballantine Books, 2004.

Benson, Robert. *The Venona Story: NSA Monograph on Venona*. Washington, DC: Center for Cryptologic History (NSA), 2001.

Browder, Bill. *Red Notice: A True Story of High Finance, Murder, and One Man's Fight for Justice*. New York: Simon and Schuster, 2015.

Campbell, Kenneth J. "Robert L. Johnson: The Army Johnnie Walker." *American Intelligence Journal* 11, no. 2 (1990): 5–10.

Central Intelligence Agency. "Shots from a Luce Cannon: Combating Communism in Italy 1953–1956," by Ronald D. Landa. Date unknown. https://nsarchive2.gwu.edu/ /NSAEBB/NSAEBB579-Defense-Department-draft-history-on-Clare-Boothe-Luce -and-US-diplomatic-intelligence-and-military-activities-in-Italy-in-1950s/Landa%20 -%20Combating%20Communism%20in%20Italy%201953-1956-Text.pdf.

Central Intelligence Agency. "The Soviets Abandon Allende." CIA Historical Review Program, September 25, 1974. https://www.cia.gov/library/readingroom/docs/DOC _0000307740.pdf.

Central Intelligence Agency–Federal Bureau of Investigation Public Affairs. Joint Press Release on the Arrest of Harold James Nicholson, November 18, 1996. Accessed at Federation of American Scientists. https://fas.org/irp/cia/news/pr111896.html.

Chambers, Whittaker. *Witness*. Washington DC: First Regnery History, 2014.

Cherkashin, Victor. *Spy Handler: Memoir of a KGB Officer; The True Story of the Man Who Recruited Robert Hanssen and Aldrich Ames*. New York: Basic Books, 2005.

Colby, William. *Honorable Men: My Life in the CIA*. New York: Simon and Schuster, 1978.

Congressional Research Service. U.S. Sanctions on Russia. January 17, 2020. Accessed at Federation of American Scientists. https://fas.org/sgp/crs/row/R45415.pdf.

Devine, Jack. *Good Hunting: An American Spymaster's Story*. New York: Farrar Straus, and Giroux, 2014.

Earley, Pete. *Comrade J: The Untold Secrets of Russia's Master Spy in America after the End of the Cold War*. New York: Penguin, 2008.

———. *Confessions of a Spy*. New York: G. P. Putnam's Sons, 1997.

Freedman, Robert O. *Moscow and the Middle East: Soviet Policy since the Invasion of Afghanistan*. Cambridge: Cambridge University Press, 1991.

Garthoff, Raymond L. "Intelligence and the Cuban Missile Crisis." *Intelligence and National Security* 13, no. 3 (1998): 18–63.

Gates, Robert M. *From the Shadows: The Ultimate Insider's Story of Five Presidents and How They Won the Cold War*. New York: Simon and Schuster, 2007.

Gessen, Masha. *The Man without a Face: The Unlikely Rise of Vladimir Putin*. New York: Riverhead Books, 2012.

Gordievsky, Oleg. *Next Stop Execution: The Autobiography of Oleg Gordievsky*. London: Macmillan, 1995.

Greene, Graham. *The Lost Childhood and Other Essays*. London: Eyre & Spottiswoode, 1951.

Grimes, Sandra, and Jeanne Vertefeuille. *Circle of Treason*. Annapolis MD: Naval Institute Press, 2012.

Haynes, John Earl, and Harvey Klehr. *Venona: Decoding Soviet Espionage in America*. New Haven: Yale University Press, 2000.

Helms, Richard, and William Hood. *A Look over My Shoulder: A Life in the Central Intelligence Agency*. New York: Random House, 2003.

Herken, Gregg. *The Georgetown Set: Friends and Rivals in Cold War Washington*. New York: Knopf Doubleday, 2014.

Heuer, Richards J., Jr. "Nosenko: Five Paths to Judgment." In *Inside CIA's Private World: Declassified Articles from the Agency's Internal Journal, 1955–1992*, edited by H. Bradford Westerfield, 379–414. New Haven: Yale University Press, 1995.

Hill, Fiona, and Clifford G. Gaddy. *Mr. Putin: Operative in the Kremlin*. Washington DC: Brookings Institution Press, 2013.

Hoffman, David E. *The Billion Dollar Spy: A True Story of Cold War Espionage and Betrayal*. New York: Doubleday, 2015.

———. *The Oligarchs: Wealth and Power in the New Russia*. New York: Public Affairs, 2011.

Jones, Nate. *Able Archer 83: The Secret History of the NATO Exercise That Almost Triggered Nuclear War*. New York: New Press, 2016.

Kalugin, Oleg, and Fen Montaigne. *The First Directorate: My 32 Years in Intelligence and Espionage against the West*. New York: St. Martin's Press, 1994.

Khrushchev, Nikita. *Khrushchev Remembers: The Glasnost Tapes*. Translated and edited by Jerrold L. Schecter with Vyacheslav V. Luchkov. Boston: Little, Brown, 1990.

Klehr, Harvey, John Haynes, and Fridrikh Firsov. *The Secret World of American Communism*. New Haven: Yale University Press, 1995.

Knightley, Phillip, and Caroline Kennedy. *An Affair of State: The Profumo Case and the Framing of Stephen Ward*. New York: Atheneum, 1987.

Kornbluh, Peter. *The Pinochet File*. New York: New Press, 2003.

Kuzichkin, Vladimir. *Inside the KGB*. London: Carlton Books, 1990.

Le Carre, John. *The Pigeon Tunnel: Stories from My Life*. New York: Viking, 2016.

Maas, Peter. *Killer Spy: Inside Story of the FBI's Pursuit and Capture of Aldrich Ames, America's Deadliest Spy*. New York: Grand Central, 1996.

Mangold, Tom. *Cold Warrior: James Jesus Angleton; The CIA's Master Spy Hunter*. New York: Touchstone Books, 1991.

Mueller, Robert S., III, Rosalind S. Helderman, Matt Zapotosky, and the U.S. Department of Justice Special Counsel's Office. *The Mueller Report*. 2 vols. New York: Scribner, 2019.

National Security Council. J. R. Scharfen, memorandum for W. Robert Pearson: The 1984 Boland Amendment. August 23, 1985. https://www.brown.edu/Research /Understanding_the_Iran_Contra_Affair/documents/d-nic-21.pdf.

Pavlov, Vitalii. *Operatsiia "Sneg": Polveka vo vneshnei razvedke KGB*. Moscow: Gaia, 1996.

Payind, Alam. "Soviet-Afghan Relations from Cooperation to Occupation." *International Journal of Middle East Studies* 21, no. 1 (1989): 107–28.

Persico, Joseph E. *Casey: From the OSS to the CIA*. New York: Viking, 1990.

Phillips, David Atlee. *The Night Watch*. New York: Atheneum, 1977.

Prados, John. *Safe for Democracy: The Secret Wars of the CIA*. Chicago IL: Ivan R. Dee, 2006.

Putin, Vladimir, with Nataliya Gevorkyan, Natalya Timakova, and Andrei Kolesnikov. *First Person: An Astonishingly Frank Self-Portrait by Russia's President*. New York: PublicAffairs, 2000.

Rasenberger, Jim. *The Brilliant Disaster: JFK, Castro, and America's Doomed Invasion of Cuba's Bay of Pigs*. New York: Simon and Schuster, 2012.

Robarge, David. "Moles, Defectors, and Deceptions: James Angleton and Counterintelligence." *Journal of Intelligence History* 3, no. 2 (2003). https://www.cia.gov/library /center-for-the-study-of-intelligence/csi-publications/csi-studies/studies/vol53no4 /pdf/JIH-Angleton-Robarge-2003.pdf.

Roosevelt, Kermit. *Countercoup: The Struggle for the Control of Iran*. New York: McGraw-Hill, 1979.

Schechter, Jerrold L., and Peter S. Deriabin. *The Spy Who Saved the World: How a Soviet Colonel Changed the Course of the Cold War*. New York: Scribner, 1992.

Schuman, Tomas D. (aka Yuri Bezmenov). *Love Letter to America*. Los Angeles: Almanac Panorama, 1984.

Shackley, Theodore and Richard A. Finney. *Spymaster: My Life in the CIA*. Sterling VA: Potomac Books, 2005.

Shevchenko, Arkady N. *Breaking with Moscow*. New York: Knopf, 1985.

Snyder, Timothy. *The Road to Unfreedom*. New York: Crown, 2018.

Sulick, Michael J. *American Spies: Espionage against the United States from the Cold War to the Present*. Washington DC: Georgetown University Press, 2013.

Summers, Anthony, and Stephen Dorril. *Honeytrap*. London: Coronet Books, Hodder & Stoughton, 1988.

U.S. Department of Treasury. "Russia-Related Directive under Executive Order of August 1, 2019 (CBW Act Directive)." August 2, 2019. https://www.treasury.gov/resource -center/sanctions/programs/documents/20190803_cbw_directive.pdf.

U.S. Senate Select Committee on Intelligence. "Report of the Select Committee on Intelligence[,] United States Senate[,] on Russian Active Measures Campaigns and Interference in the 2016 U.S. Election." 2 vols. S. Rep. No. 116-XX (2019). https://www .intelligence.senate.gov/sites/default/files/documents/Report_Volume1.pdf.

Vickers, Robert. "Intelligence and Punta Huete Airfield: A Symbol of Past Soviet/Russian Strategic Interest in Central America." *Studies in Intelligence* 60, no. 2 (2016).

Waller, Douglas. *Disciples: The World War II Missions of the CIA Directors Who Fought for Wild Bill Donovan*. New York: Simon and Schuster, 2015.

Washington, George, to Robert Hunter Morris. January 1, 1756. Founders Online, National Archives. https://founders.archives.gov/documents/Washington/02-02-02-0255. Digitized from *The Papers of George Washington*, Colonial Series, vol. 2, August 14, 1755–April 15, 1756, edited by W. W. Abbot, 249–50. Charlottesville: University Press of Virginia, 1983.

Weiner, Tim. *Legacy of Ashes: The History of the CIA*. New York: Doubleday, 2008.

Weinstein, Allen. *Perjury: The Hiss-Chambers Case*. Stanford CA: Hoover Institution Press, Stanford University, 2013.

Weinstein, Allen, and Alexander Vassiliev. *The Haunted Wood: Soviet Espionage in America— the Stalin Era*. New York: Modern Library, Penguin Random House, 2000.

Werner, Michael, and J. Kenneth McDonald. *US Intelligence Community Reform Studies since 1947*. Central Intelligence Agency, April 2005. https://www.cia.gov/library /center-for-the-study-of-intelligence/csi-publications/books-and-monographs/US %20Intelligence%20Community%20Reform%20Studies%20Since%201947.pdf.

The White House. National Security Decision Directive on Cuba and Central America. National Security Decision Directive No. 17, January 4, 1982. https://www .reaganlibrary.gov/sites/default/files/archives/reference/scanned-nsdds/nsdd17.pdf.

Wise, David. *Spy: The Inside Story of How the FBI's Robert Hanssen Betrayed America*. New York: Random House, 2003.

Wolf, Markus, with Anne McElvoy. *Man without a Face: The Autobiography of Communism's Greatest Spymaster*. New York: Public Affairs, 1999.

INDEX

Abbottabad, raid on, 156

Abel, Rudolf Ivanovich, 71, 72–73. *See also* Fisher, William August; "Mark"

Able Archer 83 (Soviet war games), 145, 146, 147

Acheson, Dean, 20

active measures, xvii, 29, 34, 35, 39, 45, 47, 51, 52, 57, 60, 62, 63, 64, 87, 155. *See also* agents of influence; covert action; *dezinformatsiya*; disinformation; elicitation; entrapment; honeytrap; influence campaigns; *mokrye dela*; propaganda; sabotage; smear campaigns; SMERSH; Swallows; wet work

Afghanistan, 5, 155, 156; buildup in, 184–85; CIA and, 182, 183–84; economic/military aid for, 179; involvement in, 27, 187; Soviet invasion of, 179, 180, 181, 182, 185, 219; war in, 26, 37, 179, 185, 217

Afghan Task Force, xvi, 179, 183, 187

Africa Division (CIA), 181

Agee, Philip, 39–40, 41

agents of influence, 8, 119

Allen, Charlie, 204, 205, 206

Allende, Salvador, 173, 174–75, 176

al-Qaeda, 4, 25, 187

Alsop, Joseph, 20

Alsop, Stewart, 20

Ambler, Eric, 80

American Farm Journal, 132

The Americans (television series), 68

Ames, Aldrich "Rick," xvi, 23, 24, 79, 82, 93, 95, 102, 195; addiction problems for, 78, 80–81; betrayal by, 98, 99, 100, 114; investigating, 13, 96–97; KGB and, 94, 97, 101

Ames, Carlton, 78

Ames, Robert "Bob," 194

Ames, Rosario, 96–97

Amin, Hafizullah, 180

Andropov, Yuri, 144, 145, 166, 184

Angleton, James, 19, 109, 113, 168; "The Briefing" (Phillips) and, 113; CIA penetrations and, 108; Golitsyn and, 111, 112; Helms and, 112; Office of Security and, 111; SIG and, 107. *See also* Nosenko, Yuri

Anglo-Afghanistan Wars (1838/1878/1917), 179

Arab Spring, 64

Árbenz, Jacobo, 159–60, 161

Argo (movie), xvi

Armed Forces Courier Center, 77

Army of Liberation, 160

artificial intelligence (AI), 51, 116

Ash-Shira, 206

Assad, Bashar al-, 60, 163

Astor, Lord, 49–50

Augustine, Saint, 188

Avrakotos, Gust, 181–82

Azzam, Abdullah, 187

Baburova, Anastasia, 44, 47

Baghdadi, Abu Bakr al-, 156

Baltic states, 147, 165, 218

Bandera, Stepan, 44

Bannon, Steve, 222–23

Barnes, Tracy, 19, 167

Batista, Fulgencio, 166

Bay of Pigs, 22, 141, 143, 155, 171, 201; CIA and, 166, 168, 169; legacy of, 169

Bearden, Milton, 12, 183, 185

Belarus, xvii, 143, 147, 165

Bender, Frank. *See* Droller, Gerry

Bentley, Elizabeth, 7, 114

Berezovsky, Boris, 47

Beria, Lavrenti, 8, 10–11, 14

Berkowitz, Avi, 222

Berlin Wall, 23, 35, 57, 58

Bezmenov, Yuri, 45

big power dynamics, 25, 27, 54, 156, 215, 217, 218, 220

Biden, Joe, xx

bin Laden, Osama, 4, 156, 187

Bissell, Richard, 19, 167, 168, 169

Bittman, Ladislav, 38, 39, 41, 42

blackmail, 34, 45, 48, 76, 99, 113, 125

Blake, George, 50, 108, 114, 151

Bloch, Felix, 99

Blunt, Anthony, 7. See also Cambridge Five

BND (Bundesnachrichtendienst, West German intelligence service), 109

Bohlen, Charles "Chip," 49

Bokhan, Sergei, 102

Boland Amendment, 202, 205, 206

Booz Allen, 73

Border Patrol, 11

Bortnikov, Aleksandr, 211, 212

Bosch, Juan, 172

Breach (movie), 101

Breaking with Moscow (Shevchenko), 124

Brennan, John, 211

Brezhnev, Leonid, 124, 143, 144, 163, 184; Allende and, 173; KGB and, 179

Browder, Bill, 120–21, 121–22

Bruce, David, 20

Brzezinski, Zbigniew, 180

Buckley, William "Bill," 196–97

Bulgaria, 18; influence in, 34, 125

Bundy, McGeorge, 142

Burgess, Guy, 7. See also Cambridge Five

Buryakov, Evgeny, 68

Bush, George H. W., 13, 205

Bush, George W., 24, 25

Butina, Mariia, 67, 68, 70, 73, 222

Cairncross, John, 7. See also Cambridge Five

Camargo Seixas, Angela, 40

Cambridge Five, 7, 8, 108. See also Blunt, Anthony; Burgess, Guy; Cairncross, John; Maclean, Donald; Philby, Kim; Pyatyorka (Ring of Five)

cameras, 31, 48, 49, 53, 133, 140, 150

Carabineros, 175, 176

Carter, Jimmy: Turner and, 129, 130, 132

Casey, William, 197, 199, 200–201, 202–6; Afghanistan and, 186, 187; Ames and, 195; Central America and, 200; George and, 197; Goldwater and, 201; Lebanon and, 196; Reagan and, 199; Soviet-Cuban threat and, 199; on Soviet expansionism, 201

Castillo Armas, Carlos, 160, 161

Castro, Fidel, 163, 165, 167, 173; Bay of Pigs and, 166; Grenada and, 198; propaganda and, 168; Sandinistas and, 200

CCTV, 131

Central America, 155, 186, 187, 201, 202; covert action in, 199; Soviet/Cuban expansion in, 194, 198, 200

Central American Task Force (CIA), 201

Chambers, Whittaker, 7, 114

Chamorro, Violeta, 207

Chapman, Anna, 69, 70

Chavez, Hugo, 163

Chechnya, 5, 43, 59

Cherepanov, Alexander, 127–28, 131

Cherkashin, Victor, 94, 102, 114

Chernenko, Konstantin, 184

Chicago Police Department, 78

Chile, 161, 169, 172–76; coup in, 176, 179

Chilean Communist Party, 173

Chile Task Force (CIA), 174

China, 5, 80, 139, 181, 182, 183, 184, 213, 215; big powers and, 218; competition with, 54; interference by, 34; spying for, 81; threats from, 27; Venezuelan oil and, 164

Churchill, Randolph, 49

Churchill, Winston, 8

Chuvakhin, Sergei, 93, 94, 97

CIA, 7, 13, 39, 41, 44, 48, 50, 71, 75, 80, 83, 93, 94, 95, 96, 100, 101, 102, 110, 111, 124, 127, 129, 130, 131, 133, 140, 149, 150, 156, 157, 158, 159, 160; Afghanistan and, 182, 183–84, 186, 187; analysis by, 139, 142, 170; Bay of Pigs and, 166, 168, 169; bureaucracy and, 193; "burn notice" by, 203; case officers, 76, 78, 81, 82, 152; Chilean coup and, 176; CI and, 92, 97, 98, 107; Cold War and, 11, 161; Communist Party and, 9; Contras and, 199, 202; Cuba and, 141, 165, 167; digital innovation and, 56; domestic issues and, 12; evolution of, 22–25;

FBI and, 17; Grenada and, 198–99; historical experience of, xvi, xx–xxi; intelligence
and, 143; Iran-Contra and, 207; Kennedy
and, 168; KGB and, 11, 64, 99, 113; legacy of,
194; mission of, 26; Nicaragua and, 201, 202;
OSS and, 17–21; penetration of, 108, 112; pol-
itics and, 11, 18, 21; Popov and, 151; public
image of, 188; public trust and, 206; Soviet
Division of, 12, 93–94; SVR and, 64; terror-
ism and, 25; training by, 132; Ukraine and, 35;
weapons buildup for, 183
CIC. See Counterintelligence Center (CIC) (CIA)
Clandestine Service (CIA), 168. See also Plans
Directorate (DDP) (CIA)
Clarridge, Dewey, 199, 200, 201, 202
Clay, Rick, 222
Clifford, Clark, 20
Cline, Ray, 142
Clinton, Bill, 25
Clinton, Hillary, 3, 31, 32, 36, 40, 61
CNC. See Counter Narcotics Center (CNC) (CIA)
A Coffin for Dimitrios (Ambler), 80
Cohen, Lona, 72
Cohen, Michael, 221, 223
Cohen, Morris, 72
Cold War, xvi, xviii, xxi, 4, 8, 12, 27, 34, 43, 54,
59, 69, 73, 75, 81, 87, 90, 91, 98, 102, 115, 116,
122, 123, 131, 147, 148; Berlin and, 35–38; CIA
and, 11, 161; communism and, 220; covert
action and, 35; end of, 13, 59, 103, 213; espio-
nage of, 219; intelligence lessons from, 215–
18; invisible front of, 57; morale during,
23; NATO and, 26; objectives of, 6; Russian
expansionist strategy during, 216; struggles of,
22; success during, 217; technology and, 140
Color Revolutions, 64
communication, 180; CIA, 94–95; electronic
trails of, 89; lines, 94
communism, 57, 180, 216; capitalism and, 162;
combatting, 20; spread of, 170
Communist Party Central Committee, 165
Communist Part of Chile, 173
Communist Party of Italy, 18
Communist Party of the Soviet Union (CPSU), 185
Contras, 207; arms sales to, 205–6; Boland
Amendment and, 202; CIA and, 199, 202;
support for, 201, 208

Council on Foreign Relations (CFR), 4
Countering America's Adversaries through
Sanctions Act (CAATSA) (2017), 212
counterintelligence (CI), xiv, 8, 9, 70, 79, 90,
100, 102, 123, 127, 132; CIA and, 92, 97, 98, 107;
developing, 17; FBI and, 79, 101; investigations,
89, 90, 91, 92; KGB and, 92, 94, 98, 108; maintaining, 116; next generation, 115; problems
with, 112, 114; sources of, 87; Soviet, 96, 109
Counterintelligence and Export Control Section (National Security Division of the U.S.
Department of Justice), 33, 213
Counterintelligence and Security Office (CIA), 94
Counterintelligence Center (CIC) (CIA), 96
Counter Narcotics Center (CNC) (CIA), 12, 23
CounterSpy (magazine), 40, 41
covert action, 20, 21, 22, 35, 41, 46, 51, 62, 67, 130,
155, 156, 157, 160, 165, 193, 199; CIA and, 35,
158–59, 167, 185, 188, 208; engaging in, 63, 188;
failed, 193; intelligence-gathering, 5; Iranian,
161, 162; mindless, 63; spectrum of, 43; success
of, 169; as tool of statecraft, 188; U.S., 179–88
Covert Action Information Bulletin (newsletter), 40, 41
COVID-19 pandemic, 33, 213
Cozy Bear (SVR hacking group), 31, 34, 52
Crimea, Russian annexation of, 36
Cruise missiles, 214
cryptography, 74, 77
Cuba, 5, 99, 134, 143, 161, 162, 163, 169, 199, 215;
CIA and, 141, 165, 167; Cuban Revolution,
173; Russian influence in, 176; spying for, 81
Cuban Missile Crisis, xix, 22, 141, 142, 146, 151,
219; prompting of, 143–44
culture, CIA, xvi, 19, 26, 75, 102, 107, 112, 129, 161
cyber: capability, xix, 51, 215; operations, 6, 31,
52, 114, 116, 140, 157, 219; sphere, 63, 73, 143,
217; warfare, 52, 75
cyber attacks, xx, 36, 51, 74, 156, 158, 212, 213–
14, 219; denial of service, 52; energy grid, 46,
53; hacking, 31, 53, 54; malware attacks, 52;
ransomware, 52; trolls, 32, 33, 42, 114
CyberBerkut (Russian hacker group), 52
Czechoslovak Secret Service, 39

DCLeaks, 3, 32, 40
dead drops, 14, 69, 71, 100, 101, 129, 134, 152
Dearborn, Rick, 222

Defectors (Russian), 22, 44, 75, 77, 81, 92, 93, 96, 109, 111, 113, 115, 149

Dejean, Maurice, 48

democracy, 34, 37, 43, 91, 113, 219, 220; assault on, xxi, 64, 156, 211, 216; building, 61; defense of, xxii, 35; porous nature of, 6, 218; strength/resilience of, 220

Democratic Congressional Campaign Committee (DCCC), 3, 31

Democratic National Committee (DNC), 31, 42, 145; attack on, xix, 3

Department V (KGB), insight into, 46

Deutch, John, 169

Devine, Pat, 175

dezinformatsiya, 38–43

DGI, 40, 163, 173

diplomatic missions, cutting, 212–13

disillusionment (Soviet), 119–22

disinformation, 31, 34, 36, 39, 61–62; dissemination of, 38–43

Dmitriev, Kirill, 222, 223

DNC. See Democratic National Committee

Dominican Republic, invasion of, 172

domino theory, 170

Donovan, William "Wild Bill," xv, 17

Downing, Jack, 95

Dragonfly (hacker group), 53

Droller, Gerry (Frank Bender), 160, 167

drones, 53, 73, 162

Dulles, Allen, 107, 160, 165, 167, 168, 169, 170; Georgetown Set and, 21; Lenin and, 19; OSS and, 18

Dulles, John Foster, 49, 160, 165

Dunlap, Jack, 75

Dunn, Bert, 203

Dzerzhinsky, Felix, 10, 11, 12, 13, 14

Eastbound (Soviet deception agent), 95

East Germany, 71, 145, 146, 150, 199; influence in, 125

Eisenhower, Dwight D., 18, 49, 151, 159, 160, 161, 165, 167; Iran and, 162

election interference, 9, 27, 121; Russian, 24, 31–38, 42, 62, 63, 64, 89, 90, 91, 103, 158, 211–16

elicitation, 47–51, 123

Eliot, T. S., 107

Energetic Bear (Russian hacker group), 53

"The Enterprise" (NSC nickname), 202

entrapment, 34, 47–51, 123, 130

Erickson, Paul, 222

Escobar, Pablo: death of, 23

espionage, 20, 25–27, 67, 92, 113, 155, 158, 169, 217, 219, 220; cyber, 73; network, 72; purview of, 87; stakes for, 98

Estemirova, Natalia, 47

Esterline, Jake, 160, 167–68

European Union (EU), 37, 61, 165

Europe Division (CIA), 202

exfiltration plans, 149–50

extrajudicial killings, 43

Facebook, 3, 32, 33, 42

fake news, 3, 37, 38, 42

Fancy Bear (GRU hacker group), 31–32, 34

FARC, 173

"The Farm" (CIA training facility), 80, 81, 82, 111, 132

Farm Journal. See American Farm Journal

FBI, 11, 13, 59, 68, 88, 92, 93, 94, 96, 97, 124, 158, 171; alert by, 46; CIA and, 17; counterintelligence and, 79, 101; Hanssen and, 100–101; investigation by, 99; Russian spies within, 24; surveillance by, 150

Felfe, Heinz, 108–9

Filaret, Patriarch, 35, 37

Filatov, Anatoly: execution of, 130

"Finlandia" (Sibelius), 150

First Chief Directorate (KGB), 148

First Intelligence Directorate (HVA), 57

Fisher, William August, 72. See also Abel, Rudolf Ivanovich; "Mark"

Fitzgerald, Desmond, 19, 168

Fleming, Ian, 167

Flynn, Michael, 222

foreign policy, 4, 5, 48, 139, 155, 162, 208; change in, 215; goals of, 157; intelligence and, 63, 75; Russian, 57, 60, 62, 211–12; terrorism and, 156

Foxtrot (source), 110. See also Nosenko, Yuri

France: disinformation about, 38; Russian meddling in, 211

FSB, 12, 24–25, 43, 57, 59, 60, 212

FSLN. See Sandinista National Liberation Front

Fuchs, Klaus, 90

Gaddafi, Muammar, 200

Galey, Priscilla Sue, 79

Garbler, Paul, 127–28
Gates, Rick, 221
Gates, Robert, 24, 25, 200
Geneva Accords (1988), 185
George, Clair, 181, 197, 203, 204
Georgetown Set, 20, 21
Gerasimov, Valery, 64; Gerasimov Doctrine, 64
Gerber, Burton, 7, 93
Germany: disinformation about, 38; Russian meddling in, 211
"Geronton" (Eliot), 107
Ghorbanifar, Manuchehr, 203, 204, 205, 206
glasnost, 58, 124, 185
Gold, Harold, 90
Goldwater, Barry, 201
Goleniewski, Michael, 108, 114
Golitsyn, Anatoliy, 108, 109, 111–12, 114; Golitsyn Syndrome, 112
Good Hunting (Devine), 35, 164
Gorbachev, Mikhail, 12, 13, 101, 147, 185
Gordievsky, Oleg, 102, 125, 126, 146, 149–50
Gordievsky, Vasily, 125, 126
Gordon, J. D., 222
Gorkov, Sergei N., 71, 222
Graham, Philip, 20
Great Britain, 121, 181; Russian meddling in, 211
Greenglass, David, 90
Grenada, 198–99
Gribaud, Louis, 48
Grimes, Sandy, 96, 97
Gromyko, Andrei, 124
GRU, xvii, xx, 11, 14, 17, 31, 32, 33, 42, 43, 47–48, 49, 51, 63–64, 75, 79, 81, 89, 91, 92, 93, 98, 110, 114, 123, 128, 129, 133, 134, 139, 144, 216; operation methods of, 88
Guaidó, Juan, 163
Guatemala, 159, 160, 161; operation in, 22, 167–68; story of, 162–63
Guccifer 2.0, 32, 40, 42, 222
Guerrillas (Cuban), 173, 200–201
Guevara, Che, 173
Gulags (Soviet), 10

Haas, Kenneth, 194
Hakim, Albert, 205
Hale, Nathan, xv
Hall, Virginia, xvi
Hanssen, Robert, xvi, 13, 78, 81, 82, 94, 95, 99,

102; FBI and, 100–101; GRU and, 79, 93; KGB and, 14, 101; personality of, 79; spying by, 100–101, 114
Hard Targets Branch (CIA), 80
Harriman, Averell, 20
Haspel, Gina, xvi
Hawkins, Jack, 168
Häyhänen, Karel (codename Vik), 70–71, 72. *See also* Maki, Eugene
Helms, Richard, xvi, 19, 107, 168–69, 202; Angleton and, 112; Bay of Pigs and, 169
Helsinki summit (2018), xix, 42, 121, 213
Hiss, Alger, 7, 8, 9, 114
Hitler, Adolf, 57
Hizballah, 81, 195, 196–97
Ho Chi Minh, 170
Holt, Jim, 96
honeytrap, 48, 95
hostages, 203, 204, 206; arms for, 197, 198, 202
Howard, Edward Lee, 93, 102, 114
human rights, abuses of, 119, 121, 206
human rights leaders/activists, 44, 47, 61
Hungary, 145, 165, 166; disinformation about, 38; influence in, 34, 125
Hunt, Howard, 168
Hussein, Saddam, 25, 26

Illegals (NOCs), 7, 50, 68, 69, 70, 71, 72, 132; Russian, 67, 92, 99, 125, 126, 133
Illegals Section, 132
INF, 147
influence campaigns, 31, 32, 34, 47, 89
information, 83, 91; classified, 34; compartmentalizing, 103; confrontation, 51–54; conspiracy theories and, 40; vetting/validating, 40; weaponizing, 39
Inside the Company: CIA Diary, 40
Instagram, 3, 33, 42
Intelligence Directorate (CIA), 204
Intelligence Identities Protection Act (1982), 41
intelligence officers, 88; deployment of, 87; Polish, 108; Russian, 43, 67, 87, 108, 218; types of, 67; West German, 48
Internet Research Agency (IRA), 32, 34, 42, 51, 114
Inter-Service Intelligence (ISI) Pakistan, 181, 182

Iran, 5, 18, 54, 60, 115, 143, 161, 162, 172, 193, 194, 195, 213, 215, 216, 220; arms for hostages and, 197, 198, 202, 205, 206; covert actions in, 22; interference by, 34; missiles for, 198; nuclear program of, 162; regime change in, 159, 166; relations with, 198; spying for, 81

Iran Branch (CIA), 194, 202, 203

Iran-Contra Affair, 194–98, 202, 206–7

Iranian Revolution, 197

Iran-Iraq War, 197

Iraq, 156, 180; spying for, 81; war in, 26, 217

IRBMS, 141

ISI. See Inter-Service Intelligence (Pakistan)

ISIS, 25, 54, 156

Islamabad, 182, 183

Islamic Amal, 196

Islamic Jihad, 195

Ivanov, Yevgeny, 49, 50

Javelin antitank weapons system, 37

Johnson, Lyndon B., 170, 172

Johnson, Robert Lee, 77–78

Juniewicz, Ed, 205

just war, principles of (St. Thomas Aquinas), 188–89

Kalugin, Oleg, 40, 46

Kaspersky security software, 73

Keeler, Christine, 49–50

Kennan, George, 20, 165

Kennedy, John F., 109, 111, 134, 167, 169, 170, 172; Bay of Pigs and, 166; CIA and, 168; Cuban Missile Crisis and, 142, 143; Khrushchev and, xix

Kerch Strait, 36

KGB, xvii, xviii, xix, 3, 5, 13, 22, 24–25, 34, 40, 43, 48, 57, 58, 59, 60, 75, 77, 81, 93, 95, 96, 112, 123, 125, 128, 129, 134, 139, 140, 143, 144, 146, 147, 149, 150, 158; Afghanistan and, 179–80; Ames and, 94, 97, 101; CIA and, 11, 64, 99, 113; contingency program of, 44; counterintelligence and, 92, 94, 98, 108; defections and, 111; Felfe and, 109; Hanssen and, 14, 101; infiltration of, 145, 157; leadership of, 11; Line X of, 157; operations of, 35, 45–46, 88, 151; Oswald and, 110; power for, 12; recruitment and, 111; sources for, 95, 100; tracers by, 127. See also FSB; NKVD; SVR; Vacheka ("Checka")

Khan, Abdur Rahman, 182

Khodorkovsky, Mikhail, 47, 120

Khokhlov, Nikolai, 44

Khrushchev, Nikita, 11, 110, 163, 165; coup against, 143; Cuban Missile Crisis and, 141, 142; Kennedy and, xix

Khusyaynova, Elena, 33, 213

kidnappings, 19, 46, 125, 174, 196, 197, 203, 208

Kilimnik, Konstantin V., 221

Kipling, Rudyard, 182

Kisevalter, George, xiii, 132, 133, 150

Kislyak, Sergei, 71, 222

Kissinger, Henry, 139, 172, 173, 174

Koechner, Karl, 130

Kolokol (source), 97. See also Ames, Aldrich "Rick"

Kommersant, 34

Korean War, 7, 75

Korobov, Igor, 212

Korotkov, Aleksandr, 71

Kostov, Vladimir, 44

Krogers, 72. See also Cohen Lona; Cohen, Morris

Kryuchkov, Vladimir, 12–13

Kulak, Aleksei, 157

Kushner, Jared, 221, 222, 223

Langelle, Russell, 150–51

La Prensa, 207

Latin American Division (CIA), 24, 41, 113, 169, 174, 194, 201; Grenada and, 198–99

law enforcement, role of, 12, 89, 113, 116

Lazaro, Juan, 69

Lebanon, 194, 195, 196; Bekaa Valley, 195; Beirut, 194, 195; Beirut bombing, 147; civil war in, 196; hostages in Beirut, 202, 204

Ledeen, Barbara, 206

Ledeen, Michael, 203, 206

Lee, Jerry Chun Shing, 76

Lenin, Vladimir, 10, 18, 19, 44

Leonov, Nikolai, 174, 176

Line X (SVR), 157

Litvinenko, Alexander, 43, 44, 47

Lonetree, Clayton, 95

Love Letter to America (Bezmenov), 45

Lukashenko, Alexander, xvii–xviii

Lyalin, Oleg, 45, 46

Maclean, Donald, 7, 8. See also Cambridge Five

Macmillan, Harold, 49, 50

Maduro, Nicolás, 163, 164, 176, 213

Magnitsky, Sergei, 47, 120–21

Magnitsky Act (2012), 119, 120

Maki, Eugene, 70. *See also* Häyhänen, Karel (codename Vik)

Malaysia Airlines Flight 17: downing of, 42

malware attacks, 52

Manafort, Paul, 221

Manhattan Project, 7

Maude Report, 7

"Mark": arrest/interrogation of, 71. *See also* Abel, Rudolf Ivanovich; Fisher, William August

Markelov, Stanislav, 44, 47

Markov, Georgi, 44

Martin, Hal, 73

Martin, William, 74

Marxist Afghan Army, 180

Maude Report, 7

McCarthy, Joseph, 9

McCone, John, 142

McMahon, John, 205

medium range ballistic missiles (MRBMS), 133, 141, 142

Mendez, Tony, xvi

Metka (Soviet "spy dust"), 128

MI5, 45, 46, 49, 50

MI6, 45, 161. *See also* SIS

Middle East, 60, 159, 162, 194, 195; influence in, 5; involvement in, 27

Middle East Division (CIA), 202

Milan antitank missile system, 37, 186

Milburn, Jim, 96

Military Diplomatic Academy (GRU training school), 128

Ministry of State Security (MSS), xiii

Mister X (Soviet deception agent), 94, 95

Mitchell, Bernon, 74

Mitrokhin, Vasiliy, 148; Mitrokhin Archives, 46, 145

Mitterand, François, 157

mokrye dela, 43–47. *See also* active measures

moles, hunting for within the CIA, 91–98

Molotov-Ribbentrop Pact (1939), 7

Montenegro, influence in, 34, 211

Montgomery, Hugh, 134–35

Mosaddeq, Mohammed, 159

Moscow Rules, xvii–xxiii, 61, 63, 64, 211; resetting, xxii, 212, 218–20

Mossack Fonseca (law firm), 61

Mossad, xiii, 165

Motorboat (source), 80. *See also* Ames, Aldrich "Rick"

Mountbatten, Lord, 133

MRBMs. *See* medium range ballistic missiles

MSS, xiii, 76

Mubarak, Hosni, 183–84

Mueller, Robert, III, xxi, 88; investigation by, 3, 32, 33, 116; report by, xxi, 88, 89, 91, 206, 213, 223; Russian interference and, 24

Mujahideen (Afghan), 180, 182, 183, 185; weapons for, 181

Naryshkin, Sergei, 212

National Assembly (Venezuela), 163

nationalism, 6, 38, 54, 170, 217

National Opposition Union (UNO) Nicaragua, 207

National Rifle Association (NRA), 8, 67, 222

National Security Act (1947): CIA and, 17

National Security Agency (NSA), 73–76, 181, 207

National Security Council (NSC), 35, 158, 187, 197, 202, 203, 204, 206, 222; policy formation and, 207

National Security Decision Directive 17 (NSDD-17), 199

National Security Division (U.S. Department of Justice), 33, 213

National Security Strategy, 212

nation-states, 54, 189, 195, 217, 220; attacks by, 213–14

NATO, 4, 6, 36, 61, 115, 125, 144, 146, 147, 158, 212, 218, 219; Cold War and, 26; expansion of, 165; military exercises and, 145; plans of, 77; Star Wars and, 214; war games and, 213; Warsaw Pact and, 57

Navalny, Alexei, 44, 47

Near East Division (CIA), 182, 204

Nemtsov, Boris, 44, 47

Neptune 80 (Soviet chemical agent), 127–28

nerve agents, 43, 212

New Economic School (Moscow), 221

New Jewel Movement (Grenada), 198

New York Times, 165

Nicaragua, 161, 162, 199; arm sales and, 206, 207; CIA and, 201, 202; Sandinistas and, 173; Soviet expansionism in, 200, 201

Nicholson, Harold James, 24, 81–82, 83, 102

Nicholson, Jeremiah, 83

Nicholson, Nathan, 83

Nikolaev, Konstantin, 67

Nikolai II, Tsar, 10

Nitze, Paul, 20

Nixon, Richard, 172–73; China and, 139; CIA and, 112

NKVD, 10, 11, 17, 43, 44, 125, 127. *See also* KGB; SVR; Vachecka ("Cheka")

nongovernmental organizations (NGOs), 61, 214

nonstate actors, 54, 74, 187, 195, 196

North, Oliver "Ollie," 202, 203, 205

North Korea, 5, 54, 143, 213, 220; interference by, 34; nuclear weapons and, 146; spying for, 81

Nosenko, Yuri, 77, 111, 128; assessing, 112–13; defection of, 109; exoneration of, 113; information from, 110. *See also* Angleton, James

Novichok (Russian nerve agent), 43, 44, 212

NRA. *See* National Rifle Association

NSA. *See* National Security Agency

NSC. *See* National Security Council

nuclear war, 145, 146, 147, 152

nuclear weapons, 7, 90, 133, 134, 141–47, 220

Obama, Barack, 212

Office of Foreign Missions (U.S. Department of State), 100

Office of Policy Coordination (OPC) (CIA), 19

Office of Security (CIA): Angleton and, 111

Office of Special Operations (OSO) (CIA), 19

Office of Strategic Services (OSS), xv, xvi, 17, 18, 107, 134, 159, 168, 199; CIA and, 17–21; veterans of, 19, 22, 160

Ogorodnik, Aleksandr, 130

Okhota, 93

Okhrana, 10

Olson, Jim, 96

OPC (CIA). *See* Office of Policy Coordination

Operation Absorb (CIA), 92

Operation Ajax (CIA), 159

Operation Anadyr (Soviet), 141, 142

Operation Fortune (CIA), 159

Operation JMATE (CIA), 166

Operation Neptune (Czech intelligence service), 38

Operation PBFortune (CIA), 160

Operation RYaN (Soviet), 144–45, 146–47

Operations Directorate (CIA), 19, 25, 204

Operation Success (CIA), 159

Opus Dei, 79

"Organization 1," 222. *See also* WikiLeaks

Ortega, Daniel, 207

OSS. *See* Office of Strategic Services

Oswald, Lee Harvey, 110, 111

Page, Carter, 68, 221, 222

Pakistan, 156, 181, 182, 184, 186

Palaez, Vicky, 69

Panama Papers, 61

Papadopoulos, George, 221

paramilitary activities, 6, 25, 155, 175, 187

Pavlov, Vitali, 71

Payne, Dan, 96

Penkovskiy, Oleg Vladimirovich, 49, 108, 123, 126, 128–29, 132, 143; CIA and, 142; Cuba and, 142; fate of, 151–52; GRU and, 129; Khrushchev and, xix; remuneration for, 133–34; sources of, xx

perestroika, 58, 185

Perroots, Leonard, 146, 147

Pershing missiles, 214

Peskov, Dmitri: Trump Organization and, 221

Peterson, Martha, 130

Petróleos de Venezuela, S.A. (PDVSA), 163

Philby, Kim, 7, 78, 108–9, 114. *See also* Cambridge Five

Philip, Prince, 49

Phillips, Dave, 113, 160, 168, 174

Pierre (Soviet illegal), 99

Pipek, Hedwig "Hedy," 77

Pitts, Earl Edwin, 24, 100, 102

Plans Directorate (DDP) (CIA), 18, 167

Plans Operations (DDO) (CIA), 18

Platt, Jack, 98

Podobnyy, Victor, 68, 221

Poindexter, John, 204, 205

Poland, 18, 145, 147; disinformation about, 38; influence in, 125; nuclear weapons in, 145

Polgar, Thomas, 168, 171, 172

Politburo, 47, 124, 125, 140, 144

politics, xviii, 47, 91, 115, 123, 218; CIA and, 11; European, 60; fringe, 36; polarization of, 26–27; Ukraine and, 35

Politkovskaya, Anna, 44, 47

polonium-210 (Russian poison): poisoning with, 43, 44

Polyakov, Dmitri (codename Top Hat), xvi, 92–93, 123, 124, 126, 139, 141, 150, 157; as Russian patriot, 148

polygraph tests, 75, 80, 82, 83, 93, 100–101, 112, 204

Popov, Pyotr, 49, 108, 123, 126, 127, 132; CIA and, 151; death of, 152; Langelle and, 150–51

Poroshenko, Petro, 52, 53

Portland Spy Ring, 60

Poteyev, Aleksandr, 69

power, 12; dynamics, 122; economic, 220; military, 217, 220; reasserting, 64, 214; soft, 61–62. See also big power dynamics

Powers, Gary, 71, 142

Prague Spring, 39, 125, 126

Prigozhin, Yevgeny V. ("Putin's Cook"), 32

Prince, Erik, 222

Profumo, John, 50

Project Lakhta, 32. See also "Translator" department (IRA)

propaganda, 34, 155, 160, 161, 168. See also active measures

PSYOPS (CIA), 144

Putin, Vladimir, xvii, xix, xx, 23, 42, 83, 88, 91, 115, 120, 140, 143, 147, 163, 164, 176, 216, 218–19, 221, 222, 223; border states and, 146; China and, 215; control by, 47; cyber operations and, 24, 114; dealing with, 26–27, 43, 215; democracy and, 64, 215, 220; election interference and, 62, 64; escalations by, 37; foreign policy and, 62; FSB and, 59; KGB and, 5, 14, 57, 59; leadership of, 6, 61, 141; Magnitsky Act and, 119; Moscow Rules and, 211; policy-making by, 89; relationship with, xviii, 64; rise of, 12, 59–60; Russian greatness and, 60–61; sanctions and, 213; Sobchak and, 59; strategy of, 3, 141, 216; Trump and, 121, 213; Ukraine and, 36, 37–38, 147; Wolf and, 58; Yeltsin and, 59

Pyatyorka (Ring of Five), 108. See also Cambridge Five

Radio Agricultura (Chile), 176

Radio Free Europe (RFE), 165

Reagan, Ronald, 140, 144, 145, 157, 204, 205; Buckley and, 197; Casey and, 199; Central America and, 198; Gorbachev and, 147; hostages and, 198; Iran-Contra and, 206; Nicaragua and, 199; NSC and, 197; show of strength and, 214; Soviet expansion and, 194

Reagan Doctrine, 214

Rebet, Lev, 44

Redmond, Paul, 96

Red Scare, 8–9

Republican National Committee (RNC), 145

Republican National Convention, 222

Research and Counter-Propaganda Department (KGB), 45

Reston, James, 20

Ricin (poison), 44

Roeber, Marty, 81, 82

Roosevelt, Franklin D., 8

Roosevelt, Kermit "Kim," 19, 159

Rosenberg, Ethel, 72, 90

Rosenberg, Julius, 72, 90

Rosneft, 164, 213

Rostow, Walter, 20

Russia: economic problems for, 58, 60; global clout of, xvii; oil/gas income for, 60; reemergence of, 61; relations with, xxii; responding to, 220; strategic weaknesses of, 158; struggle with, 3, 36, 54

Russian Central Bank, 71

Russian Federation, 43, 69

Russian Orthodox Church: Ukrainian Orthodox Church and, 35, 37

Russian Revolution (1917), 10, 18, 32, 88, 115, 179

Russian State Investigative Committee, 120–21

"Ryzhiy" (Redhead, KGB nickname for Edward Ellis "Little Guy" Smith), 49

SA-2 missiles, 133

S Directorate (KGB), 68

sabotage, 46, 52, 53. See also active measures

Sanchez, Nestor, 199

Sanctions (U.S.), 53, 61, 64, 119, 163, 164, 181, 212, 213, 216, 218

Sanders, Bernie, 32

Sandinista National Liberation Front (FSLN), 207

Sandinistas, 173, 199, 200, 201, 207

Santiago station (CIA), 62, 64, 175

Sasha (spy in the CIA), 109, 111, 112. See also Angleton, James; Golitsyn, Anatoliy

Sater, Felix, 221

Savchuk, Lyudmila, 114

Scavino, Dan, 223

Schneider, René: death of, 174

Scoon, Paul, 198

Seborer, Oscar, 90

Second Directorate (KGB), 110

Secord, Richard, 205

Secret Intelligence Service (SIS), xiii, 7, 95, 129, 133, 146, 149

secret police, 10, 127

Secret Service (U.S.), 11

security, 74, 143, 149, 196, 218; digital/cyber, 23, 219; information, 53; national, 7, 26, 35, 54, 73, 77–78, 83, 98, 122, 174, 188, 193, 199, 218; operational, 107, 128; protocols, 100; threat to, 6–7, 212

Security Council (UN), 163. See also United Nations

Sellers, Mike, 92

Semichastny, Vladimir, 143, 144

September 11th, 4, 25, 26, 156, 175, 180, 217

Sessions, Jeff, 222

Shackley, Ted "The Blond-Ghost," 171

Shah, 159; fall of, xvi

Shakespeare, William, 149

Shelepin, Alexander, 143, 144

Shevchenko, Arkady, 124, 125, 126, 140, 141, 149

Shultz, George, 195, 198, 206, 207

Sibelius, Jean, 150

Sidorkov, Konstantin, 223

SIS (UK). See Secret Intelligence Service (SIS)

Sites, Erik, 95

Skripal, Sergei, 43, 47, 212

smear campaigns, 34, 45. See also active measures

SMERSH, 44. See also active measures

Smith, Edward Ellis "Little Guy," 48–49. See also "Ryzhiy" (Redhead)

Smith, Walter Bedell, 18, 160

Snowden, Edward, 73, 74, 75

Snyder, Timothy, 204

Sobchak, Anatoly, 59

Sobell, Morton, 72

social media, 3, 32, 33, 47, 51

Soleimani, Qassem, 162

Solzhenitsyn, Alexandr, 10

Somoza, Anastasio, 160, 199

Somoza National Guard, 201

Soviet Division (CIA), 12, 78, 93–94, 111, 131

Soviet expansion, 73, 140, 161, 193, 194, 198, 201, 216

"Soviet Policies and Activities in Latin America and the Caribbean," 200

Soviet Union: collapse of, xvii, 6, 58, 133; competition with, 200; as Evil Empire, 214; intelligence advantage over, 134; R&D and, 158; sanctions on, 181; spying on, 122; stability/legitimacy of, 184; transformation of, 184

Spaso House (U.S. Ambassador's residence in Moscow), 134–35

Special Counsel's Office (U.S. Department of Justice), 89

Special Forces (U.S.), 11, 188

Special Investigations Group (SIG) (CIA): Angleton and, 107

Special National Intelligence Estimate (U.S.), 200

Spetsnaz (KGB), 145, 180

spies, xiii, xvi, xxi, 13, 18, 23, 24, 27, 43, 45, 46, 47, 50, 51, 59, 67, 70, 72, 74, 80, 82, 83, 88, 91–92, 96, 98–103, 108, 114–15, 121, 122–26, 128, 129, 143, 156, 157, 158, 163, 164, 167, 200, 215, 216, 217, 220; deep-cover, 7, 124; identifying, 75; intelligence, 76–77, legacy of, 22, 139–41; patriot, 148–52; recruiting, 8, 73, 75, 87, 89, 99, 103, 110, 111, 132, 149; Russian, 8, 54, 87, 89, 90, 101, 112, 113; search for, 95; Soviet, 22, 71, 120, 130, 131; uncovering, 102

Sporyshev, Igor, 68

spymasters, xiii–xiv, xv–xvii, xx, 40, 114, 143, 156, 220

spy rings, 69, 73, 90

Stalin, Joseph, 7–8, 10, 18, 44, 123; cult of the personality and, 165; death of, 11

Star Wars, 214

Stashinsky, Bogdan, 44

Stasi (East German intelligence service), 48

Stein, Jill, 32

Stinger Missiles, xvi, 183, 184, 185–86, 187

Stone, Rocky, 159

Stone, Roger, 222

Strategic Defense Initiative (SDI), 214

suicide bombers, 194, 195

Sullivan and Cromwell (law firm), 160

Šumava National Park, 38

surveillance, 89, 128, 150, 151, 196–97; drone, 53; regular, 110; teams, 82; technical, 74

SVR, xiii, xvii, 14, 31, 51, 68, 73, 89, 114, 211, 212, 221, 222; assault by, 3–4; CIA and, 64; diplomatic sources for, 4; power for, 12; spying for, 81. *See also* KGB

Swallows, 48. *See also* active measures

Syria, 5, 60, 115, 126, 143, 156, 161, 162, 194, 195, 215; spying for, 81

Syrian Democratic Forces (SDF), 156

Tairova, Margarita, 150, 151

Taliban militants, 5

Taraki, Nur Mohammed, 179, 180

technology, 34, 94, 150, 214; collecting, 73; communication, 42; cyber, 91; defective, 158; military, 140, 158; nuclear, 71; scientific, 90; Soviet, 140; submarine, 71

Teplyakova, Irina, 45

terrorism, xviii, 23, 46, 74, 194, 195, 196, 208; CIA and, 25; combatting, 217; foreign policy and, 156; sponsorship of, 194; transnational, xxi, 4

Thomas Aquinas, Saint, 188

Tillerson, Rex, 223

Tito, Josip Broz, 44

Tolkachev, Adolf, xvi, 93, 114, 131, 141, 150; work of, 139–40, 148

Torshin, Alexander, 67, 71

TOW missiles, 203, 205

"Translator" department (IRA), 32. *See also* Project Lakhta

Tretyakov, Sergei (codename Comrade J), 3–4, 5, 25, 68, 124

Trident Juncture (war games), 213

Trotsky, Leon, 44

Truman, Harry S., 17, 18, 160

Truman Doctrine, 17

Trump, Donald, Jr., 221, 222, 223

Trump, Donald J., xviii, 42, 221, 222; campaign of, 8, 47–48, 68, 88, 119; National Security Strategy and, 212; nuclear treaty and, 147; Putin and, 121, 213; Russians and, 51; support for, 32–33

Trump, Ivanka, 221

Trump Tower, 221, 223

Turner, Stansfield: Carter and, 129, 130, 132

Twetten, Tom, 181, 182, 204

U-2 flights, 71, 142, 167

Ukraine, 5, 35–38, 43, 58, 62, 126, 143, 147, 165, 218; CIA and, 35; democracy in, 37; disinformation about, 38; influence in, 34, 115; Kyiv, as new Berlin, 35–38; Russian attack on, 37, 53; U.S. relations with, 35, 36

Ukrainian Central Election Commission, 52

Ukrainian Orthodox Church: Russian Orthodox Church and, 35, 37

United Fruit Company (UFC), 159–60

United Nations, 4, 68, 123, 124, 163, 185

U.S. Air Force, 82, 146

U.S. Congress, 40–41, 186, 189

U.S. Cyber Command, 219

U.S. Defense Department, 53, 89, 158

U.S. Department of Homeland Security, 46

U.S. House Intelligence Committee, 201

U.S. Department of Justice, 33, 206, 213, 222

U.S. Marine Corps barracks, bombing of, 195

U.S. Senate Intelligence Committee, xvii, 33, 201, 213

U.S. State Department, 9, 19, 31, 49, 89, 99, 100, 127, 171

U.S. Treasury Department, 213

Vacheka ("Cheka") 10, 43. *See also* KGB; NKVD

VAJA (Iran), xiii

Vasenkov, Mikhail, 69

Vasilenko, Gennadi (codename Monolight), 98, 99

Vassall, John, 50

VEB. *See* VneshEconomBank

Vekselberg, Victor, 223

Venezuela, 5, 115, 143, 162, 163, 215, 216; dealing with, 164; Russian influence in, 176; spying for, 81

Venona Project, 7, 90

Vertefeuille, Jeanne, 96

Veselnitskaya, Natalia, 221

Vetrov, Vladimir (codename Farewell), 157, 158

Viaux, Roberto, 174

Vietnam, 140, 161, 170, 171, 172, 180

virtual private networks (VPNs), 69

Vkontakte (VK), 223

VneshEconomBank (VEB), 68, 71, 222

Walker, John Anthony, Jr., 171

war criminals, prosecution of, 38

war games, 145, 146, 147, 171, 213

Ward, Stephen, 49–50
Warsaw Pact, 57, 58
Washington Post, 20
Wauch, Mark, 100
weapons of mass destruction (WMDs), 25, 26
Webster, William, 23
Weinberger, Caspar, 195, 198, 207
Weir, Benjamin, 203
Weiss, Gus, 158
Welch, Richard "Dick," 41
wet work, 43–47. *See also* active measures
White, Dick, 133
Who's Who in the CIA, 39
WikiLeaks, 3, 32, 40, 222. *See also* "Organization 1"
Wilson, Charlie, 182, 183–84, 186
Wisner, Frank, Sr., 19, 156, 160
WMDs. *See* weapons of mass destruction

Wolf, Markus, xiii, 48, 57, 58
World War II, xvi, xxi, 6, 8, 10, 17, 18, 19, 20, 46, 72, 76, 90, 123, 165
Worthen, Diana, 96

Yagoda, Genrikh, 10
Yalta Conference, 8, 165
Yandarbiev, Zelimkhan, 43
Yarosh, Dymtro, 52
Yatskov, Anatoly, 90
Yeltsin, Boris, 59
Yezhov, Nikolai, 10
"The Young British Soldier" (Kipling), 182
Yurchenko, Vitali, 92, 93, 114

Zahedi, Fazlollah, 159
Zapad war games, 147
Zelensky, Volodymyr, 36
Zhomov, Aleksandr, 95

Printed in the USA
CPSIA information can be obtained
at www.ICGtesting.com
LVHW041208151223
766489LV00003B/271